KEY TO HARDINESS ZONES

This map shows eleven geographical zones based on the average annual minimum temperatures recorded for the years 1974 to 1986. The zone numbers accompanying the plants in this book indicate their lower limits of winter-cold hardiness. Extreme summer heat and humidity also play a part in a plant's adaptability; many plants hardy in colder zones grow poorly in warmer, wetter ones.

1	BELOW -50°F BELOW -46°C
2	-50° TO -40°F -46° TO -40°C
3	-40° TO -30°F -40° TO -34°C
4	-30° TO -20°F -34° TO -29°C
5	-20° TO -10°F -29° TO -23°C
6	-10° TO 0°F -23° TO -18°C
7	0° TO 10°F -18° TO -12°C
8	10° TO 20°F -12° TO -7°C
9	20° TO 30°F -7° TO -1°C
10	30° TO 40°F -1° TO 4°C
11	ABOVE 40°F ABOVE 4°C

What
Plant
Where

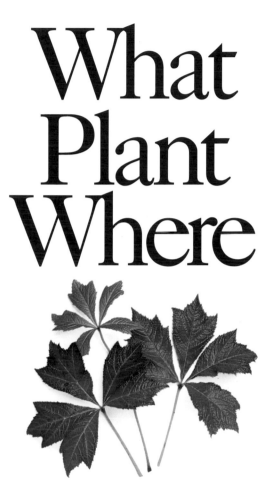

What Plant Where

ROY LANCASTER

A DK PUBLISHING BOOK

PROJECT EDITOR Lesley Malkin
PROJECT ART EDITOR Colin Walton
MANAGING EDITOR Mary-Clare Jerram
MANAGING ART EDITOR Amanda Lunn
US EDITOR Ray Rogers
PRODUCTION Meryl Silbert
TREE ILLUSTRATIONS COMMISSIONED BY Mustafa Sami

First American Edition, 1995
2 4 6 8 10 9 7 5 3

Published in the United States by DK Publishing, Inc.,
95 Madison Avenue, New York, New York 10016

Library of Congress Cataloging-in-Publication Data
Lancaster, Roy
    What plant where / by Roy Lancaster. -- 1st American ed.
        p.   cm
    Includes index.
    ISBN 0-7894-0151-7
        1. Plants, Ornamental.   2. Plants, Ornamental–Location.
        3. Landscape gardening.   4. Gardening   I. Title
    SB407.L25 1995
    635.9--dc20   95-8172
                                                        CIP

Computer page makeup by Colin Walton, Great Britain • Text film output by The Right Type, Great Britain
Reproduced by grb EDITRICE, Italy • Printed and bound in Great Britain by Butler and Tanner

CONTENTS

Plant Finder

IF YOU HAVE a specific site, condition, or decorative effect in mind, refer to the condensed index below. The page numbers alongside each entry take you to visual lists of plants that thrive there, or to what the author recommends to achieve the desired effect. The color-coded bands match the section markers.

	PERENNIALS	CLIMBERS	SHRUBS	CONIFERS	TREES
Crevices and between paving	54				
Fences, walls, and other vertical supports	106	102, 107			
Groundcover	28, 30		118, 121	190	
Rock gardens, raised beds, and screes	56, 58		142	188	
Trees and shrubs, training into		102			
Wet soil, streambanks	44, 46		134		210
Wild areas	60				

SEASONAL FEATURES

	PERENNIALS	CLIMBERS	SHRUBS	CONIFERS	TREES
Spring interest	78				
Summer interest	80				
Autumn interest	82		156		222, 224
Winter interest	84, 85		166, 168		224, 226
Evergreen	66	104	146		216

COLOR

	PERENNIALS	CLIMBERS	SHRUBS	CONIFERS	TREES
Blue-gray or silver leaves	72		152	193	220
Golden or yellow leaves	70		150	192	219
Purple, red, or bronze leaves	74		154		221
Variegated leaves	68		148	191	218

OTHER PLANT FEATURES

	PERENNIALS	CLIMBERS	SHRUBS	CONIFERS	TREES
Berries for birds			161, 162		224
Butterflies, flowers attractive to			164		
Fragrance	76	105	158, 160		
Hedging and screening			140	186	215
Herbs	86, 88				
Multipurpose trees					228
Ornamental fruits			161,162		224
Rabbitproof	90		170		
Self-clinging climbers		107			
Specimen plants	18		110, 112		196
Thorny shrubs			169		

INTRODUCTION

THE DIVERSITY OF PLANTS available to gardeners today is so wide that we need never again suffer the disappointment of watching a recently acquired plant struggling and even dying because it was planted in the wrong place, or it was not a good plant for the job.

A great many people acquire plants for their garden on impulse. You see a plant that takes your fancy, or a fellow gardener offers you an offset or cutting. With little regard for its suitability, you take it home and lose no time in planting it, usually wherever a space beckons.

Sometimes the site proves just right and your plant thrives. More often than not, though, the site is vacant for a very good reason: it is too wet or too dry, too shady, too shallow, or filled with the roots of other plants. When a plant fails for one of these reasons, you may shrug it off and keep trying or, with your confidence gone, give up and switch your attentions elsewhere.

Don't you ever ask yourself how the glorious gardens you see down your street, on television, and in magazines are achieved? Of course you do, and although it is easy to dismiss them as the gardens of experts, you suspect that if you had the time and means to check out plants before acquiring them, you too could enjoy the same success.

GARDENERS' QUESTIONS

I worked for a major British nursery for many years, advising customers on the choice of plants for their gardens. I dealt with a variety of people; some were professionals or gardening enthusiasts who already had a good idea of the plants likely to grow in their gardens, but were seeking something new or special. Most people, however, were first-time gardeners who had little knowledge or experience of plants and their uses, but were eager to learn and anxious to make the best choice for their money.

On the whole, my inquirers belonged to one of two categories: those who had seen a plant they liked and wanted to know if it would grow in their garden, or those who had no specific idea of what they wanted but knew what purpose they wanted it for. This confirmed my belief that most people seeking help simply want to know what plants will grow in a given situation, taking factors such as soil, sun, and exposure into account, or what plants will create a desired effect, such as seasonal features, color, fragrance, and ultimate size or shape.

△ GARDEN CENTER TEMPTATIONS
It is tempting to buy a plant for the initial impact of its flowers, fruit, or foliage, instead of its suitability for your garden.

△ AUTHOR'S GARDEN *My own garden, in Hampshire, England, is filled with plants of all kinds for year-round effect. The walls of the house are densely planted with both climbers and shrubs.*

◁ ORIGIN OF A SPECIAL PLANT
I am particularly proud of Hypericum lancasteri, *which flowers its heart out in late summer. It was raised from a seed I collected in the hills above Kunming, City of Eternal Spring, in China.*

GARDENERS' ANSWERS

Many years of visiting gardens and interviewing people for television programs about gardening have convinced me that poor or adverse conditions can often be improved. If this is not practical, some choice usually exists for most sites and situations as they stand.

What Plant Where is a guide to selecting the best plants for given conditions and ornamental effects. It will assist beginners in finding plants suited to their gardens, and hopefully remind more seasoned gardeners of excellent contenders they may have overlooked. Never before have so many ornamental plants been available to gardeners. Among those in this book are a host of old favorites, as well as many newer, sometimes rare or unusual, ones. Success with these should inspire you to try to grow more challenging plants. Let *What Plant Where* be your guide.

LILY, WILD AND IN THE GARDEN △ ▷
An experience I cherish was first seeing Lilium regale *growing wild on a sun-drenched, rocky mountainside in China. It is one of the easiest, loveliest, and most satisfying lilies for the garden, and is delightfully fragrant, too.*

▽ THE POWER OF FOLIAGE
Conifers, ferns, bergenias, irises, and shrubs surround this small pool; their diverse foliage combines to create an effect that is dramatic, yet easy on the eye.

How This Book Works

IN THIS BOOK, my aim is to help you choose the most suitable plants for a given garden situation, taking account of the local growing conditions, different plant characteristics, and any special ornamental effects. The book is divided into five sections by plant type: Perennials, Climbers, Shrubs, Conifers, and Trees. Within each section, I suggest possible plants suitable for different types of site and decorative effects. All woody plants listed, with the exception of conifers, are deciduous unless specified evergreen. Conifers are deciduous only where specified. Perennials are herbaceous unless described as evergreen.

PLANT NAMES

Currently accepted botanical names are used throughout. Well-known synonyms appear in the index and are cross-referenced. Common names in general use are given, and where none exists, the generic name is repeated, or else an English name common to the whole genus is given. In the case of specialist groups such as roses, the category is specified.

KEY TO pH ACIDITY SYMBOL

The majority of plants will grow in most soils. Those that require acid soil are highlighted with this symbol (see p.12).

PH   *Requires acid soil*

UNDERSTANDING HARDINESS

Hardiness is a measure of a plant's ability to survive and grow under local environmental conditions, especially winter cold. The United States Department of Agriculture has produced a map of 11 hardiness zones based on average annual minimum temperatures recorded from 1974 to 1986; this hardiness map appears on the endpapers of this book. Knowing your region's hardiness zone is a very useful guide and can help you determine if a plant will grow in your garden. However, many other factors, such as summer heat and humidity, soil fertility and drainage, and protection from strong winds, also influence plant hardiness. Many plants will grow beyond their listed hardiness zones if they are provided with extra winter protection, or if other care is taken to modify its environment.

BOTANICAL AND COMMON PLANT NAMES •
Below each plant's botanical name is the common name or, if none exists, the generic name.

SYMBOLS FOR •
LIGHT LEVEL, HARDINESS, AND ACIDITY
Light level and hardiness are given for all plants. The pH symbol appears only if a plant requires acid soil (see boxes).

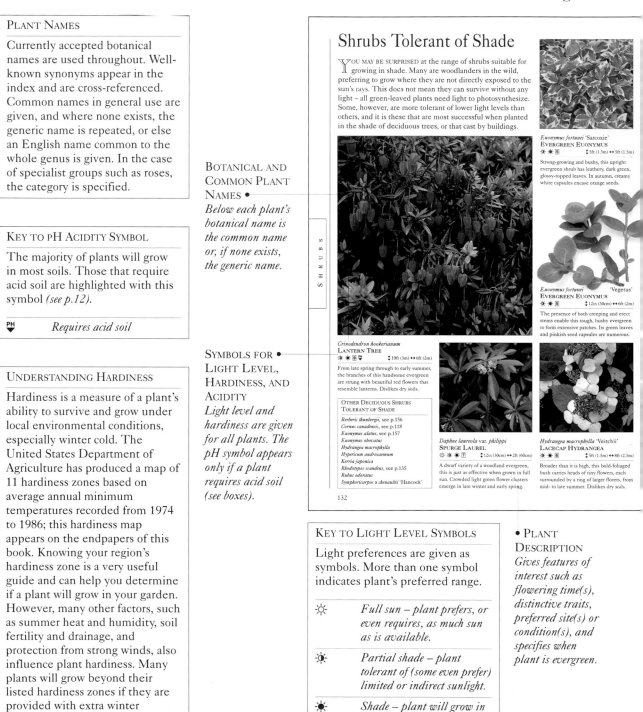

Shrubs Tolerant of Shade

YOU MAY BE SURPRISED at the range of shrubs suitable for growing in shade. Many are woodlanders in the wild, preferring to grow where they are not directly exposed to the sun's rays. This does not mean they can survive without any light – all green-leaved plants need light to photosynthesize. Some, however, are more tolerant of lower light levels than others, and it is these that are most successful when planted in the shade of deciduous trees, or that cast by buildings.

Euonymus fortunei 'Sarcoxie'
EVERGREEN EUONYMUS
☼ ☀ 5 ‡ 5ft (1.5m) ↔ 5ft (1.5m)
Strong-growing and bushy, this upright evergreen shrub has leathery, dark green, glossy-topped leaves. In autumn, creamy white capsules encase orange seeds.

Crinodendron hookerianum
LANTERN TREE
☼ ☀ 9 PH ‡ 10ft (3m) ↔ 6ft (2m)
From late spring through to early summer, the branches of this handsome evergreen are strung with beautiful red flowers that resemble lanterns. Dislikes dry soils.

Euonymus fortunei 'Vegetus'
EVERGREEN EUONYMUS
☼ ☀ 5 ‡ 12in (30cm) ↔ 6ft (2m)
The presence of both creeping and erect stems enable this tough, bushy evergreen to form extensive patches. Its green leaves and pinkish seed capsules are numerous.

OTHER DECIDUOUS SHRUBS TOLERANT OF SHADE
Berberis thunbergii, see p.156
Cornus canadensis, see p.118
Euonymus alatus, see p.157
Euonymus obovatus
Hydrangea macrophylla
Hypericum androsaemum
Kerria japonica
Rhodotypos scandens, see p.135
Rubus odoratus
Symphoricarpos x chenaultii 'Hancock'

Daphne laureola var. *philippi*
SPURGE LAUREL
☼ ☀ 7 ‡ 12in (30cm) ↔ 2ft (60cm)
A dwarf variety of a woodland evergreen, this is just as effective when grown in full sun. Crowded light green flower clusters emerge in late winter and early spring.

Hydrangea macrophylla 'Veitchii'
LACECAP HYDRANGEA
☼ ☀ 6 ‡ 5ft (1.5m) ↔ 8ft (2.5m)
Broader than it is high, this bold-foliaged bush carries heads of tiny flowers, each surrounded by a ring of larger florets, from mid- to late summer. Dislikes dry soils.

132

• PLANT DESCRIPTION
Gives features of interest such as flowering time(s), distinctive traits, preferred site(s) or condition(s), and specifies when plant is evergreen.

KEY TO LIGHT LEVEL SYMBOLS

Light preferences are given as symbols. More than one symbol indicates plant's preferred range.

☼   *Full sun – plant prefers, or even requires, as much sun as is available.*

☀   *Partial shade – plant tolerant of (some even prefer) limited or indirect sunlight.*

☀   *Shade – plant will grow in a site receiving low light, such as under a tree canopy.*

PLANT DIMENSIONS

Plant dimensions vary depending on growing conditions. Sizes are a guide to ultimate size in average conditions. The height includes flowering stems in perennials.

↕	*Average height*
↔	*Average spread*
↕↔	*Average height and spread*

NOTE ON ANNUALS

Hardiness zones are not given for annuals, because most are grown for one season and then die. Many, however, produce seeds that over-winter and germinate the following spring, or germinate in autumn and overwinter as small plants. Others are tender perennials that may be overwintered and planted out again in spring, or started from cuttings.

WHAT IS A PERENNIAL?

I have defined perennials in this book as nonwoody plants that live for several to many years. Most are herbaceous, dying down below ground level usually in winter; some are evergreen, retaining their foliage throughout the winter months. A few, such as bamboos for example, do have woody stems and evergreen leaves.

WHAT IS A CLIMBER?

Plants that are grown to climb in a variety of ways, such as into or over trees and shrubs, or trained to cover walls, fences, and other structures, are considered climbers here. The most commonly grown climbers are woody-stemmed perennials or shrubs that are trained. Climbers may be evergreen, deciduous, or even herbaceous.

WHAT IS A SHRUB?

Shrubs are woody plants, often with a bushy habit, that usually produce more than one main stem. Many are capable of reaching heights and spreads in excess of 10ft (3m). They may be evergreen or deciduous, depending on the species. Subshrubs have a woody base, but their top growth is often killed by cold.

WHAT IS A CONIFER?

Conifers are a botanically distinct group of primitive woody plants. Most are trees, typically with a single upright stem or main leader, but myriad smaller, shrubby kinds include dwarf and slow-growing selections. A minority – always stated in the text – are deciduous; the majority are evergreen with needlelike or scalelike leaves.

WHAT IS A TREE?

A tree is a woody plant that has a single main stem supporting an elevated crown of branches. Most trees grow in this way naturally, but others produce several main stems, and they will consequently develop a bushy habit that can be changed if preferred by careful pruning and training when the tree is young. Trees may be deciduous or evergreen.

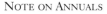

SHRUBS TOLERANT OF SHADE

Hydrangea serrata 'Bluebird'
LACECAP HYDRANGEA
☀ ☀ 6   ↕ 4ft (1.2m) ↔ 5ft (1.5m)

The pointed leaves of this dense, bushy shrub often color well in autumn. Violet-blue, lacecap flowers in summer have pale marginal florets. Dislikes dry soils.

Pachysandra terminalis
JAPANESE SPURGE
☀ ☀ 4   ↕ 4in (10cm) ↔ 8in (20cm)

This evergreen, suckering shrublet likes moist soils and makes a superb ground-cover for shade. Its dark green leaves back little white flower spikes in spring.

Skimmia japonica 'Fructu-albo'
SKIMMIA
☀ ☀ 7   ↕ 30in (75cm) ↔ 30in (75cm)

This spring-flowering cultivar will produce an abundance of white berries if you plant a male variety of this dense, low evergreen nearby to effect pollination.

• HEIGHT AND SPREAD
Gives the average ultimate size of the plant, in imperial and metric.

Lonicera pileata
SHRUBBY HONEYSUCKLE
☀ ☀ 6   ↕ 24in (60cm) ↔ 6ft (2m)

Its low and wide-spreading habit makes this an excellent evergreen groundcover. Tiny, inconspicuous, late spring flowers are occasionally followed by violet berries.

Prunus laurocerasus 'Otto Luyken'
CHERRY LAUREL
☀ ☀ 6   ↕ 3ft (1m) ↔ 6ft (2m)

The branches of this low evergreen shrub are clothed with narrow, glossy, leathery leaves. Erect spikes of white flowers in late spring are followed by black fruits.

SHRUBS

• THUMB MARKER
Identifies each of the five sections in the book (see right).

Mahonia nervosa
CASCADES MAHONIA
☀ ☀ 6 ♥   ↕ 24in (60cm) ↔ 3ft (1m)

This evergreen, suckering shrub produces short, erect stems with handsome leaves that turn red or purplish in winter. Spikes of yellow flowers appear in early summer.

OTHER EVERGREEN SHRUBS
TOLERANT OF SHADE
Aucuba japonica
x *Fatshedera lizei*, see p.144
Fatsia japonica, see p.111
Ilex crenata
Osmanthus heterophyllus
Rhododendron catawbiense
Rubus tricolor
Ruscus hypoglossum
Sarcococca hookeriana var. *humilis*
Viburnum davidii, see p.119

Vinca major 'Variegata'
VARIEGATED LARGE PERIWINKLE
☀ ☀ 7   ↕ 12in (30cm) ↔ 5ft (1.5m)

Striking, variegated leaves are margined creamy white and form a superb ground-cover that is rampant if unchecked. Blue flowers last from spring to autumn.

133

OTHER PLANTS •
Lists more plants suitable for the site or effect, with page references given for those illustrated elsewhere in other parts of the book.

SPECIAL NOTES FOR TREES CHAPTER

Prunus serotina
BLACK CHERRY
☀ ☀ 3   Moderate growth   ↕ 50ft (15m) ↔ 43ft (13m)

This free-growing tree has an oval crown of pendulous or arching branches. Its deep green, glossy leaves are deciduous, becoming yellow or red in autumn. Small white spring flowers are carried in drooping tassels, and give way to shining black fruits.

TREES

• TREE ARTWORK
Shows typical shape of mature tree. Bare branches indicate tree is deciduous, full leaf that it is evergreen.

• GROWTH RATE
This is given as either vigorous, moderate, or slow.

215

P E R E N N I A L S C L I M B E R S S H R U B S C O N I F E R S T R E E S

Soil Guide

THE SIZE and proportion of clay, sand, or silt particles present in your garden soil influence its chemical and physical nature. They make it either heavy (wet and poorly drained), or light (dry and free-draining), and thus determine what plants will thrive on it. Its pH value, a measure of acidity or alkalinity, is measured on a scale of 1 to 14. Below neutral (7), soils are progressively acid; above neutral, they are progressively alkaline (limy). You can determine what type of soil you have by looking at the color, feeling the texture, and observing what kind of plants will grow on it or, if you prefer, by doing a soil test.

AVERAGE ideal for *Forsythia*

Different cultivation requirements and variable local conditions make average soil hard to define. Usually, it is moist but well-drained, with a reasonable humus content, neutral to slightly acid pH, and suits the widest range of plants.

HEAVY CLAY ideal for *Berberis*

Minute clay particles stick together, making clay soils slow-draining after rain, sticky, and likely to bake hard in hot sun. Often highly fertile, they can be improved by draining or by adding grit or coarse organic matter.

SANDY ideal for *Potentilla*
Sand particles are much larger than clay particles, making sandy soils light, free-draining, and quick to warm up in spring. Some plants may need frequent irrigation and feeding, though fertility can be improved by adding organic matter.

ACID ideal for *Rhododendron*

Peaty or acid soils are generally dark, and rich in organic matter. Acid in nature and moisture-retentive, they are favored by plants not tolerant of alkaline soil and can be made more free-draining by adding coarse sand.

ALKALINE ideal for *Kolkwitzia*

Limy or alkaline soils are usually pale, shallow, and stony. Free-draining, they warm up quickly in spring and are moderately fertile. Like sandy soils, they benefit from the addition of organic matter.

Sunlight Guide

Ｐ LANTS NEED SUNLIGHT to photosynthesize, so receiving the proper light
level is crucial to plant growth and health.
Many plants are flexible in their light needs,
preferring one situation but tolerating
another. Most thrive when open to the sky.

• THE SUN'S POSITION
The position of the sun varies during
the year. In midwinter, the sun is
lower and the shadows much longer.
In the height of summer, the sun is
high and the shadows are short.

FULL SUN •

Oak ▷

◁ Birch

PARTIAL SHADE •

SHADE •

☼ FULL SUN
Open to the sun for the greater part of the day, fully
sunny sites are not subject to shade cast by trees or
buildings. Numerous garden plants grown for their
flowering display, including many perennials, annuals,
and shrubs *(see above)*, prefer sunny sites. Sun and
warmth ripen woody growth, encouraging flowering
and fruiting. Many plants at their best in full sun will
also tolerate a degree of shade, such as that found near
buildings and on the edge of woodland.

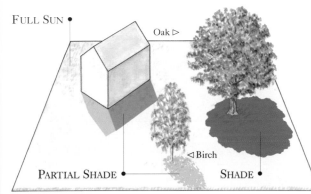

☀ PARTIAL SHADE
Sites in partial shade are subject to reduced light. They
are found near buildings that block direct sunlight, but
do not hide the sky above. Partial shade is also found
in the lee of, if not directly beneath, trees such as birch
(Betula), which cast a light, dappled shade. If the soil is
moist, these conditions suit many plants, some of
which may also be tolerant of full sun or even heavier
shade. Numerous foliage perennials, and those found
naturally in woodland sites *(see above)* thrive best here.

☀ SHADE
This defines sites subject to permanent shade or shade
during the main growing season (summer). Such sites
may be closely surrounded by tall buildings or, more
usually, beneath or in the lee of dense-canopied trees.
Even here, the degree of shade varies. If combined
with dry or compacted soil, such as that often found
beneath large conifers or similar evergreen trees, the
choice of suitable underplanting is limited to the few
shade-tolerant plants growing in such sites in the wild.

PERENNIALS

IF TREES AND SHRUBS form the bones of a garden, then perennials provide its flesh, forming the bulk of border plants and groundcover. No other plant group offers such great variety of form, flower, and foliage, from tiny rock plants to large bamboos. This section includes bulbs (with tubers and corms), and annual or biennial plants.

△ *Oenothera speciosa* 'Rosea'

△ SUN LOVING *The bold flowerheads of a superb spurge,* Euphorbia characias *subsp.* wulfenii, *enjoy a place in the sun.*

THE BEAUTY OF PERENNIALS

- Provide massed effects in borders.
- Bold single specimens or groups can create special effects in lawns.
- Ideal for carpeting rock gardens and screes, or draping retaining walls.
- Provide mass impact as spring bulbs.
- Ideal as groundcover beneath trees.
- Perfect for planting in containers for terraces, patios, or courtyards.
- Annuals or biennials give fast results.
- Offer striking waterside or bog plants.

Some perennials have evergreen foliage, which gives year-round interest, but most are herbaceous, dying to below ground level, usually in winter. Unless otherwise stated, all plants in this section are herbaceous. The pleasurable anticipation associated with their annual re-emergence is something of which we never tire, and makes them all the more exciting and valuable in the garden.

PLANTS FOR EFFECT

For many gardeners, no finer sight exists than that of a perennial bed at its best in summer. Whether we are inspired by Gertrude Jekyll's plant associations, or prefer a more haphazard mix of color, perennials abound to suit every taste. When

planting borders, foliage impact is just as important as floral display, and it is worth remembering the beautiful, nostalgic pictures that are possible in winter when certain dead seedheads are spared.

PLANTS FOR ALL PLACES

Warm, sunny sites in the garden are ideal for growing those perennials that enjoy hot, dry conditions in the wild. The abundance of plants thriving in such situations are best planted in raised beds or beneath sunny walls in cooler areas. To take advantage of shady places, consider plants native to woodland. Ferns, spring-flowering perennials, and bulbous plants such as trilliums and miniature cyclamen tolerate shade and form attractive groundcover.

△ SHADE CARPET *Miniature cyclamen* (Cyclamen repandum) *form a lovely spring carpet in a beech tree's shade.*

◁ WINTER BEAUTY *The elegance of dead seedheads and leaves in winter is further enhanced when they are coated with frost.*

▷ EARLY SUMMER SPECTACLE *This cottage garden border boasts a glorious mix of perennials, annuals, and biennials.*

Tall Perennials for the Backs of Borders

TALL PERENNIALS lend a feeling of permanence to a border, while their size alone guarantees attention. Even a small bed or border is enhanced by at least one. With few exceptions, clump-formers should be supported to prevent the stems from becoming splayed in windy weather. It is best to do this staking well before the stems are fully developed.

Eremurus himalaicus
FOXTAIL LILY
☼ 5　　　↕ 7ft (2.2m) ↔ 3ft (1m)

Clumps of strap-shaped leaves fade early in summer as dense spires of starry white flowers develop. A spectacular plant that thrives best in well-drained soils.

Aruncus dioicus
GOATSBEARD
☼ ☼ 3　　　↕ 6ft (2m) ↔ 4ft (1.2m)

Goatsbeard is worth growing for its bold mounds of leaves. These, however, are topped by equally striking plumes of tiny, creamy white flowers in midsummer.

Delphinium 'Fanfare'
DELPHINIUM
☼ 2　　　↕ 6ft (2m) ↔ 30in (75cm)

One of many cultivars differing in color, this bears tall, imposing spikes of semi-double flowers in summer. It thrives in rich, deep soils, and must be staked.

Eupatorium purpureum
JOE PYE WEED
☼ 4　　　↕ 7ft (2.2m) ↔ 3ft (1m)

Erect, leafy stems are crowned with dense, flattened heads of small, pinkish purple flowers in late summer and autumn. These are appreciated by bees and butterflies.

Campanula lactiflora
'Prichard's Variety'
☼ ☼ 5　　　↕ 4½ft (1.4m) ↔ 30in (75cm)

Clumps of upright, leafy stems sport heads crowded with bell-shaped, violet-blue flowers from summer into early autumn. Will naturalize, even in rough grass.

Echinops sphaerocephalus
GLOBE THISTLE
☼ 3　　　↕ 6ft (1.8m) ↔ 3½ft (1.1m)

The deeply cut, prickle-toothed leaves are green on the top and gray beneath. Popular with bees and butterflies, Globe Thistle supports globular flowerheads in summer.

Helianthus x multiflorus
PERENNIAL SUNFLOWER
☼ 4   ↕ 5½ft (1.7m) ↔ 3ft (1m)

This erect, leafy plant produces branched heads of large, rich yellow, daisylike flowers in late summer and early autumn. It will spread to form large patches in time.

OTHER TALL GRASSES

Arundo donax
Arundo donax 'Variegata'
Calamagrostis epigejos 'Hortorum'
Chionochloa conspicua
Cortaderia selloana 'Carnea'
Cortaderia selloana 'Sunningdale
  Silver', see p.18
Miscanthus sinensis 'Grosse Fontäne'
Miscanthus sinensis 'Morning Light'
Miscanthus sinensis 'Silberfeder'
Stipa gigantea, see p.19

Lavatera cachemiriana
LAVATERA
☼ 6   ↕ 5½ft (1.7m) ↔ 4½ft (1.4m)

A loosely branched perennial with slender stems and downy, semievergreen leaves. Its large pink mallow flowers are carried continuously throughout summer.

Miscanthus sinensis
'Zebrinus'
☼ 4   ↕ 5ft (1.5m) ↔ 5ft (1.5m)

This bold, clump-forming grass requires plenty of space to show off its elegant, arching, cream-banded green leaves. Fan-shaped flower spikes develop in autumn.

OTHER TALL PERENNIALS

Aster tataricus
Cimicifuga racemosa
Cimicifuga simplex, see p.32
Crambe cordifolia, see p.18
Cynara cardunculus, see p.18
Eryngium eburneum
Filipendula rubra
Helianthus salicifolius
Inula magnifica, see p.19
Rudbeckia 'Herbstsonne'
Verbascum olympicum, see p.73

Helianthus x multiflorus 'Loddon Gold'
PERENNIAL SUNFLOWER
☼ 4   ↕ 5ft (1.5m) ↔ 30in (75cm)

Numerous double flowers of a golden yellow are produced in loosely branched heads from late summer and into early autumn. Will form patches in time.

Macleaya microcarpa
'Kelway's Coral Plume'
☼ 3   ↕ 7ft (2.2m) ↔ 4ft (1.2m)

Spectacular clumps of boldly lobed leaves, gray-green above and whitish beneath, are topped in summer by plumes of pinkish buff flowers. These are darker in bud.

Rudbeckia laciniata 'Goldquelle'
RUDBECKIA
☼ 4   ↕ 6ft (2m) ↔ 30in (75cm)

This erect perennial is strong-growing. Bright yellow double flowers with green centers appear among leafy green foliage from late summer and into autumn.

Bold Perennials for Specimen Planting

SOME PERENNIALS are so striking in flower or foliage, or both, that it is worth planting them as a special feature. A small bed surrounded by paving or gravel will show off a single specimen, but where space and scale permit, a group will create an even more spectacular display. Choose evergreens if a year-round effect is desired.

Cortaderia selloana 'Sunningdale Silver'
PAMPAS GRASS
☼ 7 ↕ 8ft (2.5m) ↔ 5ft (1.5m)

A most popular ornamental grass, with tall, silky plumes of creamy white spikelets from late summer. The leaves are razor-edged and require careful handling.

Acanthus spinosus
BEAR'S BREECHES
☼ 6-7 ↕ 4ft (1.2m) ↔ 3½ft (1.1m)

Lush clumps of dark green, spine-toothed leaves are topped in summer with prickly spires of mauve and white hooded flowers. It will spread freely in some soils.

Beschorneria yuccoides
BESCHORNERIA
☼ 9 ↕ 6ft (2m) ↔ 10ft (3m)

This succulent evergreen, perfect in warm sites, will form huge, yuccalike clumps of spine-tipped leaves. Its tubular summer flowers are held on stout red stems.

Crambe cordifolia
CRAMBE
☼ 6 ↕ 6ft (2m) ↔ 5ft (1.5m)

Attractive mounds of wavy-edged leaves are almost eclipsed when the clouds of small, fragrant white flowers appear in summer. Good drainage is desirable.

OTHER SPECIMEN PERENNIALS

Aralia cachemirica
Arundo donax
Cynara scolymus 'Glauca'
Dierama pulcherrimum, see p.81
Eryngium decaisneanum
Eryngium eburneum
Euphorbia characias 'Lambrook Gold'
Ferula tingitana
Filipendula kamtschatica
Filipendula purpurea, see p.46
Kniphofia cultivars
Ligularia dentata 'Othello'
Osmunda regalis
Paeonia species and cultivars
Peltiphyllum peltatum, see p.47
Phormium tenax 'Purpureum'
Rodgersia pinnata 'Superba'
Yucca gloriosa, see p.67
Yucca recurvifolia

Chusquea culeou
CHILEAN BAMBOO
☼ ☼ ☼ 8 ↕ 15ft (5m) ↔ 8ft (2.5m)

A bold, distinctive bamboo with shining evergreen leaves. Huge clumps of green canes with pale sheaths create a striking banded effect. It forms colonies in time.

Cynara cardunculus
CARDOON
☼ 7 ↕ 6ft (2m) ↔ 4½ft (1.4m)

This perennial, with attractive silver-gray leaves, is as spectacular as its relative, the Globe Artichoke. The thistlelike summer flowers have wickedly spiny bracts.

Gunnera manicata
GUNNERA
☼ 7   ↕ 7ft (2.2m) ↔ 7ft (2.2m)

This striking perennial is excellent for
watersides since it enjoys moist, fertile
soils. Huge leaves rise above furry crowns,
which need protection in cold winters.

Hedychium densiflorum
GINGER LILY
☼ 10   ↕ 5ft (1.5m) ↔ 30in (75cm)

A member of the ginger family, this plant,
with exotic, lance-shaped leaves, produces
fragrant flower spikes in late summer. It is
ideal for moist, well-drained soils.

Inula magnifica
INULA
☼ 3   ↕ 6ft (2m) ↔ 3½ft (1.1m)

This stout perennial, which has upright,
hairy stems and bold leaves, may need
some support. The large, daisylike yellow
flowerheads occur in late summer.

OTHER SPECIMEN BAMBOOS
Fargesia nitida *Fargesia spathacea* *Phyllostachys nigra* *Semiarundinaria fastuosa* *Thamnocalamus tessellatus*

Rodgersia aesculifolia
RODGERSIA
☼ ☼ 5   ↕ 4ft (1.2m) ↔ 3ft (1m)

Excellent for planting near watersides,
the rough-stalked leaves are divided into
leaflets, bronze at first, later green. It has
plumes of fragrant midsummer flowers.

Rheum palmatum 'Atrosanguineum'
ORNAMENTAL RHUBARB
☼ 4   ↕ 6ft (2m) ↔ 6ft (2m)

The large, boldly lobed leaves of this
perennial are its main ornamental feature.
In early summer they are dwarfed by
impressive heads of crimson flowers.

Stipa gigantea
GIANT, OR GOLDEN, OATS
☼ 7   ↕ 5½ft (1.7m) ↔ 4½ft (1.4m)

A lovely ornamental grass with clumps of
narrow leaves, and pretty golden spikelets
with awns in summer. The sun-bleached
seed husks are an additional attraction.

Medium-height Perennials

SOME OF THE MOST ATTRACTIVE and popular perennials are found in the height range of 2–4ft (60–120cm). These plants can be used to excellent effect as companions for taller perennials or shrubs in mixed plantings, or as groups or drifts in their own right. Some are so spectacular in foliage that they are well worth planting as specimens. Many of the plants in this range are sturdy and self-supporting, but those with slender stems carrying large or heavy heads of flowers may require some staking to prevent them from splaying out in the wind.

Galega orientalis
GALEGA
☼ 5   ↕ 4ft (1.2m) ↔ 30in (75cm)

A compact, bushy perennial with erect stems and attractive, rich green leaves. Spikes of violet pea flowers occur in early summer. It spreads in suitable conditions.

Aconitum x *cammarum* 'Bicolor'
MONKSHOOD
☼ ☼ 3   ↕ 4ft (1.2m) ↔ 20in (50cm)

Although poisonous, monkshoods have long been valued in the garden. This handsome hybrid bears striking heads of violet-blue and white summer flowers.

Chrysanthemum 'Clara Curtis'
KOREAN CHRYSANTHEMUM
☼ 4   ↕ 30in (75cm) ↔ 18in (45cm)

This bushy perennial flowers all through summer and autumn. It has aromatic leaves and masses of beautiful, daisylike flowers. Divide every few years.

PERENNIALS GROWN FOR BOTH FLOWERS AND FOLIAGE

Acanthus hungaricus
Astilbe 'Ostrich Plume', see p.90
Euphorbia griffithii 'Dixter'
Gentiana lutea, see p.87
Hosta 'Tall Boy'
Persicaria campanulata
Phlomis russeliana
Phlox paniculata 'Harlequin'
Polygonatum odoratum 'Variegatum'
Rodgersia pinnata 'Superba'

Baptisia australis
FALSE INDIGO
☼ 3   ↕ 4ft (1.2m) ↔ 24in (60cm)

Pretty blue-green foliage in early summer turns gray, then green later. Spikes of summer pea flowers are replaced by seed pods, ideal for dried winter decorations.

Geranium psilostemon
CRANESBILL
☼ 5   ↕ 4ft (1.2m) ↔ 4ft (1.2m)

Magenta flowers with black eyes create a spectacular effect in midsummer. The long-stalked, deeply cut leaves will often color richly in autumn. Needs support.

Heliopsis 'Light of Loddon'
HELIOPSIS

☼ ③   ↕ 4½ft (1.4m) ↔ 30in (75cm)

This erect perennial has branched heads of rich orange dahlia-like flowers that last for weeks during late summer and early autumn. Its toothed leaves are dark green.

Lupinus 'Inverewe Red'
LUPINE

☼ ③   ↕ 3½ft (1.1m) ↔ 24in (60cm)

Bold perennial with beautifully fingered leaves and erect, cylindrical spikes of red pea flowers in early summer. There are many other cultivars of varying colors.

Penstemon 'Garnet'
BEARDTONGUE

☼ ④   ↕ 26in (65cm) ↔ 24in (60cm)

One of the hardiest and most reliable of a colorful genus. It bears narrow, semi-evergreen leaves and spires of red flowers from midsummer to early autumn.

Hemerocallis 'Golden Chimes'
DAYLILY

☼ ③   ↕ 30in (75cm) ↔ 24in (60cm)

From early to midsummer, thin branched heads of golden yellow trumpet flowers are carried above bold clumps of grasslike leaves. Each flower lasts for one day.

Lythrum virgatum 'The Rocket'
PURPLE LOOSESTRIFE

☼ ③   ↕ 3ft (1m) ↔ 18in (45cm)

Erect clumps of slender, leafy stems bear long spikes of rich rose-red flowers in summer. This plant thrives in rich, moist soils, and may invade natural areas.

Sidalcea 'William Smith'
GREEK MALLOW

☼ ⑤   ↕ 4ft (1.2m) ↔ 3ft (1m)

Worthy of widespread use, this perennial has handsome clumps of deeply cut leaves and erect stems bearing warm salmon-pink mallow flowers in summer.

Kniphofia 'Percy's Pride'
RED-HOT POKER

☼ ⑥   ↕ 3ft (1m) ↔ 24in (60cm)

Dense, pokerlike spikes of canary yellow flowers rise above clumps of strap-shaped leaves in late summer. A striking plant to brighten a border late in the season.

Paeonia 'Bowl of Beauty'
PEONY

☼ ③   ↕ 3ft (1m) ↔ 3ft (1m)

Huge pink flowers with cream petaloids are borne above lush clumps of leaves in early summer. The leaves of this peony color well in autumn. Needs support.

OTHER MEDIUM-HEIGHT PERENNIALS

Aster cordifolius 'Silver Spray'
Centaurea pulcherrima
Echinacea purpurea 'Robert Bloom'
Gillenia trifoliata
Knautia macedonica
Linaria purpurea 'Canon J. Went'
Phlox maculata 'Omega', see p.77
Salvia nemorosa 'May Night'
Veronica spicata 'Romiley Purple', see p.49

Medium to Large Annuals and Biennials

HOWEVER THOROUGHLY you plant a bed or border, you can be sure that gaps will occur. Plants may fail or grow more slowly than expected, so you are left with unwanted spaces. An ideal solution is to fill these gaps with a temporary display of annuals or biennials to tide you over until the permanent planting makes good, or dead plants are replaced.

Consolida ambigua
LARKSPUR
☼ ↕ 4ft (1.2m) ↔ 12in (30cm)

Larkspur is a robust, free-growing annual with finely divided, feathery foliage and erect spikes of spurred summer flowers, in white or shades of pink and blue.

Alcea rosea
HOLLYHOCK
☼ 3 ↕ 6ft (2m) ↔ 24in (60cm)

This biennial herb is a long-standing cottage garden favorite. Its spikes of large saucer-shaped flowers tower above bold foliage in summer and early autumn.

Amaranthus caudatus
LOVE-LIES-BLEEDING
☼ ↕ 4ft (1.2m) ↔ 18in (45cm)

Striking tassels crowded with tiny red flowers drape the branches of this robust, bushy annual from summer into autumn. The large leaves are a light green color.

OTHER LARGE ANNUALS
Amaranthus caudatus 'Viridis'
Amaranthus tricolor 'Illumination'
Atriplex hortensis var. *rubra*, see p.88
Celosia 'Apricot Brandy'
Centaurea cyanus
Cosmos 'Sensation'
Helianthus 'Italian White'
Impatiens balsamina
Mirabilis jalapa
Nicotiana alata 'Grandiflora'
Perilla frutescens
Ricinus communis
Salvia farinacea 'Victoria'
Salvia splendens
Tagetes erecta
Tithonia rotundifolia 'Torch'
Verbena patagonica, see p.37
Zea mays 'Gracillima Variegata'
Zinnia Zenith Series

Cleome hassleriana 'Colour Fountain'
SPIDER FLOWER
☼ ↕ 4ft (1.2m) ↔ 24in (60cm)

This bushy annual has elegant, fingered leaves held on long stalks. In summer, each stem is crowned by a loose, spidery head of narrow-petaled flowers.

Digitalis purpurea 'Sutton's Apricot'
FOXGLOVE
☼ 4 ↕ 5ft (1.5m) ↔ 18in (45cm)

Tall spikes of nodding, bell-shaped flowers rise from bold rosettes of crinkly leaves in summer. 'Sutton's Apricot' is a lovely selection of a popular biennial.

Papaver somniferum
OPIUM POPPY

☼   ↕ 30in (75cm) ↔ 12in (30cm)

Both the stems and foliage of this lush, leafy, fast-growing annual have a grayish tint. Its large summer flowers are available in pink, red, purple, or white.

Papaver somniferum
Peony-flowered Series

☼   ↕ 30in (75cm) ↔ 12in (30cm)

The large, rounded flowers of this most spectacular selection resemble peonies and have frilled, crowded petals. This popular annual comes in a range of colors.

OTHER LARGE BIENNIALS

Alcea rosea 'Chater's Double'
Campanula medium
Digitalis Excelsior Hybrids
Digitalis purpurea f. *alba*
Hesperis matronalis, see p.77
Lunaria annua var. *alba*
Matthiola 'Giant Excelsior'
Onopordum acanthium
Rudbeckia hirta
Silybum marianum, see p.89
Smyrnium perfoliatum

Lunaria annua 'Variegata'
VARIEGATED MONEY PLANT

☼ ☼ 4   ↕ 30in (75cm) ↔ 24in (60cm)

This vigorous biennial is worth growing for its leaves alone. Its purplish flowers in spring and early summer are followed by attractive, disklike seed capsules.

Eryngium giganteum 'Silver Ghost'
MISS WILLMOTT'S GHOST

☼ 4   ↕ 4ft (1.2m) ↔ 30in (75cm)

This striking upright biennial has heart-shaped basal leaves and stiff, silvery stems with prickly leaves. These support domed summer flowerheads on a ruff of bracts.

Nicotiana langsdorfii
FLOWERING TOBACCO

☼   ↕ 5ft (1.5m) ↔ 24in (60cm)

Leafy at its base, this ornamental flowering tobacco is an elegant annual that bears many small, drooping, pale green, bell-shaped flowers from summer into autumn.

Salvia sclarea var. *turkestanica*
CLARY SAGE

☼ 5   ↕ 30in (75cm) ↔ 24in (60cm)

Clary sage, a fast-growing biennial with bold rosettes of downy, aromatic leaves, is topped by branching stems with clusters of small lavender-purple summer flowers.

Small Perennials for Fronts of Borders, and Small Beds

SOME OF THE MOST GORGEOUS and reliable perennials fall in the small-size range, with flowering stems in the region of 24in (60cm) or less. They are ideally suited for planting in groups, or alone where space is limited, as it is in smaller beds. They can be equally valuable for fronting taller perennials or even shrubs in large beds and borders. All the following are relatively easy to cultivate, and many have both attractive flowers and foliage.

Digitalis x *mertonensis*
STRAWBERRY FOXGLOVE
☼ ☼ ③   ‡ 30in (75cm) ↔ 12in (30cm)

This unusual foxglove bears erect stems that carry full spikes of nodding, rose-mauve summer flowers over clumps of soft, hairy evergreen leaves.

Astilbe simplicifolia 'Sprite'
ASTILBE
☼ ③   ‡ 20in (50cm) ↔ 24in (60cm)

Low clumps of divided, glossy leaves are topped by feathery plumes of tiny star-shaped summer flowers. Thrives in soils that do not dry out in summer.

Coreopsis verticillata
THREADLEAF COREOPSIS
☼ ③   ‡ 20in (50cm) ↔ 12in (30cm)

The erect stems of this cheerful, highly reliable perennial are clothed with finely divided, feathery leaves. Its bright yellow flowers appear throughout summer.

Buphthalmum salicifolium
YELLOW OX-EYE
☼ ③   ‡ 24in (60cm) ↔ 3ft (1m)

Bright yellow daisylike flowers top loose clumps of hairy stems with narrow leaves throughout summer. Yellow Ox-eye may require support, especially in a windy site.

OTHER SMALL FLOWERING PERENNIALS

Aster lateriflorus 'Horizontalis'
Astrantia maxima
Brunnera macrophylla
Dianthus gratianopolitanus 'Tiny Rubies'
Dicentra eximia
Epimedium x *versicolor* 'Sulphureum'
Eryngium bourgatii, see p.36
Geranium sanguineum var. *striatum*, see p.28
Helleborus argutifolius
x *Heucherella alba* 'Bridget Bloom'
Iris cristata
Lathyrus vernus
Liatris spicata 'Kobold'
Penstemon 'Apple Blossom'
Primula vulgaris
Sedum 'Vera Jameson'

Erysimum 'Bowles Mauve'
PERENNIAL WALLFLOWER
☼ ⑦   ‡ 24in (60cm) ↔ 3ft (1m)

One of the best little evergreen perennials for sunny sites, this produces tall flower spikes above blue-gray foliage over an extended period from early spring.

Euphorbia polychroma
CUSHION SPURGE
☼ 4 ↕ 20in (50cm) ↔ 20in (50cm)

A reliable, justifiably popular perennial, this forms low mounds of leafy stems, and star-shaped yellow flowerheads lasting for several weeks in spring.

Omphalodes cappadocica
BLUE-EYED MARY
☼ 6 ↕ 8in (20cm) ↔ 12in (30cm)

Loose sprays of rich blue, forget-me-not flowers appear among low tufts of neat, oval leaves from spring into early summer. Prefers soils that are moist in summer.

Geranium 'Johnson's Blue'
CRANESBILL
☼ 4 ↕ 12in (30cm) ↔ 24in (60cm)

This outstanding perennial forms clumps of long-stalked, deeply divided leaves. Its branched lavender-blue flowerheads are produced in summer.

> **OTHER SMALL FOLIAGE PERENNIALS**
>
> *Alchemilla mollis*
> *Asarum europaeum*, see p.30
> *Festuca glauca* 'Elijah Blue'
> *Hakonechloa macra* 'Aureola'
> *Heuchera micrantha* 'Palace Purple', see p.74
> *Hosta* 'Kabitan'
> *Persicaria virginiana* 'Painter's Palette'
> *Pulmonaria saccharata*, see p.33
> *Stachys byzantina* 'Silver Carpet'

Schizostylis coccinea 'Sunrise'
KAFFIR LILY
☼ 7 ↕ 24in (60cm) ↔ 12in (30cm)

This relative of gladiolus has upright stems rising from clumps of grassy leaves. They carry spikes of starry flowers through autumn, sometimes into early winter.

Helichrysum 'Schweffellicht'
HELICHRYSUM
☼ 5 ↕ 20in (50cm) ↔ 12in (30cm)

In summer, the softly downy stems bear terminal clusters of fluffy, everlasting sulfur-yellow flowerheads above mats of similarly coated silver-gray leaves.

Prunella grandiflora
SELFHEAL
☼ 5 ↕ 6in (15cm) ↔ 12in (30cm)

The low, semievergreen mats of foliage provide a pleasant foil for the short, erect spikes of two-lipped, funnel-shaped purple flowers borne in summer.

Stachys macrantha 'Superba'
BETONY
☼ 2 ↕ 18in (45cm) ↔ 24in (60cm)

In summer, eye-catching spires crowded with purple-violet hooded flowers top low clumps of large, heart-shaped, prominently veined and crinkly leaves.

Small Annuals and Biennials

A RICH VARIETY of small annual and biennial plants is suitable and widely available for the garden. Many are colorful and attractive, and are especially useful for filling temporary seasonal gaps in perennial plantings. The following selection contains less familiar examples as well as some old favorites. Most are easy to grow from seed.

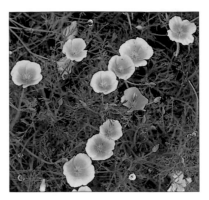

Eschscholzia californica
CALIFORNIA POPPY
☼ ↕12in (30cm) ↔6in (15cm)

This popular, fast-growing annual has blue-green, feathery leaves and cup-shaped flowers in shades of yellow, cream, orange, and red in summer and early autumn.

Brachyscome iberidifolia
SWAN RIVER DAISY
☼ ↕18in (45cm) ↔18in (45cm)

Masses of small, fragrant blue, mauve, pink, or white flowers cover this bushy, slender-stemmed annual with finely cut leaves in summer and early autumn.

Gypsophila elegans
ANNUAL BABY'S BREATH
☼ ↕24in (60cm) ↔12in (30cm)

A bushy annual, this has erect, slender stems and gray-green, paired leaves. Many tiny, white, starlike flowers form branched heads from summer into early autumn.

Agrostemma githago 'Milas'
CORN COCKLE
☼ ↕30in (75cm) ↔12in (30cm)

Slender and fast-growing, this annual has erect stems and narrow, paired leaves, and freely produces its purplish pink flowers with darker lines in summer.

Cheiranthus cheiri 'Fire King'
WALLFLOWER
☼ ☀ 7 ↕15in (38cm) ↔12in (30cm)

This evergreen perennial, commonly grown as an annual or biennial, bears fragrant spring flowers in many colors, including red, yellow, white, and orange.

Iberis amara
CANDYTUFT
☼ ↕12in (30cm) ↔6in (15cm)

Candytuft has long been an old favorite annual; it is bushy with erect stems and narrow leaves, and has flattened heads of sweet-scented white flowers in summer.

Nemophila maculata
FIVE-SPOT
☼   ↕6in (15cm) ↔ 8in (20cm)

Five-spot is a charming, spreading annual with deeply lobed leaves and a long succession of striking flowers. Each petal is purple-veined with a violet tip.

Nigella damascena 'Persian Jewels'
LOVE-IN-A-MIST
☼   ↕18in (45cm) ↔ 8in (20cm)

This slender, upright annual has feathery leaves and showy summer flowers in blue, pink, and white. Its attractive red-green seed pods, suitable for drying, follow.

Reseda odorata
SWEET MIGNONETTE
☼   ↕20in (50cm) ↔ 12in (30cm)

From summer into autumn, this upright, branching, leafy annual produces dense, conical heads of small, starry white, fragrant flowers with orange-brown stamens.

Tropaeolum majus 'Alaska'
NASTURTIUM
☼ ☼   ↕12in (30cm) ↔ 12in (30cm)

Fast-growing and bushy, this annual has fleshy stems and long-stalked, variegated leaves. Spurred red and yellow flowers last all through summer and into autumn.

OTHER SMALL ANNUALS AND BIENNIALS
Dyssodia tenuifolia
Lobularia maritima
Malcolmia maritima
Sanvitalia procumbens

Papaver rhoeas Shirley Series
SHIRLEY POPPY
☼   ↕24in (60cm) ↔ 12in (30cm)

Nodding buds in summer reveal delicate single flowers in many colors. Erect and slender-stemmed with pale green leaves, there is also a double strain of this annual.

Xeranthemum annuum (double)
IMMORTELLE
☼   ↕24in (60cm) ↔ 18in (45cm)

Heads of daisylike summer flowers, in shades of pink, mauve, purple, or white, are excellent for drying. This is an erect annual with narrow silvery leaves.

Perennials for Groundcover in Sun

THERE IS NO REASON why soil in the garden should remain bare, given the number of plants with low spreading or carpeting growth. Many of these grow well on problematic banks, and most have ornamental foliage or flowers. Some spring- or early summer-flowering plants can be trimmed after flowering to encourage a second display later in the season.

Geranium endressii 'Wargrave Pink'
CRANESBILL

☼ 4   ‡ 20in (50cm) ↔ 24in (60cm)

Of dense, leafy habit, this evergreen is free flowering. Attractively lobed leaves form a carpet above which the warm salmon pink flowers bloom throughout summer.

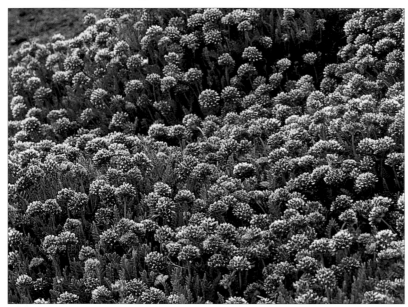

Anthyllis montana
ANTHYLLIS

☼ 5   ‡ 8in (20cm) ↔ 12in (30cm)

Prettily divided leaves create downy mats, and rounded heads of pale pink and red flowers appear in late spring and early summer. Does best in well-drained soils.

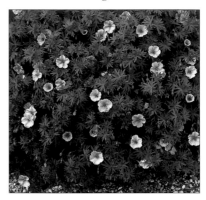

Geranium sanguineum var. *striatum*
BLOODY CRANESBILL

☼ 3   ‡ 5in (13cm) ↔ 12in (30cm)

Better known as var. *lancastriense*, this low, mound-forming perennial has small, attractively fingered leaves and pale pink flowers over many months in summer.

Cerastium tomentosum
SNOW-IN-SUMMER

☼ 2   ‡ 3in (8cm) ↔ indefinite

A reliable groundcover favorite that has carpets of silvery gray leaves and stems. Star-shaped flowers occur from late spring into summer. Invasive if conditions suit.

Asarina procumbens
CLIMBING SNAPDRAGON

☼ ☼ 6   ‡ 2in (5cm) ↔ 12in (30cm)

This softly hairy semievergreen has trailing stems, rounded leaves, and pale snapdragon flowers through summer into early autumn. It dislikes winter moisture.

OTHER PERENNIALS FOR GROUNDCOVER IN SUN

Acaena 'Blue Haze'
Achillea clavennae
Anthemis punctata subsp. *cupaniana*, see p.50
Arabis caucasica 'Rosabella', see p.54
Aubrieta 'Joy', see p.54
Euphorbia cyparissias
Euphorbia myrsinites, see p.36
Globularia cordifolia
Gypsophila repens
Hippocrepis comosa
Oenothera missouriensis
Persicaria vacciniifolia, see p.55
Phlox douglasii 'Boothman's Variety', see p.57
Potentilla alba
Prunella grandiflora, see p.25
Silene schafta

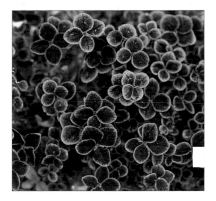

Glechoma hederacea 'Variegata'
VARIEGATED GROUND IVY
☼ 3   ↕ 6in (15cm) ↔ indefinite

The slender, trailing stems of this ground ivy form extensive carpets of heart-shaped, toothed, evergreen leaves. The flowers are small and generally hidden from view.

Persicaria affinis 'Donald Lowndes'
KNOTWEED
☼ 3   ↕ 4½in (11cm) ↔ 18in (45cm)

Dense flower spikes occur in summer and early autumn; the pink flowers darken with age. The mats of evergreen leaves will color attractively in winter when old.

Trifolium repens 'Purpurascens'
PURPLE-LEAVED CLOVER
☼ 3   ↕ 4in (10cm) ↔ 18in (45cm)

An easy and attractive form of clover worth growing for its carpets of pretty bronze or purple leaves with a bright green edge. White flowerheads are borne in summer.

Helianthemum 'Wisley Pink'
ROCK ROSE
☼ 5   ↕ 12in (30cm) ↔ 18in (45cm)

Dense evergreen carpets of gray-green leafy stems bear saucer-shaped flowers in early summer. Other cultivars in a range of flower colors are just as good.

Saponaria ocymoides
ROCK SOAPWORT
☼ 2   ↕ 2in (5cm) ↔ 18in (45cm)

A long-established favorite in the garden, reliable for its low mounds of trailing leafy stems covered in pale to dark pink flowers in summer. There is also a white form.

STONECROPS AND HOUSELEEKS

Sedum acre 'Aureum'
Sedum album 'Coral Carpet'
Sedum kamtschaticum
Sedum obtusatum
Sedum spathulifolium 'Purpureum'
Sedum spurium 'Schorbuser Blut'
Sempervivum arachniodeum
Sempervivum ciliosum
Sempervivum 'Commander Hay'
Sempervivum 'Othello'
Sempervivum tectorum

Phuopsis stylosa
CAUCASIAN CROSSWORT
☼ 6-7   ↕ 12in (30cm) ↔ 24in (60cm)

The stems and foliage of this plant form low mounds and have a pungent aroma. Its small summer flowers, however, have a sweet scent. Vigorous once established.

Veronica peduncularis 'Georgia Blue'
CAUCASIAN SPEEDWELL
☼ ☼ 6   ↕ 5in (13cm) ↔ 18in (45cm)

A fast-creeping perennial with wiry stems and tiny evergreen leaves, bronze-purple when young. Flowers plaster the growth in spring, and often again later in the year.

Perennials for Ground-cover in Shade

A SHADY SITE will support a wide selection of perennials, including many that make ideal groundcover, providing that it is not in the dry shade of an evergreen canopy, nor filled by tree roots. To cover an area quickly, plant in large numbers, even with creeping perennials. All these plants need some moisture in the soil during summer.

Galium odoratum
SWEET WOODRUFF
☼ ☼ 4   ↕6in (15cm) ↔ indefinite

The stems of this strong-growing, aromatic perennial are clothed in whorls of narrow leaves. Clusters of tiny star flowers open in summer. Thrives in alkaline soils.

OTHER EVERGREEN PERENNIALS FOR GROUNDCOVER IN SHADE

Asarum caudatum
Carex morrowii
Epimedium grandiflorum
Euphorbia amygdaloides
  subsp. *robbiae*, see p.53
Hexastylis shuttleworthii 'Callaway'
Lamium maculatum 'Beacon Silver'
Luzula sylvatica 'Marginata'
Saxifraga x *urbium*
Vinca minor

Acanthus mollis
BEAR'S BREECHES
☼ ☼ ☼ 7   ↕4ft (1.2m) ↔ 3ft (1m)

One of the boldest groundcovers, this has semievergreen leaves and mauve-pink summer flowers. The leaves of *A. mollis* 'Latifolius' are more attractive.

Anemone nemorosa 'Robinsoniana'
WOOD ANEMONE
☼ ☼ 3   ↕6in (15cm) ↔ 8in (20cm)

A beautiful form of a charming perennial, this forms carpets of ferny leaves and star-shaped lavender-blue flowers in spring. Plants die down by midsummer.

Aegopodium podagraria 'Variegatum'
VARIEGATED GOUTWEED
☼ ☼ 3   ↕4in (10cm) ↔ indefinite

No one would dream of planting invasive Goutweed, but this less vigorous form makes an attractive groundcover with its boldly variegated, creamy white leaves.

Asarum europaeum
EUROPEAN WILD GINGER
☼ ☼ 4   ↕5in (12.5cm) ↔ indefinite

Plants bear handsome, evergreen mats of kidney-shaped, glossy, dark green leaves, which conceal small, brownish purple, bell-shaped flowers in spring.

Hosta 'Shade Fanfare'
PLANTAIN LILY
☼ ☼ 3   ↕30in (75cm) ↔ 3ft (1m)

This clump-forming perennial bears large, heart-shaped, light green leaves, each with a bold, creamy margin. Erect stems carry nodding lavender flowers in summer.

Lamium galeobdolon 'Florentinum'
VARIEGATED ARCHANGEL
☀ ☀ 4   ↕ 10in (25cm) ↔ indefinite

This scrambling semievergreen forms a dense carpet of nettle-shaped, silver-striped leaves, borne in pairs. Its whorls of two-lipped yellow flowers open in summer.

Tiarella cordifolia
FOAM FLOWER
☀ ☀ 3   ↕ 8in (20cm) ↔ indefinite

Delicate, fluffy spires of tiny white flowers rise above evergreen carpets of lobed, heart-shaped, bright green leaves from late spring into early summer.

Waldsteinia ternata
BARREN STRAWBERRY
☀ ☀ 4   ↕ 4in (10cm) ↔ indefinite

Three-parted, toothed, strawberry-like leaves form mats and are semievergreen. Potentilla-like yellow flowers are borne in late spring and early summer.

Saxifraga spathularis
SAINT PATRICK'S CABBAGE
☀ ☀ 7   ↕ 10in (25cm) ↔ indefinite

Evergreen rosettes of dark green, toothed leaves form low carpets. Tiny, starry white flowers are held in airy, branched clusters in summer. Dislikes dry soils.

Symphytum grandiflorum
DWARF COMFREY
☀ ☀ 5   ↕ 10in (25cm) ↔ indefinite

Cream-colored tubular flowers, reddish when in bud, are carried in clusters above the rich green leaves in spring. The foliage quickly forms low clumps and patches.

Tolmiea menziesii 'Taff's Gold'
PIGGYBACK PLANT
☀ ☀ 7   ↕ 24in (60cm) ↔ 18in (45cm)

Clumps of long-stalked, yellow-speckled, hairy leaves are either evergreen or semi-evergreen. Tall spikes carrying tiny green and brown flowers are borne in spring.

OTHER HERBACEOUS PERENNIALS FOR GROUNDCOVER IN SHADE

Geranium macrorrhizum 'Ingwersen'
Liriope muscari, see p.43
Polystichum acrostichoides
Trachystemon orientalis

Perennials for Heavy Clay Soils

EVERYONE WHO GARDENS on heavy clay soils knows they are usually wet and sticky in winter, and hard and dry in summer. They are at least fertile, and if their structure is improved, they can support a wide range of ornamental plants. Many perennials will grow anyway, provided there is enough moisture in summer and the soil is not waterlogged in winter.

Astrantia major
MASTERWORT
☼ ☀ 4   ↕ 24in (60cm) ↔ 18in (45cm)

The leaves of this tough and reliable clump-forming plant are long-stalked. Its flowers are greenish white or pink-tinted, and appear from summer into autumn.

Aster novae-angliae 'Alma Pötschke'
NEW ENGLAND ASTER
☼ 4   ↕ 30in (75cm) ↔ 24in (60cm)

Erect clumps of leafy stems produce large, branching heads of daisylike flowers with yellow centers in autumn. Provides a most striking color for late in the season.

Cimicifuga simplex
BUGBANE
☼ ☀ 3   ↕ 5½ft (1.7m) ↔ 24in (60cm)

Erect plant with glossy, divided leaves that may color attractively before they wither. Tiny, slightly fragrant flowers are carried on tall, slender spikes in autumn.

Aster novi-belgii 'Carnival'
NEW YORK ASTER
☼ 4   ↕ 30in (75cm) ↔ 18in (45cm)

Like many asters, this one is ideal for clay soils. It has an upright habit and brilliantly colored autumn flowers. Susceptible to mildew in dry conditions.

Astilbe 'Montgomery'
ASTILBE
☼ ☀ 4   ↕ 30in (75cm) ↔ 14in (35cm)

Tapering plumes of deep red flowers rise above clumps of delicate, glossy, fernlike leaves in summer. There are many other cultivars with red, pink, or white flowers.

CREEPING PERENNIALS THAT
COLONIZE HEAVY CLAY SOILS

Cirsium rivulare var. *atropurpureum*
Epimedium x *perralchicum*, see p.42
Geranium macrorrhizum
   'Ingwersen's Variety'
Houttuynia cordata 'Flore Pleno'
Mentha x *gentilis* 'Variegata'
Mentha longifolia
Peltiphyllum peltatum 'Nanum'
Persicaria bistorta 'Superba', see p.47
Saponaria officinalis

Helenium 'Moerheim Beauty'
SNEEZEWEED
☼ 3   ↕ 3ft (1m) ↔ 24in (60cm)

This is an old and reliable border plant. Upright and close-packed clumps of leafy stems bear rich bronzy red flowerheads with brownish centers in late summer.

Monarda 'Cambridge Scarlet'
BEE BALM
☼ 4   ↕ 3ft (1m) ↔ 30in (75cm)

A popular and handsome bee balm with dense clusters of rich red, tubular flowers throughout summer. Its leaves are aromatic when bruised. It thrives in moist soils.

Rudbeckia fulgida
'Goldsturm'
☼ 3   ↕ 30in (75cm) ↔ 18in (45cm)

This black-eyed Susan is one of the most reliable and attractive of all perennials, flowering in late summer and autumn. The leaves will wilt in dry conditions.

Heliopsis 'Ballet Dancer'
OX EYE
☼ 3   ↕ 3½ft (1.1m) ↔ 30in (75cm)

This perennial is of upright habit and has bold foliage. In late summer it carries a profusion of large, daisylike flowerheads with frilled, rich yellow petals.

Polemonium reptans
'Lambrook Mauve'
☼ ☼ 2   ↕ 18in (45cm) ↔ 12in (30cm)

A low, mound-forming relative of Jacob's Ladder, this has similarly much-divided leaves and loose lilac-blue flowerheads in late spring and early summer.

Solidago 'Goldenmosa'
GOLDENROD
☼ 4   ↕ 3ft (1m) ↔ 24in (60cm)

A smaller and superior version of the old-fashioned tall Goldenrod. Sturdy clumps of leafy stems bear handsome plumes of yellow flowers in late summer.

Kirengeshoma palmata
KIRENGESHOMA
☼ 5 ᴾᴴ   ↕ 3ft (1m) ↔ 30in (75cm)

A handsome perennial, both in flower and leaf. The sprays of waxy flowers occur from late summer into autumn. Thrives best in a moist, acid, but well-drained soil.

Pulmonaria saccharata
LUNGWORT
☼ ☼ 3   ↕ 12in (30cm) ↔ 24in (60cm)

Low mounds and hummocks of pointed leaves are covered with whitish spots and speckles. Spring flowers, borne in clusters, open pink then turn blue as they age.

OTHER PERENNIALS FOR HEAVY CLAY SOILS

Aconitum 'Bressingham Spire'
Anemone x *hybrida* 'Honorine Jobert', see p.52
Brunnera macrophylla
Chelone obliqua
Crocosmia 'Lucifer'
Eupatorium maculatum 'Atropurpureum'
Ligularia stenocephala 'The Rocket'
Prunella grandiflora 'Loveliness'
Rodgersia podophylla, see p.47

Perennials for Acid Soils

RELATIVELY FEW garden perennials prefer or thrive best in acid soils; those that do are natives of woodland or mountain areas, especially in Asia and North America. Of the following, many are suited to raised beds and rock or peat gardens, and most need a constant supply of moisture in summer, although not boggy conditions.

Iris innominata
PACIFIC COAST IRIS HYBRIDS
☼ 8 PH ↕ 8in (21cm) ↔ 18in (45cm)

These evergreen iris are superb for the edge of beds or as groundcover in well-drained soils. Delicately veined flowers of various colors occur from late spring.

Adiantum pedatum
NORTHERN MAIDENHAIR FERN
☼ 3 PH ↕ 18in (45cm) ↔ 18in (45cm)

In time, this lovely fern forms small colonies of fingered fronds on erect, wiry stalks. It thrives in moist, shady soils, especially in peat or woodland gardens.

Celmisia walkeri
NEW ZEALAND DAISY
☼ 8 PH ↕ 9in (23cm) ↔ 3ft (1m)

Dense rosettes of shiny evergreen leaves form low mounds. Above these, slender stems each bear a daisylike flower in summer. Needs moist, well-drained soil.

Lewisia Cotyledon Hybrids
LEWISIA
☼ 5 PH ↕ 10in (25cm) ↔ 6in (15cm)

This evergreen, with attractive rosettes of strap-shaped leaves, is suitable for cracks in rocks or stone walls. Erect heads of pink to purple flowers appear in early summer.

OTHER PERENNIALS FOR ACID SOILS

Blechnum spicant
Celmisia coriacea, see p.66
Celmisia spectabilis
Cryptogramma crispa
Epigaea gaultherioides
Galax urceolata
Gentiana x *macaulayi* 'Edinburgh'
Gentiana sino-ornata
Kirengeshoma koreana
Kirengeshoma palmata, see p.33
Linnaea borealis
Lithodora diffusa 'Grace Ward'
Maianthemum canadense
Phlox adsurgens 'Red Buttes'
Phlox x *procumbens* 'Millstream'
Phlox stolonifera 'Blue Ridge'
Shortia galacifolia
Viola pedata

Gentiana x *macaulayi* 'Well's Variety'
GENTIAN
☼ 5 PH ↕ 2in (5cm) ↔ 8in (20cm)

A striking gentian, forming mats of narrow evergreen leaves. Gorgeous, upturned blue trumpet flowers appear in late summer. Needs moist soil in a rock or peat garden.

Lithodora diffusa 'Heavenly Blue'
LITHODORA
☼ 6 PH ↕ 6in (15cm) ↔ 24in (60cm)

An evergreen carpeting perennial, with small, hairy gray-green leaves, prized for its small, star-shaped early summer flowers. It is ideal for banks or wall tops.

Luzula nivea
SNOWY WOODRUSH
☀ 4 PH   ↕ 24in (60cm) ↔ 20in (50cm)

Evergreen clumps of narrow, whiskery-edged, grasslike leaves surround erect, slender stems bearing loose clusters of glistening white spikelets in early summer.

Meconopsis betonicifolia
BLUE POPPY
☀ 7 PH   ↕ 4ft (1.2m) ↔ 18in (45cm)

A plant famed for its blue flowers in late spring or early summer. The leaves decrease in size up the stem from a basal rosette. Dislikes dry soils.

Phlox adsurgens 'Wagon Wheel'
PHLOX
☀ 6 PH   ↕ 4in (10cm) ↔ 12in (30cm)

Branched heads of small, wheel-shaped pink flowers rise above mats of evergreen leafy stems in summer. Thrives in humus-rich, but well-drained, soils.

Phlox stolonifera 'Ariane'
PHLOX
☀ 3 PH   ↕ 6in (15cm) ↔ 12in (30cm)

Low, leafy evergreen mats produce loose heads of long-tubed, saucer-shaped white flowers in early summer. This is a good companion to *P. adsurgens* 'Wagon Wheel'.

Podophyllum hexandrum
HIMALAYAN MAY APPLE
☀ 5 PH   ↕ 16in (40cm) ↔ 12in (30cm)

A white or pale pink, yellow-centered flower is borne in spring above brown and green mottled leaves. The flowers may be followed by pendent red seed pods.

NATIVE PLANTS FOR ACID SOILS

Actaea rubra
Hexastylis shuttleworthii 'Callaway'
Osmunda regalis
Sanguisorba canadensis
Trillium grandiflorum, see p.45

Smilacina racemosa
FALSE SOLOMON'S SEAL
☀ 3 PH   ↕ 34in (85cm) ↔ 18in (45cm)

This is an excellent flowering and foliage plant. Bold, arching, leafy stems end in plumes of white flowers from spring into summer. Dislikes dry soils.

Perennials for Alkaline Soils

THE DRY, TYPICALLY WELL-DRAINED conditions provided by alkaline soils suit a variety of perennials; if they are combined with a sunny exposure, so much the better. Many perennials are so content in these conditions that they seed around, giving even more spectacular displays, as well as seedlings for you to pass on to gardening friends.

Eryngium bourgatii
MEDITERRANEAN SEA HOLLY
☼ 5 ‡ 24in (60cm) ↔ 12in (30cm)

Branched, wiry stems carry many small, thistlelike flowers from mid- to late summer. Leathery, spine-toothed leaves are marbled gray-green, with white veins.

Anthericum liliago
ST. BERNARD'S LILY
☼ 5 ‡ 24in (60cm) ↔ 12in (30cm)

White, star-shaped flowers with light yellow stamens are carried on loose spires in early summer. These rise above clumps of long, narrow gray-green leaves.

Campanula glomerata 'Superba'
CLUSTERED BELLFLOWER
☼ 3 ‡ 30in (75cm) ↔ 3ft (1m)

Sturdy, leafy stems sport dense heads of bell-shaped purple flowers in summer. This vigorous, clump-forming perennial will seed itself in suitable sites.

Euphorbia myrsinites
TRAILING SPURGE
☼ 5 ‡ 3in (8cm) ↔ 12in (30cm)

This fleshy evergreen has trailing stems crowded with blue-gray leaves, and bears yellowish green spring flowers. Pinkish seed heads follow.

Asphodeline lutea
YELLOW ASPHODEL
☼ 6 ‡ 4ft (1.2m) ↔ 24in (60cm)

Tall spikes of starry yellow flowers are borne above grassy clumps of sea green leaves, which first appear in autumn. Self-seeds in well-drained soil.

Dianthus 'Gran's Favourite'
OLD-FASHIONED PINK
☼ 4 ‡ 12in (30cm) ↔ 24in (60cm)

Fragrant flowers, borne in summer, have white petals with raspberry red bases and margins. The mounds of blue-gray foliage are evergreen.

Geranium pratense
'Plenum Violaceum'
☼ 5 ‡ 30in (75cm) ↔ 24in (60cm)

Erect, branching stems carry small, deep violet, rosettelike flowers in summer. The bold clumps of finely divided leaves often have fine autumn color.

Origanum laevigatum
ORNAMENTAL OREGANO
☼ 6   ↕12in (30cm) ↔ 10in (25cm)

This aromatic, mat-forming plant sends up slender, branching stems that support numerous cerise pink summer flowers, popular with bees and butterflies.

Oxalis adenophylla
OXALIS
☼ 5   ↕2in (5cm) ↔ 4in (10cm)

A beautiful carpeting perennial, this has neat tufts of deeply divided gray-green leaves, through which large, dark-eyed, purplish pink flowers appear in spring.

Pennisetum villosum
FOUNTAIN GRASS
☼ 8   ↕3ft (1m) ↔ 20in (50cm)

In late summer and autumn, the narrow leaves of this grass give way to slender, downy shoots bearing creamy spikes with long, bearded bristles. Often annual.

Platycodon grandiflorus
BALLOON FLOWER
☼ 3   ↕24in (60cm) ↔ 18in (45cm)

Loose clumps of erect stems, with fleshy, bluish green leaves, produce balloonlike buds in summer. These expand into large blue or purple starry bells.

Pulsatilla vulgaris
PASQUE FLOWER
☼ 5   ↕10in (25cm) ↔ 10in (25cm)

Tufts of fine feathery foliage produce hairy stems, each with a single nodding bell flower, in spring. This flower opens wide and later becomes a silky seed head.

OTHER PERENNIALS FOR ALKALINE SOILS

Acanthus spinosus, see p.18
Achillea 'Coronation Gold'
Bergenia cordifolia 'Purpurea', see p.66
Campanula persicifolia 'Chettle Charm'
Cortaderia selloana 'Pumila', see p.85
Crepis incana
Gypsophila paniculata
Helenium autumnale
Iris unguicularis
Limonium latifolium
Linum narbonense
Phlomis russeliana
Salvia x *superba*
Scabiosa caucasica
Sedum 'Vera Jameson'
Stipa gigantea, see p.19
Veronica incana
Viola cornuta

Verbascum 'Gainsborough'
MULLEIN
☼ 6   ↕4ft (1.2m) ↔ 24in (60cm)

From a semievergreen rosette of leaves, tall, branching spikes of small, saucer-shaped sulfur yellow flowers rise in summer. A short-lived perennial.

Verbena patagonica
TALL VERBENA
☼ 7   ↕5ft (1.5m) ↔ 20in (50cm)

Tall, wiry stems carry narrow leaves and small, dense clusters of tiny purple flowers through summer into autumn. Often annual. Self-seeds in suitable sites.

Perennials for Dry, Sunny Sites

OVERLY DRY SOILS IN SUN are not exclusive to the warmer, drier countries of the world. One summer drought can put many garden perennials in temperate climates under stress unless water is available. Plants grown in light or sandy soils are often the first to suffer. It pays, therefore, to choose at least some perennials that tolerate warm, dry conditions.

Campanula persicifolia 'Telham Beauty'
☀ 3   ↕ 3ft (1m) ↔ 12in (30cm)

This lovely cultivar of the Peach-leaved Bellflower has upright, slender stems and narrow leaves. It is adorned by sprays of large, nodding bellflowers in summer.

Anthemis tinctoria 'E.C. Buxton'
GOLDEN MARGUERITE
☀ 3   ↕ 3ft (1m) ↔ 3ft (1m)

A colorful and reliable bushy perennial with aromatic, fernlike leaves. Branching stems bear a succession of daisylike flowers from summer into autumn.

CUSHION AND HUMMOCK PLANTS FOR DRY, SUNNY SITES

Acantholimon glumaceum
Armeria juniperina
Armeria maritima 'Vindictive'
Artemisia schmidtiana 'Nana', see p.56
Astragalus angustifolius
Aubrieta 'Elsa Lancaster'
Azorella trifurcata
Dianthus 'Pike's Pink'
Erinacea anthyllis
Phlox subulata

OTHER PERENNIALS FOR DRY, SUNNY SITES

Achillea 'Gold Plate', see p.85
Anthemis punctata subsp. *cupaniana*,
  see p.50
Anthemis tinctoria 'Kelwayi'
Asphodeline lutea, see p.36
Crepis incana
Eryngium bourgatii, see p.36
Gaillardia x *grandiflora*
Linum narbonense 'Heavenly Blue'
Oenothera odorata

Bletilla striata
BLETILLA
☀ 5   ↕ 24in (60cm) ↔ 18in (45cm)

A beautiful terrestrial orchid, well worth growing just for its attractive patches of ribbed leaves. Above these, loose flower sprays occur in late spring or early summer.

Diascia rigescens
TWINSPUR
☀ 7   ↕ 10in (25cm) ↔ 10in (25cm)

The stems of this trailing, leafy perennial curve upward to bear flower spikes from summer into autumn in cooler climates. A most spectacular groundcover.

Dictamnus albus var. *purpureus*
GAS PLANT
☼ 3   ↕ 3ft (1m) ↔ 24in (60cm)

A fabled plant, slow to establish, but well worth the wait once the loose spikes of lilac to purple-pink flowers appear above deeply divided leaves in summer.

Echinops ritro 'Veitch's Blue'
GLOBE THISTLE
☼ 3   ↕ 4ft (1.2m) ↔ 30in (75cm)

Silvery stems above handsome clumps of jagged leaves support many tight, globular blue flowerheads. They are popular with bees and butterflies in late summer.

Eryngium alpinum
ALPINE ERYNGO
☼ 4   ↕ 34in (85cm) ↔ 24in (60cm)

This spectacular perennial has basal rosettes of heart-shaped leaves and stout, branching stems carrying conical summer flowerheads with softly spiny ruffs.

Gypsophila paniculata 'Bristol Fairy'
BABY'S BREATH
☼ 3   ↕ 28in (70cm) ↔ 3ft (1m)

A splendid form of the well-known Baby's Breath that is much used by florists. Its wiry, multibranched stems produce clouds of tiny summer flowers.

Helianthemum 'Wisley Primrose'
ROCK ROSE
☼ 5   ↕ 10in (25cm) ↔ 24in (60cm)

Low hummocks of evergreen foliage are joined by a plentiful supply of saucer-shaped flowers in summer. Other varieties in different colors are available.

Hordeum jubatum
SQUIRREL-TAIL GRASS
☼ 5   ↕ 18in (45cm) ↔ 12in (30cm)

One of the most beautiful ornamental grasses. From summer into autumn, erect stems sport feathery plumes of silky spikelets, green at first, ripening to gold.

Linum flavum 'Compactum'
FLAX
☼ 5   ↕ 6in (15cm) ↔ 6in (15cm)

This small, bushy perennial has narrow green leaves and pretty heads of funnel-shaped, bright yellow flowers from late spring into summer.

Oenothera speciosa 'Rosea'
EVENING PRIMROSE
☼ 5   ↕ 18in (45cm) ↔ 12in (30cm)

The pink flowers of this lovely evening primrose are carried above deeply cut leaves. Nodding buds open in summer during the day, unusual for this genus.

Bulbs for Dry, Sunny Sites

MANY BULBS ARE FOUND in dry, often hot and arid places in the wild, or they appreciate such conditions at certain times of the year. In gardens, these bulbs will struggle if you plant them in shade or in a deep, rich soil. Although they may survive for a time, eventually they will die under such conditions. The following selections perform best in good drainage and as much sun and warmth as possible. A raised bed or a border at the foot of a sunny wall is usually perfect.

Lilium candidum
MADONNA LILY
☼ 4   ↕ 5ft (1.5m)

In summer, a large, loose head of broad, funnel-shaped, fragrant white flowers with yellow throats crowns each erect, leafy stem. Thrives in alkaline soils.

Allium christophii
STARS OF PERSIA
☼ 4   ↕ 16in (40cm)

The large, globular head of star-spangled flowers in summer makes this one of the most spectacular of all alliums. Its flowerheads are also attractive dried.

Eucomis comosa
PINEAPPLE LILY
☼ 7   ↕ 28in (70cm)

Wavy-margined, strap-shaped leaves are topped in late summer by a single purple-spotted stem with a spike of pink-flushed starry flowers and a crown of green bracts.

Triteleia laxa
TRIPLET LILY
☼ 7   ↕ 20in (50cm)

Loose umbels of funnel-shaped flowers, pale to deep blue or purple-blue, are borne above tufts of narrow green leaves in early summer. Seeds around if content.

Amaryllis belladonna
BELLADONNA LILY
☼ 7   ↕ 24in (60cm)

This lovely autumn-flowering bulb bears scented, funnel-shaped pink flowers carried elegantly on sturdy, purplish stems. The strap-shaped leaves follow in spring.

OTHER BULBS FOR DRY SUN

Allium karataviense
Allium moly
Anemone blanda
Anemone pavonina
Anomatheca laxa
Arum creticum
Colchicum agrippinum, see p.58
Crocus chrysanthus cultivars
Fritillaria imperialis, see p.79
Gladiolus communis subsp. *byzantinus*, see p.61
Hermodactylus tuberosus
Ixiolirion tataricum
Lilium x *testaceum*
Muscari armeniacum
Scilla peruviana
Tulipa clusiana
Tulipa praestans
Tulipa sprengeri

Tulipa saxatilis
TULIP
☼ 7   ↕ 14in (35cm)

In early spring, branched stems support up to four pink to lilac flowers, each with a yellow eye, above attractive, glossy green leaves. Forms patches in warm, dry soils.

Bulbs for Shady Sites

FAR OUTNUMBERED by the sun-lovers, a variety of bulbs enjoy shady conditions in soils that remain moist in summer. Many of these bulbs are woodlanders, originating from the temperate regions. They are ideal for sunless situations in the garden, provided that the shade is not too heavy and that they do not have to compete with the roots of trees growing nearby. Plant in groups to create the best effect. Many will seed around if content.

Corydalis flexuosa
BLUE CORYDALIS
☀ ☀ 6   ↕ 6in (15cm)

The striking blue flowers of this beautiful clump-forming plant open in spring. Its fernlike leaves are sometimes bronze-tinted. Several cultivars are available.

Erythronium hendersonii
TROUT LILY
☀ ☀ 3   ↕ 12in (30cm)

In spring, Trout Lily's nodding lavender-pink flowers, with gracefully swept back petals, rise above a pair of fleshy leaves, mottled green and brown.

Ornithogalum nutans
ORNITHOGALUM
☀ ☀ 5   ↕ 14in (35cm)

Star of Bethlehem produces loose spikes of large, drooping, bell-shaped flowers, translucent and green tinted, in spring. Prefers well-drained soil.

OTHER BULBS FOR SHADE

Allium moly
Arisaema sikokianum, see p.44
Arisaema triphyllum
Arum italicum 'Marmoratum'
Brimeura amethystina
Chionodoxa luciliae, see p.58
Cyclamen repandum
Eranthis hyemalis, see p.60
Galanthus nivalis 'Flore Pleno', see p.84
Leucojum vernum
Scilla siberica 'Spring Beauty', see p.59

Cyclamen coum
HARDY CYCLAMEN
☀ ☀ 6   ↕ 4in (10cm)

A charming and reliable early-flowering bulb, this has pads of small, plain green or silver-zoned, kidney-shaped leaves. These are topped by bright carmine flowers.

Hyacinthoides hispanica
SPANISH BLUEBELL
☀ ☀ 4   ↕ 12in (30cm)

This bold, clump-forming perennial has upright, fleshy stems and shining green leaves. Loose spikes of drooping white, blue, or pink bellflowers appear in spring.

Trillium sessile
TOADSHADE
☀ ☀ 3   ↕ 14in (35cm)

Red-brown flowers nestle above leaves with white, pale green, or bronze markings in spring. In time, this plant will form handsome clumps. It thrives in rich soil.

Perennials for Dry Shade

THE DRY SHADE BENEATH TREES is regarded as one of the most difficult soil situations in which to grow plants. In summer, dense leaf canopies and root systems conspire to keep available moisture to a minimum. If possible, it is worth trying to improve conditions by reducing overhead shade, regularly applying ample organic mulch, and watering. But if all else fails, the following perennials, which mainly grow wild in woodlands, are more tolerant of dry shade than most.

Epimedium x *perralchicum*
BISHOP'S HAT
☼ ☀ 5   ↕ 18in (45cm) ↔ 18in (45cm)

This mounding, wiry-stemmed plant bears semievergreen to evergreen leaves, with glossy green leaflets. The spires of short-spurred yellow flowers emerge in spring.

Geranium macrorrhizum
BALKAN CRANESBILL
☼ ☀ 3   ↕ 14in (35cm) ↔ 24in (60cm)

In most soils and situations, this carpeting semievergreen makes excellent ground-cover. Magenta flower sprays top aromatic, deeply cut leaves in early summer.

Convallaria majalis
LILY OF THE VALLEY
☼ ☀ 2   ↕ 6in (15cm) ↔ indefinite

This old favorite spreads by underground stems to form patches of erect shoots with attractive foliage and sprays of nodding, fragrant white bell flowers in spring.

OTHER HERBACEOUS PERENNIALS FOR DRY SHADE

Anemone nemorosa 'Allenii'
Dicentra cucullaria
Dicentra 'Luxuriant'
Disporum sessile
Geranium macrorrhizum 'Album'
Geranium maculatum
Geranium phaeum
Polygonatum multiflorum
Trachystemon orientalis
Vancouveria hexandra

Dicentra formosa
WILD BLEEDING HEART
☼ ☀ 3   ↕ 18in (45cm) ↔ 12in (30cm)

This clump-forming perennial has fern-like gray-green leaves and arching sprays of nodding pink or reddish, locket-shaped flowers in spring or early summer.

Geranium nodosum
CRANESBILL
☼ ☀ 7   ↕ 18in (45cm) ↔ 18in (45cm)

Excellent in shade, this clump-former gives continuous supplies of delicate lilac-mauve flowers in spring and all through summer. Long-stalked, three-lobed leaves.

Liriope muscari
LIRIOPE, LILYTURF
☼ ☀ 6　　　↕12in (30cm) ↔18in (45cm)

Dense evergreen clumps of deep green, strap-shaped leaves are joined in summer by narrow spikes crowded with tiny, purplish blue, bell-shaped flowers.

Pachyphragma macrophyllum
PACHYPHRAGMA
☼ ☀ 7　　　↕12in (30cm) ↔indefinite

In spring, heads of white, four-petaled flowers rise on long stalks above mats or carpets of heart-shaped, glossy green leaves. Makes excellent groundcover.

Iris foetidissima
STINKING IRIS
☼ ☀ 7　　　↕24in (60cm) ↔3ft (1m)

A clump of long, pointed evergreen leaves forms a backdrop to yellow-tinged, dull purple flowers in summer, and brilliant orange seed clusters throughout winter.

OTHER EVERGREEN PERENNIALS FOR DRY SHADE

Asplenium scolopendrium, see p.44
Epimedium perralderianum
Epimedium pinnatum subsp. *colchicum*
Epimedium pubigerum
Galax urceolata
Geranium endressii
Helleborus foetidus, see p.66
Polystichum acrostichoides
Polystichum munitum, see p.45
Speirantha convallarioides

Lunaria rediviva
PERENNIAL HONESTY
☼ ☀ 4　　　↕30in (75cm) ↔30in (75cm)

Clouds of white or lilac spring flowers are followed by flattened silvery seed pods, pointed at both ends. Clumps of much-branched stems bear toothed, oval leaves.

Tellima grandiflora
FRINGE CUPS
☼ ☀ 4　　　↕24in (60cm) ↔24in (60cm)

Erect stems support spires of whiskery-mouthed, bell-shaped cream flowers in spring, above a basal mound of evergreen, purple-tinted, hairy, heart-shaped leaves.

Lamium maculatum
SPOTTED DEADNETTLE
☼ ☼ ☀ 3　　　↕6in (15cm) ↔indefinite

This vigorous semievergreen perennial forms dense carpets of heart-shaped green leaves with a white central stripe. Clusters of hooded spring flowers are mauve-pink.

Meconopsis cambrica
WELSH POPPY
☼ ☀ 6　　　↕18in (45cm) ↔12in (30cm)

Single orange or yellow poppy flowers are held on slender stems in spring. Its foliage is light green and fernlike. Forms with double flowers are also available.

Viola labradorica 'Purpurea'
LABRADOR VIOLET
☼ ☀ 3　　　↕3in (7.5cm) ↔6in (15cm)

In time this reliable little perennial forms low mounds of kidney-shaped, purplish green leaves. Small purple flowers continue from spring all through summer.

Perennials for Cool, Moist Soils in Shade

Nᴜᴍᴇʀᴏᴜs ʙᴇᴀᴜᴛɪғᴜʟ ᴘᴇʀᴇɴɴɪᴀʟs, many native to woodlands, are suitable for gardens in full or partial shade. Such plants prefer a cool, reasonably moist, if well-drained, soil, particularly during the growing season (spring to early summer). If necessary, construct a raised bed filled with soil high in organic matter. Few thrive in heavy, dry shade.

Helleborus orientalis
LENTEN ROSE
☀ ☀ 4   ↕ 18in (45cm) ↔ 18in (45cm)

This is one of the most worthy garden perennials, with its evergreen leaves and nodding winter or early spring flowers. Several color selections are available.

Arisaema sikokianum
BLACK JACK-IN-THE-PULPIT
☀ ☀ 5   ↕ 20in (50cm) ↔ 12in (30cm)

The long-stalked leaves of this striking, tuberous-rooted perennial each have three beautifully marked leaflets. Single mid-spring flowers have white interiors.

Arisarum proboscideum
MOUSE-TAIL PLANT
☀ ☀ 6   ↕ 4in (10cm) ↔ 12in (30cm)

An amusing little tuberous-rooted plant that forms patches of arrow-shaped leaves under which hide curious, long-tailed, hooded flowers in spring.

Jeffersonia dubia
TWINLEAF
☀ ☀ 5   ↕ 6in (15cm) ↔ 9in (23cm)

Twinleaf is a choice perennial producing tufts of kidney-shaped, boldly toothed blue-green leaves and saucer-shaped, long-stalked, poppylike flowers in spring.

OTHER PERENNIALS FOR COOL, MOIST SHADE

Actaea rubra
Anemonella thalictroides
Dodecatheon meadia
Epimedium grandiflorum
Epimedium x *warleyense*
Galax urceolata
Glaucidium palmatum
Helleborus viridus
Jeffersonia diphylla
Omphalodes verna
Pachysandra procumbens
Podophyllum hexandrum, see p.35
Sanguinaria canadensis 'Plena'
Shortia galacifolia
Smilacina racemosa, see p.35
Tiarella cordifolia, see p.31
Trillium sessile, see p.41
Trollius europaeus, see p.91

Asplenium scolopendrium
HART'S-TONGUE FERN
☀ ☀ 5   ↕ 30in (75cm) ↔ 24in (60cm)

This distinguished, resilient fern forms bold evergreen clumps of broad, strap-shaped fronds, banded beneath with spores. It will also grow in shady walls.

Mertensia virginica
VIRGINIA BLUEBELL
☀ ☀ 3   ↕ 20in (50cm) ↔ 12in (30cm)

A charming perennial, this has a delicate appearance: blue-green stems and leaves, and nodding clusters of pink buds that open into blue flowers in spring.

Ourisia macrophylla
OURISIA
☀ ☀ 7   ‡ 24in (60cm) ↔ 8in (20cm)

A vigorous perennial, this forms mats of
evergreen, heart-shaped leaves in time,
above which spring flowerheads rise.
Thrives in rich, especially moist, soils.

Polystichum munitum
SWORD FERN
☀ ☀ 5   ‡ 36in (90cm) ↔ 36in (90cm)

In time, this handsome evergreen fern
forms bold clumps of shining, ladderlike
fronds. Good alone, or planted in groups,
especially with other woodland plants.

OTHER FERNS FOR MOIST SHADE

Adiantum pedatum, see p.34
Arachniodes standishii
Asplenium scolopendrium 'Crispum'
Athyrium nipponicum 'Pictum'
Blechnum tabulare, see p.66
Cyrtomium falcatum
Dryopteris erythrosora
Dryopteris marginalis
Polystichum acrostichoides
Polystichum setiferum 'Divisilobum',
  see p.67
Woodsia ilvensis
Woodwardia virginica

Trillium grandiflorum
WHITE TRILLIUM
☀ ☀ 4   ‡ 15in (38cm) ↔ 15in (38cm)

Few woodland perennials are more eye-
catching than this, when the large white
flowers are held above its leaves in spring.
It slowly forms substantial clumps.

Scopolia carniolica
JAPANESE BELLADONNA
☀ ☀ 5   ‡ 20in (50cm) ↔ 20in (50cm)

This uncommon, clump-forming perennial
has rich green, boldly toothed leaves and
nodding bellflowers in spring. These are
purplish brown with yellow interiors.

Tricyrtis formosana
TOAD LILY
☀ ☀ 4   ‡ 30in (75cm) ↔ 18in (45cm)

Clumps of erect, fleshy stems, rising from
a creeping rootstock, carry boldly veined
leaves and loose heads of curious, purple-
spotted flowers in early autumn.

Uvularia grandiflora
BELLWORT, MERRYBELLS
☀ ☀ 5   ‡ 24in (60cm) ↔ 12in (30cm)

A charming member of the lily family
that forms clumps of erect, slender, leafy
stems with drooping clusters of long, bell-
shaped yellow flowers in spring.

Perennials for Bog Gardens

SOILS THAT ARE permanently wet or squishy have some gardeners scratching their heads as to what plants, if any, will grow in these seemingly inhospitable conditions. The bog garden is often the best, most challenging solution. Numerous interesting and ornamental perennials will not only survive but actually thrive there. Usually associated with pond or stream-sides, bog gardens can also be planted around a natural spring or some artificial source of water. Whatever their size, these sites can support an exciting range of perennials that should be selected as much for their varied effects as for their tolerance of wet conditions.

Astilbe 'Bressingham Beauty'
ASTILBE
☼ 4   ↕ 3½ft (1.1m) ↔ 3½ft (1.1m)

The bold clumps of leaves are attractive, especially in spring, but the erect plumes of tiny flowers in summer are spectacular. Dried seedheads are a bonus in winter.

Filipendula purpurea
MEADOWSWEET
☼ 4   ↕ 4ft (1.2m) ↔ 30in (75cm)

Handsome in both foliage and flower, this has big, bold clumps of large, deeply lobed leaves above which heads of little, rosy crimson flowers rise in summer.

Euphorbia palustris
EUPHORBIA
☼ ☼ 5   ↕ 3ft (1m) ↔ 3ft (1m)

A reliable and attractive perennial with upright, leafy stems and branched heads of green and yellow spring flowers. The leaves often color richly in autumn.

Gentiana asclepiadea
WILLOW GENTIAN
☼ 6   ↕ 30in (75cm) ↔ 24in (60cm)

Lush clumps of slender, leafy stems arch gracefully under the weight of numerous blue trumpet flowers in late summer and early autumn. A white form exists.

Hosta 'Frances Williams'
PLANTAIN LILY
☼ 3   ↕ 30in (75cm) ↔ 30in (75cm)

A cultivar of the popular *H. sieboldiana*. Bold mounds of heart-shaped, bluish gray leaves have yellow margins that darken with age. It bears flowers in summer.

Mimulus luteus
MONKEY FLOWER
☼ 8 ↕12in (30cm) ↔12in (30cm)

Sometimes also known as Monkey Musk, and particularly suited to watersides, this low-spreading, fleshy plant produces many yellow flowers with red spots in summer.

Primula pulverulenta
CANDELABRA PRIMULA
☼ 5 ↕30in (75cm) ↔16in (40cm)

This striking candelabra primula forms lush, leafy clumps above which rise erect stems. In early summer these support tubular, dark-eyed crimson flowers.

Ligularia przewalskii
LIGULARIA
☼ ☼ 5 ↕5ft (1.5m) ↔3½ft (1.1m)

A striking perennial with long-stalked, large, jaggedly cut leaves above which slender-stemmed spires of yellow flower-heads rise in mid- to late summer.

Peltiphyllum peltatum
UMBRELLA PLANT
☼ ☼ 5 ↕3½ft (1.1m) ↔30in (75cm)

The creeping rhizomes of this distinctive plant send up hairy stems topped with spring flowerheads. The umbrella leaves that follow color richly in autumn.

Rodgersia podophylla
RODGERSIA
☼ ☼ 5 ↕3½ft (1.1m) ↔3ft (1m)

A bold, clump-forming perennial, this is worth growing for its striking leaves, which color richly in autumn. Creamy white flowerheads are a bonus in summer.

OTHER PERENNIALS FOR BOG GARDENS

Astilboides tabularis
Caltha palustris
Gunnera manicata, see p.19
Helianthus angustifolius
Hosta sieboldiana 'Elegans', see p.65
Iris, many beardless kinds
Ligularia dentata 'Othello'
Lobelia cardinalis
Lobelia siphilitica
Lysichiton americanum
Lysimachia clethroides, see p.91
Osmunda regalis
Primula florindae
Primula japonica
Rheum palmatum 'Atrosanguineum', see p.19
Symphytum x uplandicum 'Variegatum', see p.69

Persicaria bistorta 'Superba'
KNOTWEED
☼ 3 ↕28in (70cm) ↔24in (60cm)

This excellent knotweed forms dense clumps of large pointed leaves above which, in early summer, rise slender stems bearing conical pokers of soft pink flowers.

Trollius x cultorum 'Alabaster'
GLOBEFLOWER
☼ ☼ 3 ↕18in (45cm) ↔18in (45cm)

Beautiful and unusual, this globeflower has long-stalked, deeply divided and dissected leaves. Its branching heads of creamy yellow flowers appear in spring.

47

Perennials Tolerant of Air Pollution

IN MANY AREAS, particularly in towns, cities, and near to industrial sites, air pollution is still a problem. Over the years, however, gardeners have come to rely upon the surprisingly large number of perennials that have proved tolerant of such conditions. Fortunately, they include some of our most popular, colorful, and reliable plants.

Centaurea montana
PERENNIAL CORNFLOWER
☼ 3   ‡ 20in (50cm) ↔ 24in (60cm)

This longstanding garden favorite forms leafy clumps and produces large heads of blue flowers in early summer. Other forms have purple, pink, or white flowers.

Aster x *frikartii* 'Mönch'
ASTER
☼ 5   ‡ 3ft (1m) ↔ 18in (45cm)

This is a strong-growing perennial that may require support. Its striking daisy flowers are produced over many weeks, from midsummer well into autumn.

Anaphalis margaritacea var. *yedoensis*
PEARLY EVERLASTING
☼ 4   ‡ 30in (75cm) ↔ 24in (60cm)

Clumps of erect stems and narrow leaves are covered in a gray, woolly down. Small white flowerheads appear in late summer, and retain their color when dried.

Geranium himalayense
LILAC CRANESBILL
☼ 4   ‡ 12in (30cm) ↔ 24in (60cm)

Easy and reliable, this clump-forming perennial has deeply cut leaves and cup-shaped lilac-blue flowers in summer. Its foliage often colors richly in autumn.

OTHER PERENNIALS TOLERANT OF AIR POLLUTION

Achillea 'Coronation Gold'
Achillea ptarmica 'The Pearl'
Ajuga reptans 'Catlin's Giant'
Anaphalis triplinervis
Aster novae-angliae 'Alma Pötschke', see p.32
Astrantia major subsp. *involucrata* 'Shaggy'
Bergenia x *schmidtii*
Dicentra eximia
Echinops ritro 'Veitch's Blue', see p.39
Geranium macrorrhizum, see p.42
Lamium maculatum 'Album'
Leucanthemum x *superbum* 'Alaska'
Monarda didyma
Persicaria bistorta 'Superba', see p.47
Potentilla 'Gibson's Scarlet'
Rudbeckia fulgida 'Goldsturm', see p.33

Astrantia major 'Hadspen Blood'
MASTERWORT
☼ ☼ 4   ‡ 18in (45cm) ↔ 24in (60cm)

Loosely branched heads of dark ruby red flowers rise above eye-catching clumps of attractive, rich green, toothed, and deeply lobed leaves in summer.

Geum 'Borisii'
GEUM
☼ 3   ‡ 12in (30cm) ↔ 12in (30cm)

Loosely branched heads of single, rich orange flowers are borne in early summer above mounds of lush green leaves. This geum is an excellent groundcover.

Liatris spicata
KANSAS GAYFEATHER
☼ 3 ↕ 24in (60cm) ↔ 12in (30cm)

Kansas Gayfeather forms dense tufts of grassy foliage and bears stiff stems holding pokerlike spikes of fuzzy rose-purple flowers in late summer.

Malva moschata
MUSK MALLOW
☼ 3 ↕ 3ft (1m) ↔ 24in (60cm)

The finely divided leaves of this bushy perennial are aromatic. Spikes of saucer-shaped, pale pink flowers occur in early summer. 'Alba' is a lovely white form.

Veronica spicata 'Romiley Purple'
VERONICA
☼ 4 ↕ 4ft (1.2m) ↔ 24in (60cm)

Clumps of narrow leaves held in whorls on erect stems give rise to slender, tapering spikes of tiny purple flowers in summer. May require support.

Lupinus 'The Chatelaine'
RUSSELL LUPINE
☼ 3 ↕ 4ft (1.2m) ↔ 18in (45cm)

Bold clumps of many-fingered, long-stalked leaves are topped with tapering spikes crowded with pink and white pea flowers in early summer. Prone to slugs.

Lychnis chalcedonica
MALTESE CROSS
☼ 3 ↕ 4ft (1.2m) ↔ 18in (45cm)

Few perennials have flowers that are a richer color than this clump-forming campion. Dense, flattened vermilion-red flowerheads appear in early summer.

Solidago 'Laurin'
GOLDENROD
☼ 3 ↕ 30in (75cm) ↔ 18in (45cm)

A miniature version of the old-fashioned Goldenrod, this has sturdy, densely leafy stems, crowned with branched heads of deep yellow flowers in late summer.

JAPANESE ANEMONES TOLERANT OF AIR POLLUTION

Anemone x hybrida 'Bressingham Glow'
Anemone x hybrida 'Honorine Jobert',
  see p.52
Anemone x hybrida 'Whirlwind'

Perennials Tolerant of Coastal Exposure

FEW CONDITIONS ARE TOUGHER for plants than those found in coastal gardens, where strong winds batter them and, even in sheltered sites, salt spray may burn them. Generally, perennials are more vulnerable in spring, when new growth emerges. Fortunately, many perennials are tolerant of these conditions, some growing near the sea in their wild state.

Agapanthus praecox subsp. *orientalis*
BLUE LILY OF THE NILE
☼ 9 ↕ 3ft (1m) ↔ 24in (60cm)

Bold clumps of semievergreen, strap-shaped leaves are topped in late summer by strong-stemmed umbels of sky blue flowers. Plant in a container in cold areas.

Anthemis punctata subsp. *cupaniana*
ANTHEMIS
☼ ☼ 5 ↕ 12in (30cm) ↔ 24in (60cm)

A reliable, adaptable plant that produces masses of long-stalked daisy flowers in early summer, above mounds of silver-gray foliage that becomes green in winter.

OTHER PERENNIALS TOLERANT OF COASTAL EXPOSURE

Agapanthus Headbourne Hybrids
Allium christophii, see p.40
Catananche coerulea 'Major'
Centaurea cineraria 'White Diamond'
Centaurea gymnocarpa
Crambe maritima
Eryngium tripartitum
Limonium latifolium
Oenothera odorata
Phormium cookianum

Artemisia arborescens
WORMWOOD
☼ 9 ↕ 3ft (1m) ↔ 3ft (1m)

Well-known for its silver-gray filigree foliage, this evergreen carries clusters of small yellowish flowers from summer into early autumn. Prune hard to keep it neat.

Centranthus ruber
RED VALERIAN
☼ 5 ↕ 30in (75cm) ↔ 30in (75cm)

This long-flowering perennial is ideal for seaside gardens. Bushy, with fleshy gray-green leaves, it has crowded red, white, or pink flowerheads from spring to autumn.

Erigeron glaucus
SEASIDE ASTER
☼ 5 ↕ 10in (25cm) ↔ 3ft (1m)

One of the most satisfactory perennials for coastal areas, this plant forms dense mats of gray-green evergreen leaves, and is covered in summer with large daisies.

Osteospermum jucundum
AFRICAN DAISY
☼ 9   ↕12in (30cm) ↔12in (30cm)

Masses of large, soft pink daisy flowers
with dark eyes rise on long stalks above
neat, low mounds of evergreen foliage in
late summer. An excellent carpeter.

**CARPETING PERENNIALS
TOLERANT OF COASTAL EXPOSURE**

Armeria maritima
Erigeron glaucus 'Arthur Menzies'
Eriogonum umbellatum
Sedum, many

Kniphofia 'Royal Standard'
RED-HOT POKER
☼ 5   ↕4ft (1.2m) ↔24in (60cm)

Clumps of narrow leaves are dominated in
late summer by stout-stemmed pokers of
lemon yellow flowers, scarlet in bud. In
cold areas, protect the crowns in winter.

Othonna cheirifolia
OTHONNA
☼ 8   ↕10in (25cm) ↔12in (30cm)

This mat-forming evergreen does best in
a warm, sheltered pocket. Solitary, long-
stalked daisy flowers appear amid gray-
green, paddle-shaped leaves in summer.

Eryngium x *oliverianum*
SEA HOLLY
☼ 5   ↕3ft (1m) ↔20in (50cm)

Blue-tinted stems carrying dome-shaped
lavender-blue flowers, nestling in prickly
ruffs, rise from a basal rosette of heart-
shaped leaves in late summer.

Lathyrus latifolius
PERENNIAL PEA
☼ 5   ↕6ft (2m) ↔6ft (2m)

A strong-growing perennial, this scrambles
by means of leaf tendrils. From summer
to autumn it produces long-stalked spikes
of small pea flowers. Needs support.

Physostegia virginiana 'Vivid'
OBEDIENT PLANT
☼ 2   ↕24in (60cm) ↔18in (45cm)

This is a distinguished and reliable clump-
forming perennial, with erect stems that
carry crowded spikes of tubular flowers in
late summer and early autumn.

Perennials for Growing at the Base of Hedges

HOW OFTEN DO YOU SEE GARDENS with borders and beds filled with perennials, but the bases of the hedges are choked with grass? It is a common situation, yet it can very easily be avoided. Many ornamental perennials are sufficiently robust to compete with grass and roots, giving the hedge a colorful, interesting, and attractive edging.

Chelidonium majus 'Flore Pleno'
GREATER CELANDINE
☼ ☼ 5   ↕ 24in (60cm) ↔ 12in (30cm)

Clumps of much-divided, pale green leaves nestle below the branched heads of small, double, bright yellow flowers borne from spring into summer. Will self-seed.

Anemone x *hybrida* 'Honorine Jobert'
JAPANESE ANEMONE
☼ ☼ 4   ↕ 5ft (1.5m) ↔ 24in (60cm)

From late summer into autumn, numerous yellow-eyed white flowers are held on branching stems. In time, this vigorous perennial will form patches.

Campanula latifolia 'Brantwood'
GIANT BELLFLOWER
☼ ☼ 3   ↕ 4ft (1.2m) ↔ 24in (60cm)

A handsome and stately plant, this bold clump-former has upright, leafy stems that terminate in spikes of large, nodding violet-purple bellflowers in summer.

Crocosmia 'Bressingham Blaze'
MONTBRETIA
☼ 5   ↕ 30in (75cm) ↔ 12in (30cm)

In late summer, arching sprays of red flowers complement clumps of handsome, sword-shaped leaves. Montbretia grows from corms, which are easily detached.

Aquilegia vulgaris
COLUMBINE, GRANNY'S BONNET
☼ ☼ 3   ↕ 3ft (1m) ↔ 20in (50cm)

This old-fashioned favorite forms clumps of attractive blue-green leaves. Branched stems carry showers of nodding flowers in early summer, in a variety of colors.

Campanula poscharskyana
SERBIAN BELLFLOWER
☼ ☼ 3   ↕ 5in (13cm) ↔ indefinite

One of the most rampant, this plant soon fills gaps with its leafy stems. The stems are crowded with violet-blue, star-shaped flowers in summer.

OTHER PERENNIALS FOR GROWING AT THE BASE OF HEDGES

Anemone x *hybrida* 'Bressingham Glow'
Anemone x *hybrida* 'Margarette'
Aster divaricatus
Aster lateriflorus 'Horizontalis'
Bidens ferulifolia, see p.62
Brunnera macrophylla
Campanula lactiflora 'Prichard's Variety', see p.16
Campanula latifolia var. *macrantha alba*
Campanula rapunculoides
Chaerophyllum hirsutum 'Roseum'
Lysimachia clethroides, see p.91
Monarda didyma
Solidago sphacelata 'Golden Fleece'
Symphytum orientale
Symphytum x *uplandicum*
Tanacetum vulgare
Vinca major

Myrrhis odorata
SWEET CICELY
☼ ☼ 4   ↕ 3ft (1m) ↔ 24in (60cm)

Erect stems bear flattened heads of tiny
white flowers in early summer above
mounds of finely divided, fernlike leaves.
All parts smell of anise when bruised.

Dryopteris affinis
GOLDEN MALE FERN
☼ ☼ ☼ 4   ↕ 4ft (1.2m) ↔ 3ft (1m)

The bright green, deeply divided semievergreen fronds of this distinguished fern
grow on upright, golden, scaly stalks.
Together they form a large "shuttlecock."

Euphorbia amygdaloides subsp. *robbiae*
MRS. ROBB'S BONNET
☼ ☼ ☼ 7   ↕ 24in (60cm) ↔ indefinite

This tough evergreen eventually forms a
carpet of upright stems with dark green
leaves. It carries loose heads of yellow-
green or lime green flowers in spring.

Pentaglottis sempervirens
GREEN ALKANET
☼ ☼ 7-8   ↕ 3ft (1m) ↔ 24in (60cm)

In spring, dense sprays of small, deep blue
forget-me-not flowers, held on branching
stems, top clumps of large, roughly hairy
leaves. A reliable, early-flowering plant.

OTHER FERNS FOR GROWING AT THE BASE OF HEDGES
Athyrium filix-femina
Dryopteris dilatata
Dryopteris filix-mas
Polystichum setiferum

Lysimachia punctata
SPOTTED LOOSESTRIFE
☼ ☼ 4   ↕ 30in (75cm) ↔ 30in (75cm)

The upper leaf axils of this easy, reliable
perennial are crowded with yellow flowers
in summer. It forms dense clumps of erect,
leafy stems, and is best in moist soils.

Symphytum caucasicum
CAUCASIAN COMFREY
☼ ☼ 4   ↕ 24in (60cm) ↔ 24in (60cm)

Bristly, branching stems bear loose clusters
of nodding, funnel-shaped blue flowers in
the spring, amid its bold clumps of large,
pointed, roughly hairy leaves.

Perennials for Wall Crevices and Between Paving

MANY PERENNIALS THAT ENJOY good drainage grow in rock crevices in the wild, and find garden walls and paved areas a home away from home. Sunny walls soak up the sun's heat, which encourages flowering, and trailing plants in bloom look splendid tumbling down a wall. Some plants prefer the cool, moist conditions usually provided by shady walls.

Campanula cochleariifolia
FAIRY'S THIMBLES
☼ 4   ↕3in (8cm) ↔ indefinite

This delightful creeping perennial forms low carpets of small, rounded leaves. Numerous charming little bellflowers appear above the foliage in summer.

OTHER PERENNIALS FOR WALL CREVICES AND BETWEEN PAVING

Androsace sarmentosa
Asarina procumbens, see p.28
Erigeron karvinskianus
Iberis sempervirens 'Little Gem'
Phlox 'Emerald Cushion'
Saxifraga 'Southside Seedling'
Sedum spathulifolium 'Cape Blanco', see p.73
Sempervivum tectorum
Verbascum dumulosum

Arabis caucasica 'Rosabella'
ROCK CRESS
☼ 4   ↕6in (15cm) ↔ 12in (30cm)

One of the most reliable perennials suited to walls, this forms evergreen mats of soft foliage, above which sprays of pink flowers open in spring and early summer.

Aubrieta 'Joy'
AUBRIETA
☼ 4   ↕4in (10cm) ↔ 12in (30cm)

Aubrietas are among the most reliable and popular of all rock and wall plants. This cultivar is covered by pale mauve flowers in spring above evergreen hummocks.

Arenaria balearica
SANDWORT
☼ ☼ 5   ↕½in (1cm) ↔ indefinite

This creeping perennial makes a charming carpeter for a damp, cool place. Little flowers pepper an evergreen film of tiny leaves in late spring and early summer.

Aurinia saxatilis
BASKET OF GOLD
☼ 3   ↕9in (23cm) ↔ 12in (30cm)

Along with *Arabis* and *Aubrieta*, this genus dominates the wall plant world. Mats of evergreen gray-green leaves are hidden in spring by clouds of rich yellow flowers.

Chiastophyllum oppositifolium
CHIASTOPHYLLUM
☼ ☼ 5   ↕8in (20cm) ↔ 6in (15cm)

Hummocks of fleshy evergreen leaves are topped in late spring and early summer by drooping yellow flower sprays, making this plant resemble a tiny weeping willow.

Lewisia 'George Henley'
LEWISIA
☀ 5 PH   ↕ 6in (15cm) ↔ 4in (10cm)

Loose sprays of dark-veined, deep pink
flowers appear from late spring and all
through summer above rosettes of narrow,
fleshy leaves. Best when grown in a wall.

Corydalis ochroleuca
CORYDALIS
☀ ☀ 5   ↕ 10in (25cm) ↔ 10in (25cm)

The fleshy stems of this reliable crevice
plant carry clusters of tubular flowers
in late spring and early summer, amid
clumps of fernlike evergreen leaves.

Persicaria vacciniifolia
KNOTWEED
☀ 7   ↕ 8in (20cm) ↔ indefinite

A free-growing, prostrate evergreen, this
forms dense carpets of small green leaves,
tinted red in autumn. Red-stalked flower
spikes rise in late summer and autumn.

Dryas octopetala
MOUNTAIN AVENS
☀ 1   ↕ 2½in (6cm) ↔ indefinite

Small, glossy green leaves form dense
evergreen carpets. White, anemone-like
flowers appear from late spring into early
summer. Pretty, silky seed heads follow.

Erinus alpinus
FAIRY FOXGLOVE
☀ 4   ↕ 3in (8cm) ↔ 3in (8cm)

This charming, short-lived perennial, best
in a wall, forms neat rosettes with delicate
purple, pink, or white flower spikes in late
spring and summer. It may self-seed.

Ramonda myconi
RAMONDA
☀ ☀ 6   ↕ 3in (8cm) ↔ 4in (10cm)

Evergreen rosettes of strongly veined,
crinkly leaves provide a perfect foil for the
stalked flower clusters in late spring and
early summer. Best in a cool, moist wall.

Perennials for Screes and Rock Gardens

Usually referred to as rock plants or alpines, a huge range of small or prostrate perennials are easily grown and best displayed in a rock garden. They generally need full sun and good drainage, although there are some exceptions. You can also grow them in scree beds, specially prepared with a well-drained medium topped by a layer of gravel or chips.

Gentiana verna
SPRING GENTIAN
☀ **5-6**   ↕ 2in (5cm) ↔ 2in (5cm)

A beautiful, but often short-lived, gentian with tuffets of evergreen leaves. Erect, long-tubed flowers of an intense blue with a white throat appear in early spring.

Aethionema grandiflorum
PERSIAN STONE CRESS
☀ **4**   ↕ 12in (30cm) ↔ 10in (25cm)

This shrubby semievergreen perennial, with tiny, narrow blue-green leaves, has loose flower clusters in late spring and early summer. Needs good drainage.

Artemisia schmidtiana 'Nana'
SILVER MOUND
☀ **3**   ↕ 3in (8cm) ↔ 8in (20cm)

A lovely little hummock with silvery gray, aromatic, filigree-like foliage that shines in the sun. Flowers are few and insignificant. Thrives in a well-drained situation.

Geranium cinereum var. *subcaulescens*
CRANESBILL
☀ **4**   ↕ 5in (13cm) ↔ 12in (30cm)

This cranesbill forms low mats of small, rounded, deeply divided leaves, and loosely branched heads of saucer-shaped magenta flowers, each with a black eye.

Arenaria purpurascens
SANDWORT
☀ **6**   ↕ ½in (1cm) ↔ 6in (15cm)

This mat-forming perennial, bearing dense evergreen rosettes of tiny, sharply pointed leaves, is covered in early spring with small clusters of pink, star-shaped flowers.

Dianthus 'La Bourboule'
ALPINE PINK
☀ **4**   ↕ 2in (5cm) ↔ 3in (8cm)

This alpine pink has low carpets of narrow evergreen leaves and abundant, small pink flowers, with good fragrance, in summer. Ideal in a well-drained, alkaline soil.

Leontopodium alpinum
EDELWEISS
☀ **5**   ↕ 7in (18cm) ↔ 7in (18cm)

An ever-popular alpine, this edelweiss is short lived but very reliable. It has silvery white, furry flowerheads in spring or early summer. Good drainage is essential.

Origanum 'Kent Beauty'
ORIGANUM
☼ 8   ↕8in (20cm) ↔ 12in (30cm)

Low mats of slender stems, clothed with
smooth, aromatic leaves, terminate in hop-
like clusters of pale pink flowers from
rose-tinted green bracts, in late summer.

Phlox douglasii 'Boothman's Variety'
ALPINE PHLOX
☼ 4   ↕2in (5cm) ↔ 8in (20cm)

Neat mats of narrow evergreen leaves are
covered in early summer by lovely, pale
lavender-blue flowers with a violet-blue
eye. This is a reliable beginner's plant.

Rhodohypoxis baurii 'Margaret Rose'
RHODOHYPOXIS
☼ ☼ 7   ↕3in (8cm) ↔ 2½in (6cm)

The delicate pink flowers of this tuberous
perennial, with narrow, hairy leaves, occur
from spring into early summer. Prefers a
gritty soil and to be kept dry in winter.

Tropaeolum polyphyllum
TROPAEOLUM
☼ 8   ↕3in (8cm) ↔ 30in (75cm)

Both the fingered leaves and fleshy stems
of this sprawling perennial are a smooth
blue-green color. Small yellow flowers
crowd the ends of the stems in summer.

Veronica prostrata 'Kapitan'
VERONICA
☼ 4   ↕12in (30cm) ↔ 18in (45cm)

This reliable plant forms dense clumps of
slender stems clothed in narrow, toothed
leaves and carrying a profusion of rich
blue flower spikes in early summer.

OTHER PERENNIALS FOR SCREES AND ROCK GARDENS
Androsace sarmentosa
Campanula carpatica
Corydalis solida
Erodium reichardii
Geranium cinereum 'Ballerina'
Gypsophila cerastioides
Nierembergia repens
Oxalis adenophylla, see p.37
Phlox bifida
Saponaria x *olivana*
Saxifraga x *apiculata*
Tanacetum argenteum, see p.73

Viola tricolor 'Bowles' Black'
VIOLA
☼ 5   ↕4in (10cm) ↔ 2½in (6cm)

A short-lived, tufted perennial with loose,
leafy stems and exquisite, small blackish
violet flowers, each with a gold eye. These
occur from spring through to autumn.

Bulbs for Rock Gardens, Raised Beds, and Screes

S OME OF THE MOST satisfying bulbous plants are the dwarf kinds ideal for rock gardens or raised beds, where they can be admired without being crowded by any more robust neighbors. Many hail from mountainous or dry places, so they need good light and sharp drainage. They like moisture during the growing season, usually in spring or summer.

Colchicum agrippinum
AUTUMN CROCUS
☼ ⑦   ↕ 5in (12cm)

Funnel-shaped flowers, checkered dark purple on a paler background, appear in early autumn. The wavy, shining green leaves develop the following spring.

Allium cyathophorum var. *farreri*
ORNAMENTAL ONION
☼ ⑤   ↕ 9in (22cm)

Slender stems bearing nodding clusters of bell-shaped, reddish purple flowers rise through tufts of narrow leaves in summer. Thrives in moist but well-drained soils.

Anemone blanda 'Radar'
GRECIAN WINDFLOWER
☼ ☼ ④   ↕ 3in (7cm)

This is a reliable tuberous perennial that produces lobed, fernlike leaves. Spring brings its vibrant magenta, multipetaled flowers with white centers.

Crocus biflorus
CROCUS
☼ ⑤   ↕ 3½in (9cm)

This exquisite crocus produces tussocks of narrow leaves, each with a white stripe. White or purple flowers, striped purple on the outside, emerge in early spring.

Allium oreophilum
ORNAMENTAL ONION
☼ ③   ↕ 4in (10cm)

An easy and reliable bulb with a pair of long, thin leaves in winter. These usually wither by the time the flowers bloom from late spring into early summer.

Chionodoxa luciliae
GLORY OF THE SNOW
☼ ☼ ④   ↕ 4in (10cm)

A beautiful spring-flowering bulb, which has strap-shaped leaves and a loose spray of brilliant blue, star-shaped flowers. It will spread by seed or by division.

Iris reticulata 'J.S. Dijt'
MINIATURE IRIS
☼ ⑤   ↕ 5in (12cm)

One of a group of charming miniature bulbous iris with long, upright, gray-green leaves. Its solitary, fragrant, rich reddish purple flowers open in early spring.

58

Muscari aucheri
GRAPE HYACINTH
☼ 5   ↕ 4in (10cm)

Erect stems above strap-shaped leaves
support dense spikes of bright blue spring
flowers. The top of the spike is usually
paler, giving a distinct two-tone effect.

**OTHER BULBS FOR ROCK GARDENS,
RAISED BEDS, AND SCREES**

Allium karataviense
Arum creticum
Crocus 'E.A. Bowles'
Fritillaria pallidiflora, see p.79
Iris histrioides 'Major'
Leucojum autumnale, see p.83
Muscari latifolium
Narcissus bulbocodium
Ornithogalum balansae
Sternbergia lutea

Puschkinia scilloides 'Alba'
PUSCHKINIA
☼ 4   ↕ 8in (20cm)

A lovely white form of the normally blue-
flowered spring bulb, this produces pairs
of strap-shaped leaves and loose spikes of
star-shaped flowers. Dislikes dry soils.

Narcissus cyclamineus
MINIATURE DAFFODIL
☼ 7   ↕ 6in (15cm)

This popular miniature daffodil has a
single golden yellow flower with upswept
petals and a slender, crinkly-mouthed
trumpet in late winter or early spring.

Scilla siberica 'Spring Beauty'
SIBERIAN SQUILL
☼ 2   ↕ 5in (13cm)

Tufts of strap-shaped, fleshy leaves are
topped in spring by the loose sprays of
rich blue, bell-shaped flowers. A popular
and easy plant that forms colonies in time.

Tulipa tarda
TULIP
☼ 5   ↕ 6in (15cm)

One of the most satisfactory wild tulips,
this is especially good in dry soils. Star-
shaped spring flowers occur several to a
stem above narrow leaves.

Bulbs for Wild Areas

THE STIRRING SIGHT of bulbs flowering *en masse* in the wild can be re-created in your own garden by planting them in quantity where conditions are most suitable. The bulbs will naturalize, by seeding around or spreading vegetatively, to give an impressive display year after year. Bulbs that come from woodland habitats will thrive in beds or borders beneath deciduous trees or shrubs, while those that are grassland species enjoy orchards or marginal areas of grass.

Crocus tommasinianus
CROCUS
☼ ☼ 5 ↕ 4in (10cm)

Excellent for naturalizing in short grass, these will spread quickly if unchecked. The pale lavender to purple flowers open in late winter and early spring.

Anemone blanda 'Atrocaerulea'
GRECIAN WINDFLOWER
☼ ☼ 4 ↕ 3in (7cm)

Deep blue, early spring flowers carpet the ground above prettily divided leaves. Particularly well-suited to alkaline soils in woodland margins, or beneath shrubs.

OTHER BULBS FOR WILD AREAS IN LIGHT SHADE

Arum italicum 'Marmoratum'
Chionodoxa luciliae, see p.58
Colchicum 'Lilac Wonder'
Colchicum 'The Giant'
Cyclamen coum, see p.41
Cyclamen repandum
Erythronium oregonum
Erythronium 'Pagoda', see p.79
Galanthus elwesii
Galanthus nivalis
Galanthus nivalis 'Flore Pleno', see p.84
Galanthus plicatus
Hyacinthoides hispanica, see p.41
Leucojum aestivum
Leucojum vernum
Narcissus pseudonarcissus
Ornithogalum nutans, see p.41
Scilla siberica

Camassia leichtlinii 'Alba'
CAMASSIA
☼ ☼ 5 ↕ 4ft (1.2m)

This striking summer-flowering bulb has long, narrow leaves and upright spires of star-shaped flowers. It is most suitable for moist soils or damp grassland.

Cyclamen hederifolium
IVY-LEAVED CYCLAMEN
☼ ☼ ☼ 5 ↕ 4in (10cm)

A charming, reliable miniature cyclamen, ideal for woodland margins and shady areas that remain moist in summer. The flowers occur in abundance in autumn.

Eranthis hyemalis
WINTER ACONITE
☼ 3 ↕ 3in (8cm)

These bright flowers with leafy collars are a heartening sight in late winter and early spring. Enjoys soil rich in leaf mold in woodland or short grass beneath trees.

Fritillaria meleagris
CHECKERED LILY
☀ **3**   ↕ 12in (30cm)

Nodding, maroon- or white-checkered
bells on slender stems in spring make this
a favorite for naturalizing in damp grassland that remains moist in summer.

Gladiolus communis subsp. *byzantinus*
GLADIOLUS
☀ **7**   ↕ 3ft (1m)

This early summer-flowering perennial
soon spreads in warm, well-drained soils.
It has spikes of funnel-shaped magenta
flowers and sword-shaped leaves.

Narcissus pseudonarcissus
subsp. *obvallaris*
☀ ☀ **5**   ↕ 9in (22cm)

This lovely form of the Lent Lily makes
a very impressive spring show when
planted in short grass or on woodland
edges, in soils that are moist in spring.

Nectaroscordum siculum
subsp. *bulgaricum*
☀ ☀ **6**   ↕ 3ft (1m)

Clusters of bell-shaped flowers in late
spring and early summer give this reliable
ornamental onion a stately appearance.
It will spread freely in grass or borders.

Galanthus caucasicus
SNOWDROP
☀ **5**   ↕ 10in (25cm)

A striking snowdrop of robust growth, this
has broad blue-green leaves and nodding
flowers in late winter and early spring. The
inner flower segments have a green tip.

**OTHER BULBS FOR WILD
AREAS IN SUN**

Camassia esculenta
Colchicum autumnale
Crocus 'Dutch Yellow'
Crocus tommasinianus 'Ruby Giant'
Crocus vernus
Narcissus bulbocodium
Narcissus 'Peeping Tom'
Narcissus 'Spellbinder'
Tulipa kaufmanniana
Tulipa tarda, see p.59

Lilium martagon
MARTAGON LILY
☀ **4**   ↕ 5ft (1.5m)

This lily is excellent for naturalizing in
woodland glades beneath deciduous trees
and shrubs, and in grass. The fragrant,
nodding flowers appear in summer.

Tulipa sylvestris
WOODS TULIP
☀ **5**   ↕ 18in (45cm)

Worthy of more widespread use, this tulip
will thrive in well-drained grassland,
particularly in orchards and open woodland, where it flowers in spring.

Flowering Perennials for Containers

ONTAINERS PROVIDE the opportunity to cultivate a wide range of hardy perennials in hard-surfaced or small gardens; most flowering perennials will grow well in such conditions. In cold areas, pots and tubs also give the exciting opportunity of growing tender perennials, since you can move them under glass for protection during the winter.

Chrysanthemum 'Pennine Flute'
QUILL CHRYSANTHEMUM
☼ **5**   ↕ 4ft (1.2m) ↔ 30in (75cm)

This erect, much-branched perennial has aromatic foliage and, in early autumn, a profusion of large pink daisylike flowers, each with a yellow center.

Argyranthemum 'Mary Wooton'
MARGUERITE DAISY
☼ **10**   ↕ 3ft (1m) ↔ 3ft (1m)

All through summer, this bushy evergreen, with its attractive, finely divided, fernlike leaves, carries large, pink daisylike flowers with anemone centers on slender stems.

Bidens ferulifolia
BIDENS
☼ **8**   ↕ 3ft (1m) ↔ 4ft (1.2m)

From late summer into autumn, many golden yellow flowers cover this slender-stemmed, sometimes scrambling, perennial with finely cut leaves.

OTHER TENDER FLOWERING PERENNIALS FOR CONTAINERS

Agapanthus Headbourne Hybrids
Argyranthemum 'Chelsea Girl'
Eucomis bicolor
Hedychium gardnerianum
Heliotropium arborescens
Osteospermum 'Silver Sparkler'
Pelargonium 'Bird Dancer'

Begonia sutherlandii
BEGONIA
☼ ☼ **7**   ↕ 18in (45cm) ↔ 18in (45cm)

One of the hardiest of all begonias, this is a tuberous-rooted species forming clumps of bright green, toothed leaves, and loose clusters of orange summer flowers.

Canna 'Assaut'
CANNA
☼ **7**   ↕ 4ft (1.2m) ↔ 24in (60cm)

A dense head of large scarlet flowers with purple bracts is borne on an erect stem above lush foliage. Different cultivars have flowers of other colors. Dislikes dry soils.

Lotus berthelotii
CORAL GEM
☼ **10**   ↕ 6in (15cm) ↔ 24in (60cm)

Summer clusters of scarlet pea flowers are a bonus, since Coral Gem is worth growing for its semievergreen, trailing silver foliage alone. Effective in hanging baskets.

Osteospermum 'Buttermilk'
AFRICAN DAISY

☼ 9   ↕ 24in (60cm) ↔ 18in (45cm)

From summer into autumn, large, pale yellow, daisylike flowers with dark centers are supported on erect stems above toothed evergreen leaves that are gray-green.

Pelargonium 'Bredon'
REGAL GERANIUM

☼ 10   ↕ 18in (45cm) ↔ 12in (30cm)

In summer, this robust evergreen sub-shrub or perennial carries clusters of large maroon flowers above its rich green, lobed and toothed, aromatic foliage.

Strelitzia reginae
BIRD-OF-PARADISE

☼ 10   ↕ 3ft (1m) ↔ 30in (75cm)

Exquisite orange and blue spring flowers are reminiscent of the heads of exotic cranes. The blue-green evergreen leaves are erect and form bold clumps.

HARDY FLOWERING PERENNIALS FOR CONTAINERS

Allium schoenoprasum, see p.86
Astilbe x *arendsii* cultivars
Bergenia 'Silberlicht'
Caltha palustris
Coreopsis 'Moonbeam'
Dicentra spectabilis f. *alba*
Lilium regale, see p.81
Liriope muscari, see p.43
Platycodon grandiflorus
Polygonatum odoratum

OTHER TRAILING FLOWERING PERENNIALS FOR CONTAINERS

Diascia rigescens
Phlox subulata
Saponaria 'Bressingham'
Verbena 'Silver Anne'

Pelargonium 'Red Cascade'
IVY-LEAVED GERANIUM

☼ 10   ↕ 18in (45cm) ↔ 18in (45cm)

This evergreen, a charming miniature of *P.* 'Ivy-leaf', has fleshy, ivy-shaped leaves and trailing stems. Clusters of red flowers open all year long in mild areas.

Verbena 'Sissinghurst'
VERBENA

☼ 8   ↕ 8in (20cm) ↔ 18in (45cm)

Low, with a wide-spreading habit, this verbena has small, aromatic, deeply cut leaves and charming heads of bright pink flowers throughout summer.

Foliage Perennials for Containers

MANY PERENNIALS are worth growing in containers solely for their attractive leaves. Some have the added bonus of attractive flowers, but the selection here has been chosen mainly for foliage effect. Treating them as container plants allows greater flexibility in their placement, and also enables you to shelter those tender plants liable to winter damage.

Aloe arborescens 'Variegata'
ALOE
☼ 10   ↕ 6ft (2m) ↔ 6ft (2m)

Succulent, spine-toothed evergreen leaves are blue-green with cream margins and stripes. Long-stalked spikes of red flowers are a bonus in late winter and spring.

Carex flagellifera
SEDGE
☼ ☼ 7   ↕ 24in (60cm) ↔ 20in (50cm)

This tough, little, grasslike evergreen perennial forms a dense tuffet of slender, arching leaves that are tinged red, and often darken in winter. Dislikes dry soils.

Agave americana 'Variegata'
VARIEGATED CENTURY PLANT
☼ 9   ↕ 5ft (1.5m) ↔ 5ft (1.5m)

Spine-toothed, pointed leaves, each with a yellow margin, eventually form a large evergreen rosette. In maturity, statuesque white flower spikes appear in summer.

Aeonium 'Zwartkop'
AEONIUM
☼ 9   ↕ 24in (60cm) ↔ 3ft (1m)

The branches of this evergreen succulent are topped with bold rosettes of polished, dark purple leaves. Its conical heads of yellow flowers appear in spring.

OTHER HARDY FOLIAGE PERENNIALS FOR CONTAINERS

Acorus gramineus 'Ogon'
Athyrium nipponicum 'Pictum'
Bergenia 'Bressingham Ruby'
Hakonechloa macra 'Aureola'
Helictotrichon sempervirens
Heuchera micrantha 'Palace Purple',
  see p.74
Hosta 'Gold Standard'
Hosta 'Wide Brim'
Houttuynia cordata 'Chamaeleon'

Dicksonia antarctica
AUSTRALIAN TREE FERN
☼ 9   ↕ 15ft (5m) ↔ 12ft (4m)

A magnificent, treelike fern, this has a stout, fibrous "stem" which is crowned by a huge rosette of big, beautifully dissected fronds. Dislikes exposure and dry soils.

Phormium 'Sundowner'
NEW ZEALAND FLAX
☼ 9   ↕6ft (1.8m) ↔4ft (1.2m)

This vigorous evergreen plant, excellent
for a large container, has tufts of glossy,
sword-shaped bronze-green leaves, edged
dark rose-pink and fading to cream.

Hosta sieboldiana var. *elegans*
PLANTAIN LILY
☼ ☼ 3   ↕3ft (1m) ↔5ft (1.5m)

The large, heart-shaped, blue-gray leaves
of this big, bold perennial are puckered
and strongly veined. Drooping, pale lilac
trumpet flowers open in early summer.

**OTHER TENDER FOLIAGE
PERENNIALS FOR CONTAINERS**

Agave americana
Asparagus densiflorus 'Meyers'
Aspidistra elatior
Canna cultivars
Cycas revoluta
Cyrtomium falcatum
Melianthus major
Musa acuminata 'Dwarf Cavendish'
Pelargonium 'Skies of Italy'
Phormium tenax 'Yellow Wave', see p.66

Pelargonium 'Royal Oak'
SCENTED-LEAVED GERANIUM
☼ 10   ↕15in (38cm) ↔12in (30cm)

Bushy and spicily fragrant, this compact
evergreen has boldly lobed, slightly sticky
leaves with brown central zones. Mauve-
pink summer flowers have dark blotches.

Ricinus communis 'Impala'
CASTOR BEAN
☼ 10   ↕5in (1.5m) ↔3ft (1m)

The leaves of this vigorous evergreen are
large, deeply lobed, and a striking deep
bronze. Usually treated as an annual, it
carries autumn clusters of spiky red fruit.

Pelargonium 'Dolly Varden'
ZONAL GERANIUM
☼ 10   ↕12in (30cm) ↔9in (23cm)

Eye-catching, aromatic evergreen foliage
is basically green with purplish brown
and crimson zoning and irregular cream
margins. Summer flowers are scarlet.

Pelargonium tomentosum
PEPPERMINT GERANIUM
☼ 10   ↕24in (60cm) ↔3ft (1m)

Bold, lobed evergreen leaves are covered,
as are the stems, in velvety down. Bushy
and spreading, they smell of mint when
rubbed. Bears white flowers in summer.

Tradescantia pallida 'Purple Heart'
PURPLE HEART
☼ 9   ↕16in (40cm) ↔12in (30cm)

Low in habit, this distinctive evergreen
forms patches of dark, glowing purple
stems and leaves and produces small,
pink, three-petaled flowers in summer.

Evergreen Perennials

FOLIAGE THAT REMAINS fresh and alive in winter is a valuable attribute in any perennial, given that so many either disappear entirely below ground or are left with leaves that look tired, if not withered. Green foliage in winter is welcome enough, but if red, purple, or any other colors are available, this only adds to the visual variety. Evergreens also provide an excellent foil for winter- and early spring-flowering bulbs. Many make impressive specimens.

Helleborus argutifolius
CORSICAN HELLEBORE
☼ ☀ 5 ⬍24in (60cm) ↔18in (45cm)

This bold, stout-stemmed hellebore has large, three-parted leaves. Its impressive clusters of cup-shaped, apple green flowers open from late winter into spring.

Bergenia cordifolia 'Purpurea'
PIGSQUEAK
☼ ☼ ☀ 3 ⬍20in (50cm) ↔20in (50cm)

The erect stems of this tough plant carry sprays of bell-shaped rose-pink flowers in late winter and early spring above bold clumps of fleshy, heart-shaped leaves.

Celmisia coriacea
NEW ZEALAND DAISY
☼ ☀ 9 PH ⬍12in (30cm) ↔12in (30cm)

In time, this magnificent perennial forms a striking clump of silvery, sword-shaped leaves, topped by large, single white daisy flowers in summer. Dislikes dry soils.

Phormium tenax 'Yellow Wave'
NEW ZEALAND FLAX
☼ 9 ⬍4ft (1.2m) ↔4ft (1.2m)

Soft yellow, sword-shaped leaves, each with a bright lime green margin, form bold arching clumps. Leaves develop chartreuse tones in autumn.

Blechnum tabulare
BLECHNUM
☼ ☀ 8 ⬍3ft (1m) ↔3ft (1m)

The deep green, much-divided fronds, which form bold clumps, are leathery, large, and arching. They may be bronze when young. Ideal for a sheltered spot.

Helleborus foetidus
STINKING HELLEBORE
☼ ☀ 5 ⬍18in (45cm) ↔18in (45cm)

Bell-shaped flowers opening in late winter and early spring are pale green with maroon markings. These and the leathery, dark green, fingered leaves are poisonous.

Phyllostachys nigra var. *henonis*
BAMBOO
☼ ☀ 7 ⬍15ft (5m) ↔10ft (3m)

Capable of twice the given height in warm, sheltered conditions, this lovely bamboo has narrow, shiny leaves and erect canes, maturing from green to yellow.

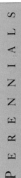

Phyllostachys viridiglaucescens
BAMBOO
☼ ☀ 7   ↕ 20ft (6m) ↔ indefinite

This vigorous bamboo forms bold clumps
of arching green canes carrying lush, shiny
green foliage. It may grow extremely tall
in warm, sheltered conditions.

OTHER EVERGREEN PERENNIALS

Asarum europaeum, see p.30
Asplenium scolopendrium 'Marginatum'
Epimedium grandiflorum
Euphorbia x *martinii*
Kniphofia caulescens
Liriope muscari, see p.43
Morina longifolia
Phlomis russelliana
Phormium cookianum 'Tricolor'
Polystichum munitum, see p.45
Shortia galacifolia

Sasa veitchii
BAMBOO
☼ ☀ ☀ 6   ↕ 4ft (1.2m) ↔ indefinite

In time, this fast-creeping bamboo forms
extensive patches of upright stems, well-
clothed with eye-catching, oblong green
leaves. These develop white margins.

Polystichum setiferum 'Divisilobum'
SOFT SHIELD FERN
☼ ☀ 6   ↕ 24in (60cm) ↔ 18in (45cm)

A lovely evergreen or, in severe winters,
semievergreen fern forming dense clumps
of finely divided, rich green fronds, pale
and scaly when young. Dislikes dry soils.

Shibataea kumasasa
BAMBOO
☼ ☀ ☀ 6   ↕ 3ft (1m) ↔ 24in (60cm)

Particularly suited to small gardens, this
bamboo forms compact clumps of upright,
slender canes that are all densely crowded
with relatively broad, pointed leaves.

Yucca gloriosa
SPANISH DAGGER
☼ 7   ↕ 6ft (2m) ↔ 4½ft (1.4m)

Rigid, spine-tipped, gray-green leaves
grow in striking clumps. A short, woody
stem eventually supports branched heads
of ivory-white bell flowers in summer.

Perennials with Variegated Leaves

CHOOSING A VARIEGATED PERENNIAL for a planting plan can be tricky since so many types exist. Blotches, spots, streaks, and stripes abound, but most common, and often most effective, are leaves with margins of a different color. Whatever their pattern, variegated plants bring interest and contrast to a border or bed.

Astrantia major
'Sunningdale Variegated'
☼ ☀ 4 ↕ 24in (60cm) ↔ 18in (45cm)

Long-stalked and deeply lobed leaves are striped and splashed cream and yellow. Loose, greenish white flowerheads are produced in summer and early autumn.

Hosta fortunei 'Aureomarginata'
PLANTAIN LILY
☼ ☀ 3 ↕ 30in (75cm) ↔ 3ft (1m)

Green, heart-shaped leaves with irregular, creamy yellow margins grow in clumps. Trumpet-shaped flowers in summer are violet. Thrives in moist or rich soils.

Mentha x *suaveolens* 'Variegata'
VARIEGATED APPLE MINT
☼ ☀ 5 ↕ 18in (45cm) ↔ 24in (60cm)

This free-growing perennial in time forms colonies. It has pale green, softly downy stems, and the leaves, splashed white and cream, are aromatic when bruised.

Phlox paniculata 'Norah Leigh'
GARDEN PHLOX
☼ 4 ↕ 3ft (1m) ↔ 24in (60cm)

Sturdy clumps of erect stems are clothed in creamy white leaves, each with an irregular green center. Conical, pale lilac flowerheads top the leaves in summer.

Brunnera macrophylla
'Dawson's White'
☼ 3 ↕ 18in (45cm) ↔ 24in (60cm)

This most effective variegated perennial has clumps of hairy, heart-shaped leaves with irregular cream-white margins. Sprays of forget-me-not flowers appear in spring.

Hosta undulata var. *univittata*
PLANTAIN LILY
☼ ☀ 3 ↕ 24in (60cm) ↔ 24in (60cm)

Vigorous and clump-forming, this hosta has glossy, oval leaves, each with a central white stripe. Mauve trumpet flowers occur in summer. Enjoys moist or rich soils.

OTHER PERENNIALS WITH WHITE- OR CREAM-VARIEGATED FOLIAGE

Cortaderia selloana 'Albolineata'
Hemerocallis fulva 'Kwanzo Variegata'
Heuchera 'Snowstorm'
Hosta 'Shade Fanfare', see p.30
Iris pallida 'Argentea Variegata'
Miscanthus sinensis 'Cabaret'
Physostegia virginiana
    subsp. *speciosa* 'Variegata'
Polygonatum x *hybridum* 'Variegatum'
Pulmonaria saccharata 'Mrs. Moon'

Sisyrinchium striatum
'Aunt May'
☼ 7　　‡24in (60cm) ↔ 12in (30cm)

The irislike clumps of semievergreen, erect gray-green leaves are striped cream. Spikes of straw yellow, purple-streaked flowers are produced in summer.

Symphytum × *uplandicum* 'Variegatum'
VARIEGATED RUSSIAN COMFREY
☼ ◐ 4　　‡3ft (1m) ↔ 24in (60cm)

Large, hairy leaves with bold margins form robust clumps. Nodding flower clusters in late spring and early summer change from pink to blue. Thrives in moist soils.

OTHER PERENNIALS WITH YELLOW-VARIEGATED FOLIAGE

Carex elata 'Aurea'
Convallaria majalis 'Aureo-variegata'
Cortaderia selloana 'Aureolineata'
Filipendula ulmaria 'Variegata'
Hakonechloa macra 'Aureola'
Hosta 'Gold Standard'
Iris pallida 'Variegata'
Persicaria virginiana 'Painter's Palette'
Pleioblastus auricomus, see p.71
Yucca flaccida 'Golden Sword'

Polemonium caeruleum 'Brise d'Anjou'
VARIEGATED JACOB'S LADDER
☼ 4　　‡18in (45cm) ↔ 12in (30cm)

This handsome perennial has mounds of neatly "laddered" leaves with numerous cream-margined leaflets. Its small bluish flowers bloom in early summer.

Pleioblastus variegatus
DWARF WHITE-STRIPED BAMBOO
☼ 6　　‡32in (80cm) ↔ indefinite

A popular dwarf bamboo, this will form evergreen clumps and colonies. Its narrow green-and-white-striped leaves clothe erect, slender, woody canes.

Scrophularia auriculata 'Variegata'
VARIEGATED WATER FIGWORT
☼ ◐ 5　　‡5ft (1.5m) ↔ 24in (60cm)

Bold clumps of leaves that are striped and splashed cream make this an impressive perennial. Its tall stems bear tiny summer flowers. Thrives in rich, moist soils.

Yucca gloriosa 'Variegata'
VARIEGATED ADAM'S NEEDLE
☼ 7　　‡6ft (2m) ↔ 4ft (1.2m)

Stiff, sword-shaped gray-green leaves are striped yellow and make a grand rosette. A magnificent creamy white flower spike tops each mature plant in late summer.

Perennials with Golden or Yellow Leaves

Most golden- or yellow-leaved forms of perennial plants originated as seedlings or bud mutations, and have been propagated vegetatively to keep them in cultivation. The strength and degree of color varies considerably, but they can bring a welcome touch of warmth to the garden, especially when contrasted with green or reddish foliage.

Lysimachia nummularia 'Aurea'
GOLDEN MONEYWORT
☼ 3   ↕ 2in (5cm) ↔ indefinite

The creeping stems of this moneywort form carpets of rounded and paired, pale yellow leaves. These are joined in summer by bright yellow, cup-shaped flowers.

Carex oshimensis hachijoensis 'Evergold'
GOLDEN JAPANESE SEDGE GRASS
☼ 5   ↕ 8in (20cm) ↔ 8in (20cm)

This bold, tufted sedge is evergreen. The arching, narrow, grassy leaves are glossy, and each has a conspicuous, creamy yellow central stripe. It forms a low mound.

OTHER HERBACEOUS PERENNIALS WITH GOLDEN LEAVES

Alopecurus pratensis 'Aureovargiegatus'
Campanula garganica 'Dickson's Gold'
Centaurea montana 'Gold Bullion'
Hakonechloa macra 'Aureola'
Hosta fortunei 'Aurea'
Hosta 'Golden Prayers'
Hosta 'Midas Touch'
Hosta 'Piedmont Gold'
Hosta sieboldiana 'Golden Sunburst'
Hosta 'Sum and Substance'
Hosta 'Wogon Gold'
Lamium maculatum 'Aureum'
Melissa officinalis 'All Gold'
Milium effusum 'Aureum'
Symphytum ibericum 'All Gold'
Tanacetum parthenium 'Aureum'
Tanacetum vulgare 'Isla Gold'
Thymus x *citriodorus* 'Aureus'

Filipendula ulmaria 'Aurea'
GOLDEN MEADOWSWEET
☼ ☼ 3   ↕ 24in (60cm) ↔ 30cm (12in)

Although the familiar, sweetly scented white flowers of this plant are attractive, it is the impressive golden yellow spring foliage that merits the most attention.

Hosta 'Zounds'
PLANTAIN LILY
☼ 3   ↕ 30in (75cm) ↔ 3ft (1m)

A spectacular perennial that forms a bold mound of large, rounded, and puckered yellow leaves, above which spikes of pale lavender flowers rise in early summer.

Melissa officinalis 'Aurea'
GOLDEN LEMON BALM
☼ ☼ 5   ↕ 24in (60cm) ↔ 18in (45cm)

The golden-variegated leaves of this bushy herb smell of lemon when bruised. Trim back after flowering to encourage a summer-long succession of color.

Origanum vulgare 'Aureum'
GOLDEN MARJORAM
☀ 5 ↕ 3in (8cm) ↔ indefinite

As summer advances, the dense, low pads of bright yellow, aromatic spring foliage begin to pale. At the same time, sparse clusters of tiny mauve flowers emerge.

Saxifraga moschata 'Cloth of Gold'
GOLDEN MOSSY SAXIFRAGE
☀ 5 ↕ 5in (13cm) ↔ 6in (15cm)

Neat rosettes of deeply divided golden leaves form evergreen mounds. White star-shaped summer flowers rise on thin stalks. Prefers moist but well-drained soil.

Stachys byzantina 'Primrose Heron'
LAMB'S-EARS
☀ 4 ↕ 15in (38cm) ↔ 24in (60cm)

This creeping evergreen forms mats of woolly silver-gray leaves, suffused pale yellow, especially when young. Mauve-pink flower spikes are carried in summer.

Valeriana phu 'Aurea'
VALERIAN
☀ 5 ↕ 15in (38cm) ↔ 12in (30cm)

The young spring foliage of this tufted perennial is lemon yellow and completely upstages the white, clustered flowers that follow in summer.

Pleioblastus auricomus
BAMBOO
☀ 6 ↕ 5ft (1.5m) ↔ indefinite

One of the best dwarf bamboos for color, this evergreen will form large colonies in time, but it is also good in containers. The yellow leaves are striped green.

OTHER EVERGREEN PERENNIALS WITH GOLDEN LEAVES

Acanthus mollis 'Holland's Gold'
Acorus gramineus 'Variegatus'
Carex elata 'Aurea'
Carex elata 'Bowles Golden'

Veronica prostrata 'Trehane'
VERONICA
☀ 4 ↕ 6in (15cm) ↔ 12in (30cm)

A choice and reliable little perennial that forms mats of toothed yellow leaves that turn yellowish green, and bears spikes of deep violet-blue flowers in early summer.

Perennials with Blue-gray or Silver Leaves

$\mathcal{S}$ ILVER- OR GRAY-LEAVED perennials are among the most valuable in the garden, providing a gentle foil to pastel shades or to strongly colored leaves or flowers. The grayish leaves provide a useful contrast in planting designs that contain mainly plants of interesting foliage. Here are a few of the many that are suitable and available.

Dicentra formosa 'Langtrees'
DICENTRA
☼ ☼ ③   ↕ 18in (45cm) ↔ 12in (30cm)

This vigorous perennial forms patches of erect, fleshy stems with blue-gray, ferny leaves. Arching sprays of white flowers are borne in late spring and early summer.

Hosta 'Hadspen Blue'
PLANTAIN LILY
☼ ☼ ③   ↕ 18in (45cm) ↔ 18in (45cm)

The heart-shaped and attractively veined, deep blue-gray leaves make this a striking foliage perennial. Lavender flower spikes appear in summer. Dislikes dry soils.

Artemisia ludoviciana
WHITE WORMWOOD
☼ ④   ↕ 4ft (1.2m) ↔ 24in (60cm)

Both the dense clumps of erect stems, and the willowlike, sharply toothed, aromatic leaves that clothe them, are downy. Tiny gray-white flowerheads occur in summer.

OTHER PERENNIALS WITH BLUE-GRAY OR SILVER LEAVES
Acaena 'Blue Haze'
Anaphalis triplinervis
Artemisia schmidtiana 'Nana', see p.56
Cynara scolymus
Hosta 'Blue Angel'
Iris pallida var. *dalmatica*
Lysimachia ephemerum
Macleaya cordata 'Flamingo'
Stachys byzantina 'Silver Carpet'
Thalictrum speciosissimum

Artemisia 'Powis Castle'
WORMWOOD
☼ ⑤   ↕ 3ft (1m) ↔ 4ft (1.2m)

The gray branches of this evergreen sub-shrub or perennial carry aromatic, silver, filigree foliage. Its summer flowerheads are tiny and sparsely produced.

Lychnis flos-jovis
FLOWER OF JOVE
☼ ④   ↕ 18in (45cm) ↔ 18in (45cm)

Like the leaves, the upright stems of this old-fashioned, favorite clump-former are clothed with a pelt of woolly gray down. Pretty summer flowers are rose-pink.

Onopordum acanthium
SCOTCH THISTLE
☼ 4   ↕ 7ft (2.2m) ↔ 4½ft (1.4m)

Vigorous and prickly, this stately biennial
(or short-lived perennial) has downy stems
and leaves. Its purplish pink flowerheads
appear in summer.

Ruta graveolens 'Jackman's Blue'
RUE
☼ 4   ↕ 24in (60cm) ↔ 30in (75cm)

The evergreen, fernlike, blue-gray foliage
of this aromatic perennial or subshrub may
cause an allergic rash. Clusters of small
flowers are produced in summer.

Stachys byzantina
LAMB'S-EARS
☼ 4   ↕ 15in (38cm) ↔ 24in (60cm)

One of the most popular and satisfactory
evergreen perennials, this forms dense
carpets of soft, woolly, silver-gray foliage,
with mauve-pink flower spikes in summer.

Sedum spathulifolium 'Cape Blanco'
STONECROP
☼ ☼ 6   ↕ 2in (5cm) ↔ indefinite

Evergreen rosettes of succulent, silvery
green leaves develop into dense pads and
mats. Eye-catching clusters of yellow
flowers rise above the leaves in summer.

Tanacetum argenteum
TANACETUM
☼ 5   ↕ 9in (23cm) ↔ 9in (23cm)

A low, mounding plant grown for its
charming, finely cut silver-gray leaves,
this tanacetum also produces a profusion
of white daisy flowers in summer.

Verbascum olympicum
MULLEIN
☼ 6   ↕ 6ft (2m) ↔ 3ft (1m)

This distinctive semievergreen biennial or
short-lived perennial often branches near
the base, and has woolly stems and leaves.
Summer flower spikes are yellow.

Perennials with Purple, Red, or Bronze Leaves

PERENNIALS WITH PURPLE or similarly dark leaves are most valuable in the garden, especially when contrasted with foliage that is green or yellow. Such plants are best planted in moderation, since their effect can be a little somber. Most of the following are at their darkest in spring, when young growth first appears, although there are some impressive exceptions.

Euphorbia dulcis 'Chameleon'
PURPLE-LEAVED SWEET SPURGE
☼ ☼ 7   ↕12in (30cm) ↔ 12in (30cm)

Masses of reddish purple leaves color richly in autumn, and tiny yellowish green flower clusters are a bonus in spring. The milky sap is caustic, so handle with care.

Ajuga reptans 'Atropurpurea'
PURPLE-LEAVED BUGLE
☼ ☼ ☼ 3   ↕6in (15cm) ↔ 3ft (1m)

The shining bronze-purple leaves of this evergreen, borne in lush rosettes, form a dense carpet. Short spikes of blue flowers appear in spring. Thrives in moist soil.

Clematis recta 'Purpurea'
ERECT CLEMATIS
☼ 3   ↕5ft (1.5m) ↔ 20in (50cm)

A profusion of fragrant white flowers rises above coppery purple leaves in summer. The erect, much-branched stems of this clump-forming perennial need support.

Foeniculum vulgare 'Purpureum'
PURPLE-LEAVED FENNEL
☼ 5   ↕6ft (2m) ↔ 18in (45cm)

Clumps of feathery young leaves emerge a deep mahogany purple, and pale to bronze as they mature. Tiny yellow flowers borne in umbels open in summer.

Anthriscus sylvestris 'Ravenswing'
PURPLE-LEAVED COW PARSLEY
☼ ☼ ☼ 5   ↕4ft (1.2m) ↔ 24in (60cm)

Mounds of finely divided, fernlike leaves are a rich dark purple in spring; they pale later. Umbels of tiny white, pink-bracted flowers open in late spring.

Euphorbia amygdaloides 'Rubra'
PURPLE-LEAVED WOOD SPURGE
☼ ☼ ☼ 6   ↕↔12in (30cm)

The evergreen leaves and stems of this bushy perennial are suffused purple-red. Small yellow flowers appear in spring. Be careful of its caustic, milky sap.

Heuchera micrantha 'Palace Purple'
PURPLE-LEAVED HEUCHERA
☼ 4   ↕18in (45cm) ↔ 18in (45cm)

Clumps of long-lived, heart-shaped leaves on tall stalks are a metallic copper-purple color. The clouds of tiny flowers appear in early summer. Will self-seed.

Lobelia 'Queen Victoria'
CARDINAL FLOWER
☼ 7   ↕ 3ft (1m) ↔ 12in (30cm)

Striking red flowers are carried on spikes
from summer into early autumn. Sturdy,
erect stems and narrow leaves are a deep,
reddish purple. Requires moist soils.

Ophiopogon planiscapus 'Nigrescens'
BLACK MONDO GRASS
☼ ☼ 6   ↕ 9in (23cm) ↔ 12in (30cm)

This creeping evergreen forms a dense tuft
of narrow, strap-shaped, blackish purple
leaves. Slender spikes bearing tiny lilac
flowers are produced in summer.

Penstemon digitalis 'Husker's Red'
BEARDTONGUE
☼ 4   ↕ 30in (75cm) ↔ 12in (30cm)

The young leaves and shoots of this erect
perennial are a rich purple in spring but
fade to green-tinged purple when the
tubular flowers appear in early summer.

> **OTHER EVERGREEN PERENNIALS
> WITH PURPLE OR BRONZE LEAVES**
>
> *Ajuga reptans* 'Braunherz'
> *Bergenia* 'Bressingham Ruby' in winter
> *Carex buchananii*
> *Epimedium* x *rubrum* in winter/spring,
>   see p.90
> *Galax aphylla* in winter
> *Phormium tenax* 'Purpureum'
> *Shortia galacifolia* in winter
> *Veronica peduncularis* 'Georgia Blue'
>   in spring, see p.29

Salvia officinalis 'Purpurascens'
PURPLE SAGE
☼ 3   ↕ 24in (60cm) ↔ 3ft (1m)

The downy, aromatic evergreen leaves of
this shrubby perennial are flushed purple
when new, and mature to grayish green.
Flower spikes are carried in summer.

> **OTHER HERBACEOUS PERENNIALS
> WITH PURPLE OR BRONZE LEAVES**
>
> *Artemisia lactiflora* 'Guizho'
> *Astilbe* 'Dunkellachs'
> *Cimicifuga simplex* 'Brunette'
>   *Eupatorium altissima* 'Braunlaub'
>   *Hypericum* 'Aubrey's Purple'
>   *Ligularia dentata* 'Othello'
>   *Lysimachia ciliata* 'Purpurea'
>   *Melica altissima* 'Atropurpurea'
>   *Plantago major* 'Rubrifolia'
>   *Rheum palmatum* 'Atropurpureum'

Sedum telephium subsp.
maximum 'Atropurpureum'
☼ 4   ↕ 24in (60cm) ↔ 24in (60cm)

Bold clumps of succulent stems, clothed
in large, rich dark maroon leaves, produce
flattened heads of tiny, reddish white
flowers in late summer.

Tellima grandiflora 'Purpurea'
PURPLE-LEAVED FRINGE CUPS
☼ 4   ↕ 24in (60cm) ↔ 24in (60cm)

Clumps of evergreen, boldly veined,
reddish purple leaves are heart-shaped.
Spikes of nodding, pinkish cream flowers
rise above them in late spring.

Perennials with Fragrant Flowers

PARTICULARLY ON WARM, still summer evenings, the flowers of certain perennials give off a strong fragrance, readily enjoyed by everyone nearby, even those without a keenly developed sense of smell. Closer encounters may be needed to appreciate more subtle-scented flowers, but even fleeting fragrances wafting by are a welcome asset in any garden.

OTHER PERENNIALS WITH
FRAGRANT FLOWERS

Convallaria majalis, see p.42
Crambe cordifolia, see p.18
Dianthus 'Helen'
Dianthus superbus var. *longicalycinus*
Hemerocallis citrinus
Hemerocallis middendorffii
Hosta 'Honeybells'
Iris graminea
Iris unguicularis
Iris, many bearded hybrids

Cheiranthus cheiri 'Harpur Crewe'
PERENNIAL WALLFLOWER
☼ 7   ↕ 12in (30cm) ↔ 12in (30cm)

A succession of richly scented yellow flowers rises above compact mounds of evergreen foliage in late spring. Dislikes hot, dry weather.

Hemerocallis lilio-asphodelus
LEMON LILY
☼ 3   ↕ 24in (60cm) ↔ 24in (60cm)

The fragrance of these lovely, lilylike flowers in late spring and early summer is unforgettable. The blooms rise above a striking clump of strap-shaped leaves.

Clematis recta
SHRUBBY CLEMATIS
☼ 3   ↕ 5ft (1.5m) ↔ 20in (50cm)

Long stems with deeply divided leaves carry clouds of small, sweetly fragrant summer flowers. Train this clump-former over small shrubs, or give it some support.

Dianthus 'Doris'
MODERN PINK
☼ 4   ↕ 12in (30cm) ↔ 12in (30cm)

All through summer this popular pink provides a fragrant succession of pale pink flowers, each with a dark central zone. Its evergreen leaves form a silvery mound.

MORE PERENNIALS WITH
FRAGRANT FLOWERS

Lavandula angustifolia 'Hidcote',
    see p.164
Mirabilis jalapa
Oenothera caespitosa
Paeonia, many species and cultivars
Petasites fragrans
Phlox maculata 'Alpha'
Phlox maculata 'Miss Lingard'
Phlox paniculata, many cultivars
Viola odorata

Hesperis matronalis
SWEET ROCKET
☼ ③   ↕4ft (1.2m) ↔ 24in (60cm)

This fragrant, old-fashioned cottage garden
favorite has erect, leafy stems and heads
of white or violet summer flowers. Short-
lived, it grows best in poor or stony soils.

Iris 'Early Light'
TALL BEARDED IRIS
☼ ③   ↕3ft (1m) ↔ indefinite

Swollen, creeping rhizomes produce fans
of sword-shaped gray-green leaves, and
branched stems support frilled cream and
yellow flowers in late spring.

Phlox maculata 'Omega'
PERENNIAL PHLOX
☼ ☼ ③   ↕3ft (1m) ↔ 18in (45cm)

Strong, leafy stems form an erect clump,
and each is topped by loosely cylindrical
heads of fragrant, lilac-eyed flowers. Likes
moist soils.

Hosta plantaginea 'Grandiflora'
FRAGRANT PLANTAIN LILY
☼ ③   ↕24in (60cm) ↔ 4ft (1.2m)

From late summer into autumn, slender,
white trumpet flowers, especially fragrant
in the evening, are carried above bold
mounds of glossy, pale green leaves.

Monarda 'Croftway Pink'
BEE BALM
☼ ④   ↕3ft (1m) ↔ 24in (60cm)

The dense clusters of hooded, soft pink
summer flowers are scented, and the
leaves, on strong, upright stems, are
pleasantly aromatic. Dislikes dry soils.

Primula veris
COWSLIP
☼ ⑤   ↕8in (20cm) ↔ 8in (20cm)

Umbels of nodding yellow spring flowers
with a distinctive scent crown upright
stems that rise out of small, neat rosettes
of wrinkled foliage. Dislikes dry soils.

Inula hookeri
INULA
☼ ⑥   ↕3ft (1m) ↔ 3ft (1m)

A series of woolly buds in summer opens
into large, scented, yellow daisy flowers.
Upright stems, forming a bold clump, are
densely clothed with downy leaves.

Nicotiana sylvestris
ORNAMENTAL TOBACCO
☼ ⑨   ↕5ft (1.5m) ↔ 30in (75cm)

Loose heads of long-tubed late summer
flowers are especially fragrant in the early
evening. A perennial in warm, sheltered
gardens, but an annual elsewhere.

Verbena rigida
VERBENA
☼ ⑧   ↕12in (30cm) ↔ 12in (30cm)

Neat and compact in habit, this popular,
tuberous-rooted perennial has branching
stems topped from midsummer onward
with fragrant, pale violet flower spikes.

Spring-flowering Bulbs

NO OTHER PLANTS signal the end of winter and the arrival of spring more convincingly than bulbs do. To eyes that are dulled by long winter nights and short gray days, the gradual emergence of brilliant tulips, golden daffodils, and a swarm of crocuses breathes new life into the garden. More than at other times of the year, you are aware of great variety, beauty, and charm. Whether in small groups or large drifts, there is no denying their impact on the garden landscape.

Crocus vernus 'Princess Juliana'
CROCUS
☼ ③   ↕ 3½in (9cm)

A bold-flowered, easily grown crocus that has narrow leaves. Its purple flowers have large, frilly orange or deep yellow stigmas. Excellent for naturalizing in beds or grass.

BULBS FOR SPRING BEDDING DISPLAY
Hyacinthus orientalis 'Delft Blue'
Hyacinthus orientalis 'L'Innocence'
Hyacinthus orientalis 'Pink Pearl'
Muscari armeniacum
Narcissus 'Mount Hood'
Narcissus 'Spellbinder'
Tulipa 'China Pink'
Tulipa 'Garden Party'
Tulipa 'Keizerskroon'
Tulipa 'White Dream'

Anemone blanda 'White Splendour'
GRECIAN WINDFLOWER
☼ ☼ ④   ↕ 3in (8cm)

Ferny leaves rising from knobby tubers are topped by multipetaled, early spring flowers. Once established, this reliable variety increases to form patches.

x *Chionoscilla allenii*
CHIONOSCILLA
☼ ☼ ③   ↕ 5in (13cm)

A choice, easy dwarf bulb, this has sprays of deep blue, star-shaped flowers above straplike leaves. Good in a pocket of a rock garden. It forms colonies in time.

Chionodoxa forbesii
GLORY OF THE SNOW
☼ ☼ ④   ↕ 5in (13cm)

Popular and reliable, this dwarf bulb has sprays of star-shaped flowers. It spreads by seed once established, especially beneath deciduous trees and shrubs.

Crocus dalmaticus
CROCUS
☼ ⑦   ↕ 3½in (9cm)

A charming crocus, this is suited to the rock garden or scree. It has tufts of narrow leaves and beautiful flowers in varying shades of purple with yellow centers.

Erythronium dens-canis
DOGTOOTH VIOLET
☼ ②   ↕ 8in (20cm)

Above a pair of fleshy, mottled green leaves a single flower with swept-back petals rises. Easy in a rock garden or border, this species seeds to form colonies.

PERENNIALS

Erythronium 'Pagoda'
DOGTOOTH VIOLET
☀ 5   ↕ 12in (30cm)

Dark stems rise above the lush, faintly mottled leaves of this vigorous plant. These support pendent flowers with pointed, upswept petals. Soon self-seeds.

Fritillaria imperialis
CROWN IMPERIAL
☀ 5   ↕ 4ft (1.2m)

A popular plant of robust growth, in time forming clumps of erect, leafy stems and nodding umbels of bell-shaped flowers beneath a crown of erect, leaflike bracts.

OTHER SPRING-FLOWERING BULBS

Allium narcissiflorum
Anemone pavonina
Crocus chrysanthus
Cyclamen repandum
Eranthis hyemalis, see p.60
Fritillaria persica
Galanthus nivalis
Ipheion uniflorum 'Wisley Blue'
Leucojum vernum
Muscari botryoides 'Album'
Tulipa clusiana

Fritillaria pallidiflora
FRITILLARY
☀ 3   ↕ 18in (45cm)

This vigorous bulb has attractive, fleshy leaves and several large, greenish yellow, pendulous flowers, normally checkered faintly inside. Needs good drainage.

Ipheion uniflorum 'Froyle Mill'
SPRING STARFLOWER
☀ 5   ↕ 5in (13cm)

Slender, erect stems each carry a single flower above clumps of narrow, onion-scented leaves. Perfect for planting under deciduous shrubs or in a cool border.

Narcissus 'February Gold'
DAFFODIL
☀ ☀ 4   ↕ 13in (32cm)

This is a popular daffodil for mass planting or naturalizing. The solitary flowers have clear yellow petals and a deeper-colored trumpet. A long-lasting, reliable plant.

Narcissus 'Kingscourt'
DAFFODIL
☀ ☀ 4   ↕ 18in (45cm)

A strong-growing daffodil, this is good for bedding and for naturalizing. Erect stems bear a single, flared, rich golden yellow trumpet surrounded by paler petals.

Tulipa fosteriana 'Madame Lefeber'
RED EMPEROR TULIP
☀ 4   ↕ 16in (40cm)

This bold-flowered, vigorous selection of a gorgeous wild tulip sports enormous, black-eyed, brilliant red flowers above its handsome gray-green foliage.

Tulipa praestans
'Van Tubergen's Variety'
☀ 4   ↕ 11in (28cm)

A striking tulip with downy stems and gray-green leaves, above which large orange-red flowers, yellow at their bases, are carried. Forms clumps in time.

79

Summer-flowering Bulbs

To THE LAYMAN, bulbs are evocative of late winter and spring, but a surprising number and variety of bulbous plants are available to provide color in the summer months. You can plant them on their own in clumps, between shrubs, or in herbaceous borders. Many make bold specimen plants. Those that originate in warm climates can, in cooler areas, be grown near a sheltering wall or in containers that can be brought indoors for decoration, winter protection, or both.

Crocosmia 'Citronella'
MONTBRETIA
☼ 7   ↕ 28in (70cm)

The erect, sword-shaped, gray-green leaves of this plant form clumps. Small, funnel-shaped golden flowers are produced in arching spikes. Best in well-drained soils.

Allium aflatunense
ORNAMENTAL ONION
☼ 4   ↕ 30in (75cm)

This ornamental onion bears a dense head of star-shaped flowers attractive to bees and butterflies. The basal leaves wither before it flowers. Best in well-drained soil.

Camassia leichtlinii 'Semiplena'
CAMASSIA
☼ 5   ↕ 4ft (1.2m)

A stately plant with long, erect, narrow leaves. Each stem ends in a loose spike of double, narrow-petaled flowers. Grow in a well-drained soil. May need some support.

Crocosmia 'Jackanapes'
MONTBRETIA
☼ 6   ↕ 20in (50cm)

Erect, branching stems bear orange-red and yellow bicolored flowers in spikes. The upright, sword-shaped leaves form clumps. Thrives in a well-drained site.

Alstroemeria 'Ligtu Hybrids'
ALSTROEMERIA
☼ 7   ↕ 22in (55cm)

Slow to establish, but a magnificent plant. Erect, leafy stems are crowned with heads of flared flowers, often streaked. Thrives in a sheltered, well-drained site.

Crinum x *powellii*
CRINUM
☼ 7   ↕ 30in (75cm)

This striking plant eventually forms lush clumps of shiny, strap-shaped leaves. Stout stems with loose heads of fragrant trumpet flowers rise above the leaves.

Dahlia 'Bishop of Llandaff'
DAHLIA
☼ 8-9   ↕ 3ft (1m)

A showy perennial with bronze-purple leaves and stems and bearing showy, multi-petaled flowers. It is impressive alone or in groups. Lift and store over winter.

Lilium 'Enchantment'
ASIATIC HYBRID LILY
☀ 3   ↕ 3ft (1m)

An old, reliable hybrid lily with erect, leafy stems, this bears loose heads of upward-facing, widespread orange flowers spotted with black. In time it will form clumps.

Lilium regale
REGAL LILY
☀ 3   ↕ 5ft (1.5m)

An old favorite, this produces erect stems with narrow leaves crowned by a loose umbel of trumpet-shaped, deliciously fragrant, yellow-throated white flowers.

Dierama pulcherrimum
WAND FLOWER
☀ 6   ↕ 5½ft (1.7m)

Graceful clumps of semi-evergreen, grass-like leaves mix with arching stems of drooping flower clusters. Grows best in deep, rich soils, where it may self-seed.

OTHER SUMMER BULBS
Allium christophii, see p.40
Canna cultivars
Cardiocrinum giganteum, see p.85
Eucomis comosa, see p.40
Galtonia viridiflora
Gladiolus cultivars
Gloriosa superba
Iris xiphium (Dutch Iris)
Lilium martagon, see p.61
Pancratium illyricum
Triteleia laxa, see p.40
Watsonia beatricis
Zantedeschia aethiopica 'Crowborough'

Galtonia candicans
SUMMER HYACINTH
☀ 6   ↕ 3½ft (1.1m)

Tufts of fleshy leaves form bold clumps. Above these, stout stems with pendulous, bell-shaped flowers rise. Thrives in deep, rich soils, but is attractive to slugs.

Lilium auratum var. *platyphyllum*
JAPANESE GOLD-BANDED LILY
☀ 4 PH ▽   ↕ 3½ft (1.1m)

This spectacular lily has lance-shaped leaves and upright stems that bear large, fragrant flowers. Each petal has a yellow central band and scattered red spots.

Ornithogalum narbonense
ORNITHOGALUM
☀ 7   ↕ 14in (35cm)

The strong, leafless stem of this bold clump-former is topped by a tapered head of star-shaped white flowers. Basal leaves are narrow. Needs well-drained soils.

Autumn-flowering Bulbs

$\mathcal{S}$O MUCH PUBLICITY is afforded bulbs that flower in late winter, spring, and summer that it is easy to neglect those that are at their prime in autumn. But some bulbs bring a welcome splash of color at a time when many plants are either dying down or shedding their leaves. Although few in number by comparison to their spring- and summer-blooming kin, autumn bulbs, corms, and tubers make a welcome addition to the autumn garden.

Crocus banaticus
FALL-BLOOMING CROCUS
☼ 4   ↕ 4in (10cm)

This choice little crocus has slender tubes supporting pale violet flowers with orange stigmas. The shiny green leaves, each one with a pale midrib, appear in spring.

Crocus pulchellus
FALL-BLOOMING CROCUS
☼ 6   ↕ 4in (10cm)

Ultimately forming patches by division and seed, this charming crocus has small, goblet-shaped flowers of palest blue, with darker veins and a deep yellow throat.

x *Amarcrinum memoria-corsii*
AMARCRINUM
☼ 7   ↕ 3ft (1m)

This hybrid between *Amaryllis* and *Crinum* forms an evergreen clump of strap-shaped leaves. Loose umbels of fragrant trumpet flowers open from late summer to autumn.

Colchicum speciosum 'Album'
AUTUMN CROCUS
☼ 4   ↕ 8in (20cm)

The large, goblet-shaped, slender-tubed, pure white flowers of this exquisite plant are quite weatherproof. Large, glossy basal leaves are produced in spring.

Colchicum byzantinum
AUTUMN CROCUS
☼ 6   ↕ 8in (20cm)

In early autumn, this striking perennial produces numerous goblet-shaped, pale purple flowers that open in the sun. Large, green basal leaves unfurl in spring.

Colchicum 'Waterlily'
AUTUMN CROCUS
☼ 4   ↕ 6in (15cm)

This is one of the most popular and eye-catching of all the autumn crocus hybrids. Its bold bunches of large, slender-tubed, double flowers are a rich pinkish lilac hue.

Crocus speciosus 'Oxonian'
FALL-BLOOMING CROCUS
☼ 5   ↕ 4in (10cm)

The slender-tubed, goblet-shaped flowers are a deep violet-blue, with darker veins and conspicuous orange stigmas. Ideal for naturalizing in grass or beneath shrubs.

Merendera montana
MERENDERA
☀ 9   ↕ 2in (5cm)

The flowers of this crocuslike perennial
are funnel-shaped with narrow, spreading,
pinkish purple petals, white at the base.
Glossy leaves follow the flowers.

Cyclamen hederifolium 'Album'
HARDY CYCLAMEN
☀ 5   ↕ 4in (10cm)

This delightful little clump-former bears
nodding white flowers, each with swept-
back petals and a dark, puckered mouth.
The leaves are beautifully marbled.

> **OTHER HARDY AUTUMN-**
> **FLOWERING BULBS**
>
> *Arum italicum* (fruits)
> *Colchicum autumnale*
> *Colchicum speciosum*
> *Crocus kotschyanus*
> *Crocus sativus*
> *Crocus speciosus*
> *Cyclamen hederifolium*, see p.60
> *Galanthus reginae-olgae*
> *Schizostylis coccinea* 'Major'
> *Schizostylis coccinea* 'Sunrise', see p.25
> *Scilla scilloides*
> *Sternbergia lutea*

Nerine bowdenii
NERINE
☀ 7   ↕ 24in (60cm)

This clump-forming, bulbous perennial is
popular and reliable. Its sturdy stems carry
loose umbels of bright pink, frilly-petaled
flowers. Ideal beneath a sunny wall.

> **OTHER LESS-HARDY AUTUMN-**
> **FLOWERING BULBS**
>
> x *Amarygia parkeri* 'Alba'
> *Amaryllis belladonna*, see p.40
> *Arum pictum*
> *Crinum* x *powellii*, see p.80
> *Cyclamen graecum*
> *Eucomis bicolor*
> *Habranthus robustus*
> *Nerine bowdenii* 'Pink Triumph'
> *Nerine undulata*
> *Zephyranthes candida*

Gladiolus papilio
GLADIOLUS
☀ 8   ↕ 3ft (1m)

Upright stems carry up to ten cup-shaped
flowers that are a mixture of cream, smoky
dull purple, yellow, and green. Its sword-
shaped leaves are narrow. Forms patches.

Leucojum autumnale
AUTUMN SNOWFLAKE
☀ 7   ↕ 6in (15cm)

The slender, erect stems of this charming
bulb each support up to four small white,
nodding bell flowers, tinged pink at their
bases. Leaves are equally slender.

Late-winter-flowering Bulbs

PERENNIALS THAT FLOWER out of doors during the late winter months are extremely valuable, so gardeners are fortunate in that a number of bulbous plants choose this time of year to make their display. Along with familiar favorites, a number of less well-known bulbs are available and worthy of consideration. Planted in small groups, in time all the following will spread to form patches, especially if lifted and divided every few years.

OTHER LATE-WINTER-FLOWERING BULBS

Crocus chrysanthus, many
Crocus tommasinianus, see p.60
Eranthis cilicica
Eranthis hyemalis, see p.60
Galanthus elwesii
Galanthus plicatus subsp. *byzantinus*
Leucojum vernum
Narcissus asturiensis
Narcissus cyclamineus, see p.59
Narcissus 'February Gold', see p.79

Cyclamen coum 'Album'
HARDY CYCLAMEN
☼ 5 ‡2in (5cm) ↔4in (10cm)

Where conditions suit, this attractive little tuberous perennial forms patches. Dainty white flowers with dark mouths appear above its tufts of kidney-shaped leaves.

Galanthus nivalis 'Flore Pleno'
DOUBLE SNOWDROP
☼ 3 ‡4in (10cm) ↔4in (10cm)

This is one of the most popular, reliable snowdrops, with its strap-shaped leaves and many-petaled white flowers with green markings. Dislikes dry soils.

Eranthis x *tubergenii*
WINTER ACONITE
☼ 4 ‡4in (10cm) ↔4in (10cm)

Cheerful, cup-shaped golden flowers open above the ruffs of deeply toothed green leaves, which are bronzed when young. Tuberous, they will form carpets in time.

Galanthus 'Atkinsii'
SNOWDROP
☼ 4 ‡10in (25cm) ↔4in (10cm)

Larger than the common snowdrop, this is a charming bulb with strap-shaped gray-green leaves and nodding white flowers on slender stems. Dislikes dry soils.

Narcissus romieuxii
HOOP-PETTICOAT DAFFODIL
☼ 7 ‡4in (10cm) ↔3in (7cm)

Excellent for a sheltered spot in a rock garden, this choice bulbous perennial has fragrant, skirtlike flowers and slender green leaves. Dislikes dry soils.

Decorative Seedheads in Winter

NEAT-MINDED GARDENERS who, once autumn arrives, feel the urge to cut down and clear all spent flowering stems, lose themselves the undeniable ornamental bonus of seed-heads in winter, particularly attractive when coated with frost. Not all are worth saving, but these should certainly be spared.

Phormium tenax
NEW ZEALAND FLAX
☼ 9   ↕8ft (2.5m) ↔6ft (2m)

This clump-forming evergreen plant has stiff, sword-shaped, dark green leaves and, in summer, tall stems bearing branched heads of red flowers. Dislikes dry soils.

OTHER PERENNIALS WITH DECORATIVE SEEDHEADS

Acanthus spinosus, see p.18
Baptisia australis, see p.20
Iris foetidissima, see p.43
Matteuccia struthiopteris
Phlomis russeliana
Thermopsis caroliniana

Achillea 'Gold Plate'
YARROW
☼ 3   ↕4ft (1.2m) ↔24in (60cm)

Sturdy-stemmed and clump-forming, this perennial has finely divided green leaves topped in summer by flattened yellow flowerheads that pale to brown.

Cortaderia selloana 'Pumila'
DWARF PAMPAS GRASS
☼ 7   ↕5ft (1.5m) ↔4ft (1.2m)

During late summer and early autumn, large, long-lasting plumes of creamy white spikelets appear above a mound of narrow, sharply toothed, evergreen leaves.

Cardiocrinum giganteum
GIANT HIMALAYAN LILY
☼ 7   ↕8ft (2.5m) ↔24in (60cm)

This bulb is stately and impressive in winter as well as summer, when it has a bold rosette of leaves and fragrant, creamy white trumpet flowers. It dislikes dry soils.

Miscanthus sinensis 'Kleine Fontäne'
CHINESE SILVER GRASS
☼ 5   ↕3ft (1m) ↔24in (60cm)

Brownish pink spikelets are produced in long-lasting, dense, fingerlike sprays in summer. These top bold clumps of narrow green leaves. Compact habit.

Sedum spectabile
SHOWY STONECROP
☼ 4   ↕18in (45cm) ↔18in (45cm)

Flattened heads of small, star-shaped pink flowers appear in late summer, and turn brown by winter. Fleshy gray-green leaves clothe its stout stems in summer.

Perennial Herbs for Herbaceous Borders

TOO OFTEN, plants traditionally considered as herbs are overlooked when it comes to selecting plants for a perennial garden, but many perennials traditionally grown in herb gardens make ideal additions to beds and borders. Their attractive flowers and often pungent foliage add special appeal to many plantings.

Allium schoenoprasum
CHIVES
☼ 3   ↕ 10in (25cm) ↔ 6in (15cm)

This well-known bulbous herb makes a low clump of green, grassy, onion-scented leaves. Its pink or purple summer flowers are very popular with bees and butterflies.

OTHER EVERGREEN PERENNIAL HERBS

Artemisia 'Powis Castle', see p.72
Asarum europaeum, see p.30
Chamaemelum nobile
Lavandula angustifolia 'Hidcote', see p.164
Salvia officinalis 'Purpurea'
Sempervivum tectorum
Teucrium chamaedrys
Thymus x *citriodorus* 'Silver Queen'
Thymus vulgaris, see p.165

OTHER HERBACEOUS PERENNIAL HERBS

Allium schoenoprasum 'Forescate'
Angelica archangelica
Artemisia absinthium 'Lambrook Silver'
Foeniculum vulgare 'Purpureum'
Inula helenium
Marrubium vulgare
Mentha x *suaveolens* 'Variegata', see p.68
Monarda didyma 'Cambridge Scarlet', see p.33
Myrrhis odorata, see p.53
Rumex scutatus 'Silver Shield'
Tanacetum vulgare

Althaea officinalis
MARSH MALLOW
☼ 4   ↕ 6ft (2m) ↔ 3ft (1m)

The stems and lobed leaves of this erect, branching herb are covered in a soft pelt of gray or grayish green hairs. Pale pink flowers grow in the leaf axils in summer.

Cichorium intybus
CHICORY
☼ 3   ↕ 4ft (1.2m) ↔ 18in (45cm)

Branched, wiry, willowy stems rise from basal rosettes of leaves. During summer, these stems are studded with bright blue, multipetaled, daisylike flowers.

Melittis melissophyllum
BASTARD BALM
☼ ☼ 6   ↕12in (30cm) ↔12in (30cm)

Loose clumps of erect, hairy, four-sided stems carry pairs of honey-scented leaves and pink or white, purple-blotched, two-lipped flowers early   in summer.

Foeniculum vulgare
FENNEL
☼ 5   ↕6ft (2m) ↔18in (45cm)

Dense clumps of upright, hollow, green stems have finely divided, feathery blue-green foliage. Plants are topped in spring with umbels of tiny yellow flowers.

Hyssopus officinalis
HYSSOP
☼ 3   ↕24in (60cm) ↔3ft (1m)

Bees and butterflies love this low, bushy semievergreen subshrub, with small, aromatic leaves and dense spires of blue flowers from late summer into autumn.

Meum althamanticum
BALDMONEY,   **SPIGNEL**
☼ 7   ↕12in (30cm) ↔6in (15cm)

Uncommon in gardens, this perennial herb forms a low clump of finely divided, feathery, aromatic leaves. Tiny white or purplish white flowers occur in summer.

Gentiana lutea
YELLOW GENTIAN
☼ 6   ↕4ft (1.2m) ↔24in (60cm)

This noble perennial produces a basal clump of large blue-green, boldly veined leaves. Stout leafy stems ending in dense spikes of yellow flowers arise in summer.

Levisticum officinale
LOVAGE
☼ ☼ 3   ↕6ft (2m) ↔3ft (1m)

This aromatic perennial forms generous clumps of upright, hollow stems with dark green leaves, bronze when young, and umbels of yellow-green summer flowers.

Monarda fistulosa
WILD BEE BALM
☼ 4   ↕4ft (1.2m) ↔24in (60cm)

In summer, the erect stems of this free-flowering, aromatic perennial are crowned with dense flowerheads enjoyed by bees and butterflies. Tolerates dry soils.

Annual and Biennial Herbs for Herbaceous Beds

NOT EVERYONE HAS SPACE in their gardens for a special herb garden, nor is one necessary. Many medicinal and culinary herbs are also ornamental and can be attractively and easily accommodated in mixed herbaceous borders or beds. This is especially true of annual and biennial herbs, which are extremely useful as temporary fillers.

Borago officinalis
BORAGE
☼ ↕ 24in (60cm) ↔ 12in (30cm)

This familiar clump-forming annual is covered with bristly hairs and produces a summer-long succession of nodding, star-shaped blue flowers. Will seed around.

Anethum graveolens
DILL
☼ ↕ 24in (60cm) ↔ 12in (30cm)

A member of the carrot family, this aromatic annual herb produces clumps of finely divided, feathery blue-green foliage and umbels of tiny flowers in summer.

OTHER ANNUAL HERBS

Anthriscus cerefolium
Artemisia annua
Calendula officinalis 'Fiesta Gitana'
Chrysanthemum coronarium
Cnicus benedictus
Nigella sativa
Ocimum basilicum 'Green Ruffles'
Ocimum basilicum 'Purple Ruffles'
Papaver somniferum, see p.23
Tropaeolum majus 'Alaska', see p.27
Vaccaria hispanica

Atriplex hortensis var. *rubra*
RED ORACH
☼ ↕ 5ft (1.5m) ↔ 12in (30cm)

This strong-growing annual is grown for its rich crimson, edible leaves and colorful stems. It contrasts well with gray-foliaged plants and will self-seed.

OTHER BIENNIAL HERBS

Althaea rosea
Digitalis purpurea, see p.90
Eryngium maritimum
Origanum majorana
Petroselinum crispum

Carthamus tinctorius
SAFFLOWER
☼   ↕ 3ft (1m) ↔ 12in (30cm)

The leaves of this annual are either entire or spine-toothed. Its red, orange, or yellow petals, borne on round flowerheads in late summer and early autumn, produce a dye.

Echium vulgare 'Blue Bedder'
VIPER'S BUGLOSS
☼ 3   ↕ 12in (30cm) ↔ 8in (20cm)

This bristly biennial herb is upright, with narrow leaves. Spikes of blue, bell-shaped flowers are carried during summer. It is best grown in well-drained soils.

Isatis tinctoria
WOAD
☼ 4   ↕ 4ft (1.2m) ↔ 18in (45cm)

Famous as a dye plant, this biennial has branching stems and large, loose heads of tiny yellow flowers in summer. These are followed by showers of dark seed capsules.

Eruca vesicaria subsp.*sativa*
ROCKET, ARUGULA
☼   ↕ 24in (60cm) ↔ 12in (30cm)

Small, pale yellow summer flowers, held on erect spikes, have reddish veins. This annual has both deeply lobed, radishlike leaves and smaller, toothed leaves.

Linum usitatissimum
COMMON FLAX
☼   ↕ 24in (60cm) ↔ 1in (2.5cm)

For centuries, this ancient annual herb has been grown for fiber and oil. Erect and slender-stemmed, it has narrow leaves and loose heads of summer flowers.

Coriandrum sativum
ANNUAL CORIANDER, CILANTRO
☼   ↕ 20in (50cm) ↔ 12in (30cm)

The lower leaves of this popular, aromatic, annual herb are parsleylike; its upper leaves are finely divided. Umbels of tiny, pale purple or white flowers appear in summer.

Helianthus annuus
SUNFLOWER
☼   ↕ 10ft (3m) ↔ 18in (45cm)

Popular with children, this strong-growing annual has large leaves. In summer, each plant bears a huge, golden daisy flower with a brown center on a stout, erect stem.

Silybum marianum
MILK THISTLE
☼ 7   ↕ 4½ft (1.3m) ↔ 24in (60cm)

Bold and carried in basal rosettes, the spiny green leaves of this biennial have white veins that create a marbled effect. Prickly thistle heads appear in summer.

Rabbitproof Perennials

EVERYONE DISAPPOINTED at finding a favorite perennial plant damaged or eaten to the ground by rabbits will be equally familiar with the frustration felt in attempting their control. Those who garden in country areas, or wherever there are large, open spaces, are particularly at risk. Where rabbits appear to be an insoluble problem, it might be worth growing some of the plants they find unpalatable. Many other cultivars of the genera featured here are also suitable.

Digitalis purpurea
FOXGLOVE
☼ 4   ↕ 5ft (1.5m) ↔ 24in (60cm)

This familiar, popular woodland plant is usually treated as a biennial. Its rosettes of large, downy leaves produce erect spikes of drooping, tubular flowers in summer.

Aconitum vulparia
WOLFSBANE
☼ 4   ↕ 4ft (1.2m) ↔ 24in (60cm)

Once used to poison wolves, all parts of this plant are toxic. The deeply divided leaves are dark green. Slender, hooded straw yellow flowers open in summer.

Astilbe 'Ostrich Plume'
ASTILBE
☼ 4   ↕ 3ft (1m) ↔ 3ft (1m)

Arching, feathery plumes of coral-pink flowers top mounds of fernlike leaves in summer. This and many similar cultivars enjoy rich, moist soils.

DEERPROOF PERENNIALS
Acanthus spinosus, see p.18
Aconitum carmichaelii 'Arendsii'
Dryopteris affinis, see p.53
Iris sibirica
Lychnis coronaria
Narcissus species and cultivars
Paeonia 'Bowl of Beauty', see p.21
Rudbeckia fulgida 'Goldsturm', see p.33
Sisyrinchium striatum
Tellima grandiflora, see p. 43
Veratrum viride

Aster novi-belgii 'Marie Ballard'
NEW YORK ASTER
☼ 4   ↕ 3ft (1m) ↔ 18in (45cm)

From late summer into autumn, branched, leafy stems are topped by lilac daisy flowers. Stems may need support. Other cultivars, also rabbitproof, are available.

Bergenia 'Ballawley'
BERGENIA
☼ ◐ ☼ 7   ↕ ↔ 24in (60cm)

Large, rounded evergreen leaves in low clumps turn red in winter. Its bright crimson, bell-shaped flowers are borne in sprays in spring. Prefers a sheltered site.

Epimedium x *rubrum*
BISHOP'S HAT
☼ 4   ↕ 12in (30cm) ↔ 12in (30cm)

Clumps of slender-stalked, heart-shaped leaflets are tinted brownish or reddish in spring, when the loose clusters of small, spurred flowers are produced.

Geranium sanguineum
BLOODY CRANESBILL
☀ 3   ↕10in (25cm) ↔12in (30cm)

Numerous deep magenta-pink flowers top
the low mounds and mats of rounded,
deeply divided leaves in summer. Makes
an excellent groundcover.

Lamium maculatum 'White Nancy'
SPOTTED DEADNETTLE
☀ 3   ↕6in (15cm) ↔3ft (1m)

A groundcover with semievergreen silvery
white, heart-shaped, toothed leaves. Spikes
of two-lipped white flowers appear from
spring into summer. Dislikes dry soil.

Nepeta x *faassenii*
CATMINT
☀ 3   ↕18in (45cm) ↔18in (45cm)

This familiar and widely grown aromatic
perennial forms mounds of grayish green
leaves, and carries loose spikes of small
lavender-blue flowers in early summer.

Helleborus orientalis (pink form)
LENTEN ROSE
☀ 4   ↕18in (45cm) ↔18in (45cm)

Cup-shaped flowers of a lovely dusky
pink with dark spots emerge ahead of the
new leaves in late winter or early spring.
Its dark green, fingered leaves overwinter.

Lysimachia clethroides
GOOSENECK LOOSESTRIFE
☀ 3   ↕3ft (1m) ↔24in (60cm)

This fast-spreading perennial soon forms
colonies. Its leafy stems end in curved,
tapering spikes of small white flowers in
late summer. Enjoys moist soils.

OTHER RABBITPROOF PERENNIALS

Aconitum 'Blue Sceptre'
Agapanthus Headbourne Hybrids
Anemone x *hybrida* 'Königin Charlotte'
Convallaria majalis 'Fortin's Giant'
Crocosmia 'Lucifer'
Kniphofia triangularis
Paeonia officinalis 'Rubra Plena'
Pulmonaria saccharata, see p.33
Sedum telephium subsp. *maximum*
   'Atropurpureum', see p.75
Vinca major

Tradescantia 'Purple Dome'
SPIDERWORT
☀ 4   ↕24in (60cm) ↔18in (45cm)

Clumps of fleshy stems, clothed in lance-
shaped leaves, carry terminal clusters of
rich purple flowers in summer. Numerous
other cultivars are also suitable.

Iris 'Bold Print'
BEARDED IRIS
☀ 3   ↕22in (55cm) ↔indefinite

Sheaves of gray-green, sword-shaped
leaves rise from a maze of thick rhizomes.
In late spring or early summer, branched
stems of purple and white flowers appear.

Trollius europaeus
GLOBEFLOWER
☀ 4   ↕24in (60cm) ↔18in (45cm)

This reliable, clump-forming perennial
has long-stalked, deeply divided leaves
and branching heads of beautiful spring
flowers. 'Superbus' is an excellent form.

CLIMBERS

THE MOST COMMON climbers are woody-stemmed perennials or shrubs with scrambling or otherwise long, slender stems. Self-clinging by adhesive tendril tips or aerial roots, or in need of artificial support from wire or a trellis, they may be trained into trees and shrubs, and to cover walls or other structures.

△ Abutilon megapotamicum

THE BEAUTY OF CLIMBERS

- Useful as cover on tree stumps or unsightly buildings.
- Offer interest for every season.
- Versatile shrubs double as climbers.
- Provide bold or decorative foliage.
- Offer fragrant flowers.
- Give shelter or nesting sites for birds.
- Provide brilliant leaf tints in autumn.
- Offer decorative fruit or seedheads.
- Create multiseason effects if one plant is used as support for another.

All plants recommended in this section are either true climbers, or shrubs suitable for training against walls. They offer a large variety of attributes, from colorful or prolific flowers to decorative or unusual fruits. Many have attractive leaves, and some deciduous climbers are also noted for their autumn tints. Once established, both wall shrubs and climbers can support further plants, creating, when planned, a continuous, multiseason feature. All the climbers recommended on the following pages are deciduous unless specified as evergreen.

CLIMBING TO THE SUN
Numerous climbers grown for their flowering qualities thrive best in a sunny site, such as most climbing roses and honeysuckles. Two popular favorites, clematis and wisteria, prefer to have their heads in the sun and their roots shaded (place a large stone or tile over their roots). When grown against a wall, climbers benefit from the reflected heat, which helps ripen growth and initiate flower bud formation.

WOODLAND SHADE
The cooler conditions of shady walls, often combined with moist but well-drained soils, are a perfect home for many natural woodland climbers. Ivies are a good example, especially colored-leaved varieties, which flourish on shady or partially shaded walls, as do those lovely South American woodlanders, *Lapageria* and *Berberidopsis*.

△ IVY-CLAD SHED *This bold-leaved ivy (Hedera colchica* 'Dentata Variegata'*) is perfect for covering an unsightly wall.*

△ SUPPORT IN DISGUISE *Evergreen spring-flowering ceanothus and twining honeysuckle beautifully decorate this pole.*

◁ PRETTY WINDOW *Wisteria, rose, and two clematis varieties combine to provide a delightful frame for this window.*

▷ SUMMER SENSATION *Luxuriant early summer growth of clematis, purple grapes, and golden hops clothes this wall.*

Climbers for Warm, Sunny Walls and Fences

SUNNY WALLS AND FENCES are excellent for climbers. When carefully selected and matched, several can be trained to grow into one another to give a continuous display. The surface, especially of a brick or stone wall, absorbs heat, and this helps promote growth and encourages flowering. All the climbers featured here require support from wires or netting.

Lonicera x *americana*
HONEYSUCKLE
☀ 6   ↕↔ 22ft (7m)

This free-flowering climber has clusters of fragrant, long-tubed, creamy yellow flowers from summer into early autumn. Its leaves are purplish when young.

Actinidia kolomikta
ACTINIDIA
☀ 5   ↕↔ 13ft (4.5m)

This striking climber is slow to establish but it is well worth the wait. It has bold, heart-shaped leaves, often splashed cream and pink, and white flowers in summer.

Passiflora caerulea
BLUE PASSION FLOWER
☀ 8   ↕↔ 30ft (10m)

Fast-growing with fingered leaves, this climber bears beautiful, unusual flowers from summer into autumn. They may be followed by attractive seed pods.

Clematis 'Bill Mackenzie'
CLEMATIS
☀ 5   ↕↔ 22ft (7m)

Vigorous and scrambling, this clematis has beautiful, lanternlike, nodding flowers in late summer and autumn. These are followed by pretty, silky seedheads.

Clematis 'Jackmanii'
CLEMATIS
☀ 3   ↕↔ 10ft (3m)

A long-established garden favorite, this climbs by twining leaf stalks. Masses of large, velvety, dark purple flowers, turning violet with age, appear in summer.

Rosa 'Dublin Bay'
CLIMBING ROSE
☀ 5   ↕↔ 7ft (2.2m)

'Dublin Bay' is a climbing floribunda rose of dense growth, with glossy, dark green leaves and clusters of cupped, fragrant flowers from summer to early autumn.

Vitis vinifera 'Purpurea'
CLARET VINE
☼ 6   ↕ ↔ 22ft (7m)

A vigorous form of the grape vine, with young leaves that mature to wine purple. These color richly in autumn, when small bunches of blue-black grapes ripen.

SELF-CLINGING CLIMBERS FOR SUNNY WALLS AND FENCES

Campsis radicans
Cissus striata
Decumaria sinensis, see p.105
Ficus pumila
Hydrangea anomala subsp. *petiolaris*, see p.107
Parthenocissus tricuspidata 'Lowii'
Trachelospermum asiaticum, see p.107
Trachelospermum jasminoides 'Variegatum'

Rosa 'Mme. Gregoire Staechelin'
CLIMBING ROSE
☼ 5   ↕ ↔ 10ft (3m)

One of the most beautiful climbing roses, this is vigorous, with shining green leaves and abundant clusters of rounded, slightly fragrant flowers in summer.

OTHER CLIMBERS FOR SUN

Aristolochia macrophylla
Campsis x *tagliabuana* 'Madame Galen'
Celastrus orbiculatus
Clematis armandii, see p.104
Jasminum officinale 'Affine'
Lonicera periclymenum
  'Graham Thomas', see p.103
Lonicera sempervirens
Parthenocissus quinquefolia
Rosa banksiae 'Lutea'
Solanum jasminoides, see p.95
Sollya heterophylla
Wisteria sinensis, see p.105

Rosa 'Maigold'
CLIMBING ROSE
☼ 5   ↕ ↔ 12ft (4m)

This vigorous climber has thorny stems and lush foliage. Fragrant bronze-yellow blooms, reddish in bud, appear in early summer and less profusely in autumn.

Solanum jasminoides 'Album'
POTATO VINE
☼ 8   ↕ ↔ 20ft (6m)

Semievergreen and slender-stemmed, this climber will grow vigorously through any support. Loose clusters of starry flowers occur from summer into autumn.

Wisteria floribunda 'Alba'
WHITE JAPANESE WISTERIA
☼ 5   ↕ ↔ 28ft (9m)

The handsome leaves of this powerful climber are compound. Long spikes of white pea flowers emerge in early summer. Thrives in neutral to slightly acid soils.

Climbers for Shady Walls and Fences

THE COOLER CONDITIONS normally found in places that do not receive the sun's glare directly suit a good number of climbers, many of which grow naturally in woodland, or similarly shaded places in the wild. Most need to be tied to a wire or trellis support, and even the self-clinging ones, such as ivy, benefit from this for a year or two after planting.

Hedera colchica 'Dentata Variegata'
PERSIAN IVY
☼ ☼ 7   ↕ ↔ 15ft (5m)

A spectacular evergreen with broad-based, leathery leaves, each irregularly margined creamy white. Shoots have aerial roots that cling to the surface of a support.

Berberidopsis corallina
CORAL PLANT
☼ ☼ 8 PH   ↕ ↔ 14ft (4.5m)

Coral Plant's long, rambling stems bear heart-shaped evergreen leaves. Pendent, globular flowers are carried from summer into autumn.

Clematis montana f. *grandiflora*
CLEMATIS
☼ ☼ 6   ↕ ↔ 30ft (10m)

In time, this vigorous climber will produce blankets of leafy growth, bronze-purple when the leaves are young. Large white spring flowers are borne in abundance.

OTHER DECIDUOUS CLIMBERS FOR SHADY WALLS
Actinidia arguta
Akebia quinata, see p.102
Akebia trifoliata
Hydrangea anomala subsp. *petiolaris*, see p.107
Parthenocissus henryana, see p.107
Parthenocissus quinquefolia
Parthenocissus tricuspidata 'Lowii'
Schizophragma hydrangeoides 'Moonlight'
Schizophragma hydrangeoides 'Roseum'

Clematis x *jouiniana* 'Praecox'
CLEMATIS
☼ ☼ 6   ↕ ↔ 10ft (3m)

Vigorous and sprawling, this dense-growing climber should be trained to a support. Its coarse foliage backs masses of small, fragrant, tubular flowers in late summer.

Clematis 'Nelly Moser'
CLEMATIS
☼ ☼ 4   ↕ ↔ 11ft (3.5m)

Large, single, pale mauve flowers, with a carmine stripe on each petal, cover this popular twining clematis in early summer. Their color fades in strong sunlight.

Hedera colchica 'Sulphur Heart'
PERSIAN IVY
☼ ☼ 6   ↕ ↔ 15ft (5m)

This dramatic ivy with its boldly splashed leaves is similar in growth to *H. colchica* 'Dentata Variegata' *(above)*. They are most effective when grown together.

Hedera helix 'Eva'
ENGLISH IVY
☀ ☀ 6   ↕↔4ft (1.2m)

The evergreen leaves of this variegated
English ivy cultivar are green and gray-
green with broad, creamy white margins.
It is self-clinging.

Lapageria rosea
CHILEAN BELLFLOWER
☀ ☀ 9   ↕↔15ft (5m)

Strongly twining stems support leathery
evergreen leaves and, from summer into
late autumn, beautiful, pendulous, tubular
flowers with fleshy petals.

Lonicera japonica 'Halliana'
JAPANESE HONEYSUCKLE
☀ ☀ ☀ 5   ↕↔30ft (10m)

Evergreen or semievergreen, this prolific,
twining climber produces loose clusters of
fragrant flowers, emerging white and aging
to yellow, from late spring into autumn.

CLIMBERS

Hedera helix 'Green Ripple'
ENGLISH IVY
☀ ☀ 5   ↕↔4ft (1.2m)

This distinctive cultivar of English ivy
has deeply lobed and pointed bright
evergreen leaves with pale veins. Self-
clinging, it is ideal for low walls.

Humulus lupulus 'Aureus'
GOLDEN HOPS
☀ ☀ 5   ↕↔20ft (6m)

A strong-growing herbaceous climber, this
has hairy, twining stems and boldly lobed
yellow-green leaves. Clusters of green
fruits (hops) are produced in autumn.

**OTHER EVERGREEN CLIMBERS
FOR SHADY WALLS**

Clematis armandii, see p.104
Euonymus fortunei 'Coloratus'
Ficus pumila
Holboellia coriacea

Schizophragma integrifolium
SCHIZOPHRAGMA
☀ ☀ 6   ↕↔40ft (12m)

In time, this slow-growing, self-clinging
climber will reach great heights. Flattened
heads of creamy white flowers appear in
summer among pointed green leaves.

Shrubs for Warm, Sunny Walls and Fences

SUNNY WALLS AND FENCES are a bonus to the gardener since they offer both the warmth and shelter necessary for less hardy plants. They are also ideal for shrubs with trailing or fragile stems that need some support. Most will greatly increase their average height when grown against a wall. Careful pruning and training onto wires or a trellis may be necessary.

MBERS

Abutilon megapotamicum
FLOWERING MAPLE
☀ 8   ↕ ↔ 10ft (3m)

This free-growing shrub is of virtually pendulous habit. From late spring to autumn it produces flowers that resemble colorful Chinese lanterns.

Callistemon pallidus
BOTTLEBRUSH
☀ 9 PH ↓   ↕ ↔ 10ft (3m)

In flower, bottlebrushes are among the most exotic of evergreen shrubs. This is certainly no exception, with its brushes of creamy yellow flowers borne in summer.

Ceanothus arboreus 'Trewithen Blue'
CATALINA CEANOTHUS
☀ 9   ↕ ↔ 20ft (6m)

This vigorous evergreen shrub is ideal for covering a large surface. It flowers for many weeks in late winter and spring. Prefers well-drained, acid soils.

Buddleia crispa
BUTTERFLY BUSH
☀ 8   ↕ ↔ 8ft (2.5m)

The oval leaves of this choice shrub are all covered in a woolly pelt of soft, grayish white down. Its small, fragrant flowers are carried in dense clusters in summer.

OTHER DECIDUOUS SHRUBS FOR WARM, SUNNY WALLS AND FENCES

Abelia floribunda
Abeliophyllum distichum
Buddleia globosa, see p.138
Caesalpinia japonica
Chimonanthus praecox 'Grandiflorus', see p.166
Clianthus puniceus
Edgeworthia chrysantha
Enkianthus campanulatus
Hamamelis mollis 'Pallida'
Indigofera heterantha, see p.126
Iochroma cyaneum
Prunus mume 'Peggy Clarke'
Punica granatum 'Flore Pleno'
Pyracantha coccinea
Ribes speciosum
Viburnum macrocephalum 'Sterile'
Xanthoceras sorbifolium, see p.127

Cytisus battandieri
MOROCCAN BROOM
☀ 8   ↕ ↔ 12ft (4m)

Worth growing for its leaves alone, which are divided into leaflets and covered in silky silvery hairs. Yellow pineapple-scented pea flowers appear in summer.

Feijoa sellowiana
PINEAPPLE GUAVA
☼ 8   ↕ ↔ 10ft (3m)

The summer flowers of this interesting evergreen shrub have fleshy, edible petals and crimson stamens. Edible, egg-shaped fruits are produced after a hot summer.

Robinia hispida
ROSE ACACIA
☼ 5   ↕ ↔ 8ft (2.5m)

Large rose-pink pea flowers are borne in drooping clusters in late spring. The leaves, with numerous lush green leaflets, are held on fragile stems.

Fremontodendron 'California Glory'
FLANNEL BUSH
☼ 9   ↕ ↔ 25ft (8m)

This fast-growing evergreen has beautiful yellow flowers from spring into autumn. Prune regularly if it is on a small fence or wall. Be sure the roots are not too wet.

Rosa x *odorata* 'Mutabilis'
CHINA ROSE
☼ 7   ↕ ↔ 10ft (3m)

This vigorous China rose is popular for its dark purple shoots, coppery young leaves, and lovely fragrant summer flowers. It will grow taller than usual against a wall.

OTHER EVERGREEN SHRUBS FOR WARM, SUNNY WALLS AND FENCES

Acacia dealbata, see p.158
Carpenteria californica, see p.158
Ceanothus 'Concha'
Viburnum odoratissimum

Desmodium tiliifolium
DESMODIUM
☼ 9   ↕ ↔ 6ft (2m)

From late summer into autumn, loose heads of pea flowers are borne above large, downy leaves. Except in warm areas, old growth is best pruned back every spring.

Itea ilicifolia
HOLLYLEAF SWEETSPIRE
☼ 8   ↕ ↔ 15ft (5m)

On warm evenings from late summer into autumn, long greenish catkins give off a honeylike aroma. The dark green, glossy, hollylike leaves are evergreen.

Solanum crispum 'Glasnevin'
BLUE POTATO VINE
☼ 8   ↕ ↔ 20ft (6m)

This vigorous and scrambling shrub is evergreen in warmer areas. Loose clusters of star-shaped flowers appear over a long period in summer. Needs support.

99

Shrubs for Shady Walls and Fences

SOME GARDENERS may perceive a wall or fence that does not receive direct sunlight as a curse, and consider it unsightly. It need not be a problem, however, as long as it receives some light. Many shrubs (and climbers) will thrive, and some even prefer the normally cooler conditions of such a site, while others flower freely in or out of the sun.

Forsythia suspensa
WEEPING FORSYTHIA
☼ ☼ ☼ 5   ↕ ↔ 10ft (3m)

A vigorous, rambling shrub that requires regular pruning and training to prevent it from becoming overpowering. Star-shaped flowers wreathe the branches in spring.

Chaenomeles x *superba* 'Rowallane'
FLOWERING QUINCE
☼ ☼ ☼ 5   ↕ ↔ 5ft (1.5m)

Superb in spring, when the previous year's branches are hidden beneath brilliant red flower clusters. Like 'Moerloosei', best pruned and trained close to the wall.

Garrya elliptica (male form)
SILK-TASSEL BUSH
☼ ☼ ☼ 9   ↕ ↔ 15ft (5m)

From midwinter through to early spring the branches are draped with long tassels, which tremble in the slightest breeze. This shrub has leathery evergreen leaves.

Azara microphylla
AZARA
☼ ☼ 8   ↕ ↔ 20ft (6m)

This elegant evergreen will grow to small tree size if allowed. Arching branchlets are clothed with leaves and, in late winter or spring, with tiny vanilla-scented flowers.

Chaenomeles speciosa 'Moerloosei'
FLOWERING QUINCE
☼ ☼ ☼ 5   ↕ ↔ 8ft (2.5m)

A reliable, adaptable, and vigorous shrub, this carries large flower clusters in spring and early summer followed by aromatic fruits. Prune regularly, and train on wires.

Euonymus fortunei 'Silver Queen'
SILVER QUEEN EUONYMUS
☼ ☼ ☼ 5   ↕ ↔ 8ft (2.5m)

A handsome evergreen shrub, low and bushy in a bed, but rising higher against a wall if trained. Glossy dark green leaves have broad, irregular creamy margins.

Illicium anisatum
CHINESE STAR ANISE
☼ ☼ 8   ↕ ↔ 8ft (2.5m)

The aromatic leaves of this slow-growing evergreen are joined by loose clusters of yellow, star-shaped flowers in spring. The wood also has a strong, agreeable aroma.

Jasminum humile
HIMALAYAN JASMINE
☼ ☼ ☀ 8   ↕↔6ft (2m)

The numerous greenish stems of this
bushy evergreen are clothed in attractive,
much-divided leaves. It sports clusters of
yellow flowers from spring into autumn.

OTHER EVERGREEN SHRUBS FOR SHADY WALLS AND FENCES
Azara serrata
Camellia japonica 'Debutante'
Camellia sasanqua
Crinodendron hookerianum, see p.132
Euonymus fortunei 'Emerald Gaiety', see p.118
Itea ilicifolia, see p.99
Jasminum humile 'Revolutum'
Ligustrum japonicum
Pyracantha 'Orange Glow', see p.169

Kerria japonica 'Pleniflora'
DOUBLE KERRIA
☼ ☼ ☀ 5   ↕↔10ft (3m)

Popular and easy to grow, this vigorous
shrub has long green shoots that need
support, along with sharply toothed leaves
and rich yellow spring flowers.

Pyracantha rogersiana
FIRETHORN
☼ ☼ ☀ 7   ↕↔10ft (3m)

The spiny branches of this vigorous
evergreen are clothed in narrow, glossy
leaves. Flower clusters in early summer
are replaced by orange-red berries.

OTHER DECIDUOUS SHRUBS FOR SHADY WALLS AND FENCES
Chaenomeles speciosa 'Cameo'
Chaenomeles speciosa 'Texas Scarlet'
Chaenomeles speciosa 'Toyo Nishiki'
Cornus alba 'Elegantissima', see p.148
Cotoneaster horizontalis
Hamamelis virginiana
Lonicera x *purpusii* 'Winter Beauty', see p.167
Rhodotypos scandens, see p.135
Viburnum acerifolium

Jasminum nudiflorum
WINTER JASMINE
☼ ☼ ☀ 6   ↕↔10ft (3m)

This is a popular and reliable winter-
flowering shrub, with long shoots bearing
yellow flowers through winter into spring.
Prune after flowering to keep plants neat.

Piptanthus nepalensis
EVERGREEN LABURNUM
☼ ☼ ☀ 9   ↕↔10ft (3m)

This strong-growing shrub has lush semievergreen or evergreen foliage. Its clusters
of bright yellow pea flowers are produced
from spring into summer.

Ribes laurifolium (male form)
BAYLEAF CURRANT
☼ ☀ 8   ↕↔6ft (2m)

A curious, slow-growing evergreen currant
that needs training to gain height. Its bold
leaves are joined by drooping flower
clusters from late winter into early spring.

Climbers to Train into Trees and Shrubs

I F YOU LACK WALLS OR FENCES, encourage climbers to grow into trees or large shrubs, where they can create spectacular effects when in flower or leaf. It is important to match each climber to its supporting plant: grow strong climbers into large trees, and weaker ones into small trees or shrubs.
Careful pruning may be necessary to control growth.

Clematis rehderiana
CLEMATIS
☼ 6   ↕ ↔ 22ft (7m)

As well as a dense growth of divided leaves, loose clusters of primrose yellow, cowslip-scented flowers cover this twining climber from late summer into autumn.

OTHER FOLIAGE CLIMBERS FOR TRAINING INTO TREES

Actinidia kolomikta, see p.94
Ampelopsis brevipedunculata
Aristolochia macrophylla
Humulus lupulus 'Aureus', see p.97
Parthenocissus quinquefolia
Vitis vinifera 'Purpurea', see p.95

Akebia quinata
CHOCOLATE VINE
☼ ☼ 4   ↕ ↔ 30ft (10m)

The clusters of vanilla-scented, brownish purple flowers in spring are followed by sausage-shaped fruits. This vigorous semi-evergreen climbs by twining.

Clematis 'Madame Julia Correvon'
CLEMATIS
☼ 5   ↕ ↔ 11ft (3.5m)

From summer to early autumn, this twining climber with slender stems freely produces magnificent, four-petaled wine-red flowers with cream-colored stamens.

Celastrus orbiculatus
ORIENTAL BITTERSWEET
☼ ☼ 4   ↕ ↔ 70ft (20m)

This vigorous climber is showy in autumn when the leaves turn yellow and clusters of orange seed capsules, which last into winter, open on pollinated female plants.

Clematis montana var. *rubens*
CLEMATIS
☼ 6   ↕ ↔ 30ft (10m)

Masses of pink flowers in spring cover the dense curtains of growth produced by this vigorous, twining climber. Many good color selections exist.

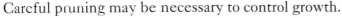

Hedera colchica
PERSIAN IVY
☼ ☼ ☼ 6   ↕ ↔ 30ft (10m)

Persian Ivy is a strong-growing, evergreen, self-clinging climber, which also makes a splendid groundcover. Its shining, dark green leaves are pointed and leathery.

Rosa 'Albertine'
CLIMBING ROSE
☀ 6   ↕↔ 15ft (5m)

An old and popular vigorous rambling
rose, 'Albertine' has thorny reddish stems
and richly fragrant, double salmon-pink
flowers, freely borne in summer.

Vitis coignetiae
JAPANESE GRAPE
☀ 5   ↕↔ 70ft (20m)

This vigorous vine climbs by means of
twining tendrils. It is chiefly grown for its
handsome, heart-shaped leaves that turn
crimson and scarlet in autumn.

Lonicera periclymenum
'Graham Thomas'
☀ 5   ↕↔ 22ft (7m)

Vigorous and dense-growing, this twining
climber has oval leaves and, in summer,
loose clusters of freely borne, fragrant
flowers that are white aging to yellow.

OTHER FLOWERING CLIMBERS FOR TRAINING INTO TREES
Clematis 'Perle d'Azur'
Clematis virginiana
Hydrangea anomala subsp. *petiolaris*, see p.107
Jasminum officinale
Lonicera x *americana*, see p.94
Rosa 'Veilchenblau'
Schisandra rubrifolia
Schizophragma hydrangeoides
Wisteria sinensis, see p.105

Rosa filipes 'Kiftsgate'
CLIMBING ROSE
☀ 6-7   ↕↔ 30ft (10m)

Rampant if unpruned, this rose has fresh,
glossy green foliage and branched heads of
fragrant, yellow-centered white flowers in
summer, followed by small red hips.

Polygonum baldschuanicum
SILVER LACE VINE
☀ 4   ↕↔ 40ft (12m)

Well known, popular, and rampant, this
twining climber has stringlike tassels of
white or pink-tinged flowers in summer
and early autumn. Dislikes dry soils.

Tropaeolum speciosum
FLAME CREEPER
☀ 7   ↕↔ 10ft (3m)

Brilliant, long-spurred flowers adorn this
climber, with fleshy, twining stems and
long-stalked leaves, from summer into
autumn. Bright blue fruits follow.

Wisteria floribunda 'Macrobotrys'
WISTERIA
☀ 5   ↕↔ 30ft (10m)

In early summer, this vigorous, twining
climber produces fragrant lilac, darker-
flushed pea flowers in handsome, pendent
tassels up to 4ft (1.2m) long.

Evergreen Climbers

OTHER EVERGREEN CLIMBERS

Cissus striata
Clematis fasciculiflora
Euonymus fortunei
Ficus pumila
Hedera canariensis 'Gloire de Marengo'
Hedera colchica 'Sulphur Heart', see p.96
Holboellia coriacea
Lapageria rosea, see p.97
Lonicera japonica 'Halliana', see p.97
Rosa bracteata
Rubus henryi

EXCEPT FOR IVIES, the number of evergreen climbers suitable for cool, temperate regions is relatively few when compared with the abundance of deciduous climbers. This makes them all the more valuable, especially in winter, when their persistent foliage provides a welcome touch of color. They can be used to hide unsightly structures, as well as providing useful shelter for wildlife. Most evergreen climbers need support, but self-clinging plants are specified here.

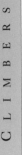

Clematis armandii
CLEMATIS
☼ 8   ↕↔ 15ft (5m)

The leaflets of this vigorous climber are dark, glossy green. Fragrant white or pink-flushed flowers are borne in bold clusters in early spring. Best in a sheltered position.

Pileostegia viburnoides
PILEOSTEGIA
☼ ☼ 7   ↕↔ 20ft (6m)

This slow-growing hydrangea relative is self-clinging, climbing by aerial roots. Its branched heads of tiny, creamy flowers open in late summer and early autumn.

Clematis cirrhosa
CLEMATIS
☼ 7   ↕↔ 10ft (3m)

Slender, twining stems and small, fernlike leaves form a dense curtain. Loose clusters of nodding, bell-shaped, creamy flowers open from late winter into early spring.

Hedera helix 'Buttercup'
GOLDEN ENGLISH IVY
☼ ☼ 7   ↕↔ 20ft (6m)

The three-lobed leaves of this self-clinging climber form a dense cover. They become a rich yellow in summer, though excessive sun can scorch them.

Trachelospermum jasminoides
CONFEDERATE JASMINE
☼ 8   ↕↔ 20ft (6m)

Best started on supporting wires, this self-clinging climber has dark green leaves that may turn red in winter. Clusters of creamy white summer flowers are fragrant.

Climbers with Fragrant Flowers

Mention fragrant climbers, and most people instantly picture honeysuckle scrambling over a hedge or framing a cottage door. No one would deny its attraction, but there are many other climbers whose flowers produce fragrances which, once experienced, are not forgotten.

Rosa 'Wedding Day'
CLIMBING ROSE
☼ 8   ↕ ↔ 25ft (8m)

The yellow buds of this climbing rose, with glossy green leaves and thorny stems, open in summer to richly scented, creamy white flowers. Blooms age to pale pink.

Clematis flammula
CLEMATIS
☼ 7   ↕ ↔ 15ft (5m)

The herbaceous stems of this vigorous climber are clothed with deeply divided green leaves and, in late summer and early autumn, almond-scented white flowers.

Jasminum officinale
'Argenteo-variegatum'
☼ 7   ↕ ↔ 15ft (5m)

Strong-growing and semievergreen, this climber has twining stems, much-divided cream-margined leaves, and richly fragrant, pink-budded, white summer flowers.

Wisteria sinensis
CHINESE WISTERIA
☼ 5   ↕ ↔ 70ft (20m)

This twining climber has fresh green leaves and crowded tassels of lilac to pale violet flowers in late spring. Pruning is required if it is grown against a wall.

Decumaria sinensis
DECUMARIA
☼ 7   ↕ ↔ 12ft (4m)

This self-clinging evergreen climber has aerial roots, fairly narrow pointed leaves, and heads of tiny, greenish white, honey-scented flowers, borne freely in spring.

Lonicera periclymenum 'Serotina'
LATE DUTCH HONEYSUCKLE
☼ ☼ 5   ↕ ↔ 15ft (5m)

In summer, the young purple shoots of this vigorous climber carry fragrant, long-tubed, purple flowers, fading to yellow within. Bears many red berry clusters.

OTHER CLIMBERS WITH FRAGRANT FLOWERS

Clematis armandii, see p.104
Clematis maximowicziana
Clematis montana
Gelsemium sempervirens
Jasminum x stephanense
Lonicera japonica 'Halliana', see p.97
Mandevilla laxa
Rosa, many
Trachelospermum jasminoides, see p.104
Wisteria floribunda

Climbing Annuals and Biennials

MOST OF THE CLIMBERS commonly grown from seed, and treated as annuals in cool gardens, are actually perennial in the wild, or when cultivated in warmer climates. When they are planted in containers, many of these can be overwintered under glass, and some may survive for several years outside in a warm, sheltered spot, especially where winters are mild.

Rhodochiton atrosanguineum
PURPLE-BELL VINE
☼   ↕ ↔ 15ft (5m)

Borne from spring to autumn, the curious, pendulous blooms of this tender perennial each have a rose-pink, bell-like calyx and a maroon-black tubular flower.

Cobaea scandens
CUP-AND-SAUCER VINE
☼   ↕ ↔ 20ft (6m)

Climbing by tendrils, this vigorous, leafy perennial grown as an annual has curious yellow-green, cup-shaped flowers that turn purple with age.

Ipomoea 'Heavenly Blue'
MORNING GLORY
☼   ↕ ↔ 10ft (3m)

Sporting lovely, large sky blue flowers from summer into autumn, this vigorous annual or tender perennial has twining stems and long-pointed, heart-shaped leaves.

OTHER CLIMBING ANNUALS

Cardiospermum halicacabum
Cucurbita pepo var. *ovifera*
Ipomoea alba
Ipomoea quamoclit
Lablab purpureus

Eccremocarpus scaber
CHILEAN GLORY FLOWER
☼ 9   ↕ ↔ 10ft (3m)

This vigorous, scrambling tender evergreen perennial climbs by means of tendrils. It has ferny leaves and spikes of orange, red, or yellow flowers in summer.

OTHER CLIMBING ANNUALS

Lathyrus odoratus
Mina lobata
Phaseolus coccineus
Tropaeolum majus
Tropaeolum peregrinum

Thunbergia alata
BLACK-EYED SUSAN VINE
☼   ↕ ↔ 10ft (3m)

A succession of striking, dark-eyed, orange-yellow flowers covers this vigorous, twining annual through summer and into autumn. It bears abundant, heart-shaped leaves.

Self-clinging Climbers

FEW SELF-CLINGING CLIMBERS, apart from the ubiquitous ivies, are hardy enough for cool, temperate gardens, especially when compared with the large number that climb by other means. Hardy, self-clinging species, therefore, have a value of their own, not only for clothing walls and fences, but also for growing up the stems or trunks of suitable trees. This selection includes climbers that cling by means of aerial roots and those that have tendrils tipped with sucker pads.

Parthenocissus henryana
PARTHENOCISSUS
☼ ☼ ☼ 6   ↕↔ 20ft (6m)

This free-growing ornamental vine clings by adhesive tendrils. Leaves are divided into silver-veined, velvety green or bronze leaflets. They color richly in autumn.

Hydrangea anomala subsp. *petiolaris*
CLIMBING HYDRANGEA
☼ ☼ ☼ 5   ↕↔ 30ft (10m)

The stems of this robust shrub, which climbs by means of aerial roots, have rich brown, peeling bark. Its white flowers, in lacecap flowerheads, open in summer.

Parthenocissus tricuspidata 'Veitchii'
BOSTON IVY
☼ ☼ ☼ 5   ↕↔ 50ft (15m)

This vigorous vine, which clings with disk-tipped tendrils, soon clothes walls with its ivylike green leaves. These color brilliantly in autumn.

Hedera helix 'Goldheart'
ENGLISH IVY
☼ ☼ ☼ 6-7   ↕↔ 10ft (3m)

Striking and easy to recognize, this ivy has dark, glossy evergreen leaves with a gold central splash. Green-leaved reversions should be removed as soon as they appear.

OTHER SELF-CLINGING CLIMBERS

Campsis radicans
Decumaria barbara
Decumaria sinensis, see p.105
Euonymus fortunei 'Coloratus'
Euonymus fortunei 'Longwood'
Ficus pumila
Hedera canariensis 'Gloire de Marengo'
Hedera colchica, see p.102
Hedera colchica 'Sulphur Heart', see p.96
Hedera helix, many
Hedera nepalensis
Hydrangea seemannii
Hydrangea serratifolia
Parthenocissus quinquefolia
Parthenocissus tricuspidata 'Lowii'
Pileostegia viburnoides, see p.104
Schizophragma hydrangeoides
Schizophragma hydrangeoides 'Moonlight'
Schizophragma integrifolium

Trachelospermum asiaticum
☼ 7   ↕↔ 20ft (6m)

Self-clinging in a wind-free situation, the slender stems of this climber twine around any support. Clusters of fragrant, creamy white flowers in summer age to yellow.

SHRUBS

ORNAMENTAL SHRUBS in the garden are the bridge between trees and perennials, forming the middle layer in mixed borders or beds. Their flexibility is legendary. Many shrubs are so distinctive in habit or impressive in flower or leaf that they make excellent single specimens in a lawn or border, where they can freely develop to their fullest potential.

△ INSECT PARADISE *The nectar-filled flowers of the Butterfly Bush* (Buddleia davidii) *attract bees and other insects, too.*

△ *Aucuba japonica* 'Crotonifolia'

The range of shrubs stretches from small carpeting plants to the larger stalwarts. Between is a host of shrubs whose habits make a substantial contribution to garden design. Horizontally extending branches such as *Viburnum plicatum* 'Mariesii', arching or weeping growth such as the brooms *(Cytisus)*, and those of upright habit such as *Viburnum sargentii* 'Onondaga' can all play a part in creating pleasing and useful architectural effects.

SOME TOUGH, SOME TENDER

Most shrubs in this section are winter hardy, but some prefer to be planted in warmer sites. In cold areas, grow tender shrubs in pots and bring them under cover for the winter. Some shrubs flourish during summer but are cut back by winter cold. These plants are known as subshrubs, and any dead growth should be removed when regrowth commences in spring.

STABILITY OR DIVERSITY

Evergreens bring an important sense of stability and continuity to the garden, most notably when deciduous or herbaceous plants are leafless or below ground. Shrubs in this section are deciduous unless described as evergreen. Numerous deciduous shrubs are worth growing for their foliage alone, especially those having bold or otherwise dramatic leaves, perhaps variegated or colored. Some produce brilliant autumn tints, of which just one can make a real impact in the garden.

△ GROUNDCOVER *The Partridgeberry* (Gaultheria procumbens) *is an attractive groundcover for acid soil.*

◁ SPRING PAGEANT *Rhododendrons and evergreen azaleas grow together in the wild and combine well in the garden.*

▷ LATE SUMMER MAGIC *This mop-headed form of* Hydrangea macrophylla *provides a reliable show late in the season.*

Large Shrubs for Specimen Planting

MOST GARDENS have at least one situation suitable for planting something particularly special – maybe in a lawn, a courtyard, or as a border feature. A tree is frequently chosen for this role, but a refreshing alternative is to consider one of the following ultimately large and impressive shrubs instead. All have character and presence as well as flowers.

Magnolia liliiflora 'Nigra'
LILY MAGNOLIA
☼ ☼ 5 PH   ↕ 10ft (3m) ↔ 10ft (3m)

One of the most satisfactory and reliable magnolias, this forms a compact mound of glossy leaves. Flowers appear from spring into summer, and in early autumn.

Aesculus parviflora
BOTTLEBRUSH BUCKEYE
☼ ☼ 5   ↕ 10ft (3m) ↔ 15ft (5m)

In time this shrub forms a bold thicket or mound of leaves, bronze-red when young and yellow in autumn. Long, tapering flower spikes are produced in summer.

Clerodendrum trichotomum
HARLEQUIN GLORYBOWER
☼ 6   ↕ 10ft (3m) ↔ 12ft (4m)

The leaves of this spreading shrub are aromatic. Pink or greenish buds open into clusters of fragrant white flowers from late summer. Turquoise blue berries follow.

Pieris formosa var. *forrestii* 'Wakehurst'
PIERIS
☼ 8 PH   ↕ 10ft (3m) ↔ 10ft (3m)

The new leaves of this handsome, mounded evergreen emerge brilliant red in spring. These follow drooping sprays of white lily-of-the-valley flowers.

Chionanthus virginicus
FRINGE TREE
☼ 4   ↕ 10ft (3m) ↔ 12ft (4m)

This large, bushy shrub bears bold, deep green leaves that turn yellow in autumn. Sprays of fragrant white flowers drape the branches in summer. Dislikes dry soils.

Ligustrum sinense
CHINESE PRIVET
☼ ☼ 7   ↕ 15ft (5m) ↔ 15ft (5m)

Upright at first, this strong-growing semi-evergreen spreads with age. Its arching, leafy branches terminate in large heads of tiny, sweet-scented white summer flowers.

OTHER LARGE SHRUBS FOR SPECIMEN PLANTING

Exochorda racemosa
Hibiscus syriacus 'Diana'
Kolkwitzia amabilis 'Pink Cloud',
  see p.126
Loropetalum chinense
Nerium oleander
Photinia serrulata
Viburnum plicatum var. *tomentosum*
Viburnum setigerum
Vitex agnus-castus

S H R U B S

Shrubs with Bold Leaves

EXPERIENCED GARDENERS sensibly choose plants as much for their foliage effect as for their attractive flowers. This is particularly important with larger plants, such as shrubs, that occupy a greater area than the average perennial. Where a shrub has both flowers and leaves worthy of attention, then give serious consideration to its inclusion; these dual-purpose plants certainly earn their place in the garden. The following is but a small selection; there are many more.

Paeonia delavayi var. *ludlowii*
TREE PEONY
☼ ☼ 5 ⬍ 8ft (2.5m) ↔ 8ft (2.5m)

Loose-stemmed, with boldly cut, bright green leaves, this shrub has yellow flowers in late spring and early summer. *P. delavayi*, with deep red flowers, is similar in leaf.

OTHER SHRUBS WITH BOLD LEAVES

Aralia spinosa
Decaisnea fargesii
Hibiscus, many
Hydrangea sargentiana
Mahonia lomariifolia
Melianthus major
Rubus odoratus
Sambucus canadensis
Tetrapanax papyrifera
Viburnum rhytidophyllum
Yucca recurvifolia

Fatsia japonica
FATSIA
☼ ☼ 7 ⬍ 10ft (3m) ↔ 10ft (3m)

This domed evergreen bears handsome, long-stalked, deeply lobed, shining green leaves. Branched clusters of white flowers in autumn precede black berries.

Eriobotrya japonica
LOQUAT
☼ 8 ⬍ 12ft (4m) ↔ 12ft (4m)

Leathery, prominently veined, dark green leaves distinguish this evergreen shrub or small tree. Fragrant white autumn flowers are followed by orange-yellow fruits.

Hydrangea quercifolia
OAKLEAF HYDRANGEA
☼ 6 ⬍ 5ft (1.5m) ↔ 8ft (2.5m)

Boldly lobed leaves that color richly in autumn cover this bushy shrub, forming a broad mound. Dense white flowerheads occur from summer into autumn.

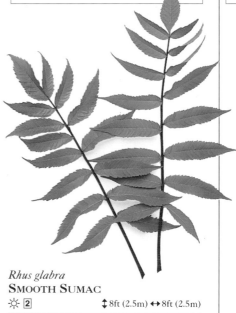

Rhus glabra
SMOOTH SUMAC
☼ 2 ⬍ 8ft (2.5m) ↔ 8ft (2.5m)

Smooth shoots support regularly divided, deep blue-green leaves that color richly in autumn. Summer flowers are followed by red-brown fruits on female plants.

SHRUBS

111

Large Shrub Roses for Specimen Planting

MOST SHRUB ROSES in the wild occur as single, scattered specimens, with space to expand and show their flowers to advantage. In gardens where space permits, shrub roses should be grown in the same way, either singly or in groups as highlights in mixed borders. Grow spreading kinds alone on the lawn, where their display can be admired from all sides.

Rosa 'Mme. Isaac Pereire'
BOURBON ROSE
☼ 6 ↕ 7ft (2.2m) ↔ 6ft (2m)

This lovely bourbon rose has a vigorous, prickly, arching growth. Richly fragrant flowers, deep rose with magenta shading, appear from summer into autumn.

OTHER SHRUB ROSES WITH FRUITS
Rosa blanda
Rosa carolina
Rosa davidii
Rosa macrophylla
Rosa moyesii
Rosa roxburghii
Rosa rugosa 'Alba'
Rosa rugosa 'Frau Dagmar Hartopp'
Rosa setipoda
Rosa sweginzowii
Rosa virginiana

Rosa 'Complicata'
GALLICA ROSE
☼ 5 ↕ 7ft (2.2m) ↔ 8ft (2.5m)

A bold, reliable gallica rose with vigorous, thorny, arching branches. Lightly scented, single, white-centered pink flowers occur in summer. May also be trained into trees.

Rosa 'Alexander'
HYBRID TEA ROSE
☼ 7 ↕ 5½ft (1.7m) ↔ 30in (75cm)

This strong-growing hybrid tea rose with erect stems makes an excellent informal hedge. Lightly fragrant, double red flowers are carried from summer into autumn.

Rosa 'Iceberg'
FLORIBUNDA ROSE
☼ 6 ↕ 5ft (1.5m) ↔ 4ft (1.2m)

'Iceberg' is a popular, reliable floribunda rose with strong, upright growth, glossy foliage, and clusters of fully double, lightly scented flowers in summer and autumn.

Rosa 'Marguerite Hilling'
SHRUB ROSE
☼ 5 ↕ 7ft (2.2m) ↔ 7ft (2.2m)

This is a vigorous shrub with dense, leafy growth. In summer, and to a lesser degree autumn, it is crowded with large, fragrant, deep pink flowers with pale centers.

Rosa moyesii 'Geranium'
SPECIES ROSE
☼ 4   ↕10ft (3m) ↔7ft (2.2m)

This tall, vigorous species rose is upright.
Its branches arch widely and sport small,
saucer-shaped summer flowers that are
followed by flask-shaped red hips.

Rosa 'Roseraie de l'Hay'
RUGOSA ROSE
☼ 4   ↕7ft (2.2m) ↔6ft (2m)

A strong-growing rugosa rose of dense
habit, this has attractive green foliage and
richly scented, velvety, deep crimson
flowers from summer into autumn.

Rosa 'Tour de Malakoff'
PROVENCE ROSE
☼ 4   ↕6ft (2m) ↔3ft (1m)

Provence rose of vigorous, open growth,
with fragrant, loosely petaled flowers in
summer. The magenta blooms fade to a
grayish purple. May require support.

Rosa 'Nevada'
SHRUB ROSE
☼ 5   ↕7ft (2.2m) ↔7ft (2.2m)

This vigorous, leafy shrub rose produces
an abundance of scented, creamy white
flowers in summer – fewer in autumn.
The flowers turn pink in hot weather.

Rosa soulieana
SPECIES ROSE
☼ 7   ↕10ft (3m) ↔10ft (3m)

The distinct stems of this rose are prickly,
and its foliage is bluish green. Numerous
scented summer flowers are yellow in bud
and open white. May need support.

Rosa
'Pink Grootendorst'
☼ 4   ↕6ft (2m) ↔5ft (1.5m)

A rugosa hybrid of bushy, upright growth,
this has prickly stems and wrinkled leaves.
Dense clusters of carnation-like flowers
occur from summer into autumn.

> **OTHER LARGE SHRUB ROSES**
> **FOR SPECIMEN PLANTING**
>
> *Rosa* 'Alba Maxima'
> *Rosa* 'Alba Semiplena'
> *Rosa* 'Blanc Double de Coubert'
> *Rosa* 'Dupontii'
> *Rosa eglanteria*, see p.169
> *Rosa* 'Frühlingsgold'
> *Rosa glauca*, see p.153
> *Rosa* 'Madame Hardy'
> *Rosa* 'White Grootendorst'
> *Rosa willmottiae*

Rosa xanthina 'Canary Bird'
SPECIES ROSE
☼ 6   ↕7ft (2.2m) ↔7ft (2.2m)

The arching branches of this vigorous
species rose carry small, fernlike foliage.
Musk-scented yellow flowers appear in
spring, with a few in autumn.

S H R U B S

Medium-sized Shrubs

S OME OF THE LOVELIEST and most desirable of all shrubs
are found in the medium-size range of 5–8ft (1.5–2.5m)
in height. Where space is no object, many of these can be
planted to glorious effect in groups, or even drifts. In smaller
gardens, where space is limited, any of the shrubs featured
here makes an impressive single specimen in the lawn. They
may also be used in combination with smaller shrubs or
groundcovers to create informal groups in beds or borders.

Hydrangea macrophylla 'Lilacina'
LACECAP HYDRANGEA
☼ 6   ↕ 5ft (1.5m) ↔ 6ft (2m)

This shrub is particularly lovely when in
flower in late summer. Its lacecap flowerheads are carried above mounds of slender,
pointed leaves. Dislikes dry soils.

Clerodendrum bungei
CLERODENDRUM
☼ 8   ↕ 6ft (2m) ↔ indefinite

From late summer into autumn, fragrant,
deep pink flowerheads nestle among the
aromatic, heart-shaped leaves. A suckering
shrub, this has erect purple shoots.

Exochorda x *macrantha* 'The Bride'
PEARLBUSH
☼ 5   ↕ 5ft (1.5m) ↔ 8ft (2.5m)

Wider than it is tall, this mounded shrub is
covered by pure white blossoms in spring
and early summer. Its arching or weeping
branches are densely leafy.

OTHER DECIDUOUS MEDIUM-SIZED SHRUBS
Cornus alba 'Sibirica', see p.168
Cytisus scoparius 'Moonlight'
Paeonia suffruticosa cultivars
Philadelphus 'Belle Etoile'
Spiraea x *vanhouttei*, see p.135
Syringa patula 'Miss Kim'
Viburnum dilatatum 'Erie'
Viburnum nudum
Viburnum opulus 'Compactum'
Weigela 'Mont Blanc'

Deutzia x *elegantissima* 'Rosealind'
DEUTZIA
☼ 6   ↕ 5ft (1.5m) ↔ 5ft (1.5m)

This is among the best flowering shrubs
for smaller gardens. Its mound of arching,
leafy branches is wreathed in clusters of
pink flowers in summer.

Hydrangea aspera
HYDRANGEA
☼ 6   ↕ 8ft (2.5m) ↔ 8ft (2.5m)

The large, downy leaves of this impressive
shrub are an excellent foil for the lacecap
flowerheads with marginal florets in late
summer and autumn. Dislikes dry soils.

Lavatera 'Rosea'
TREE MALLOW
☼ 8   ↕ 6ft (2m) ↔ 6ft (2m)

Tree mallow is one of the most continuous
and free-flowering of all garden shrubs,
with its pink blooms opening throughout
summer. The lobed leaves are downy.

SHRUBS

114

Syringa microphylla 'Superba'
LITTLELEAF LILAC
☼ 5   ↕ 6ft (2m) ↔ 6ft (2m)

Slender-stemmed and spreading, with
pointed leaves, this lilac produces fragrant
pink flowerheads, darker in bud, in late
spring and again in early autumn.

Viburnum plicatum 'Pink Beauty'
DOUBLEFILE VIBURNUM
☼ ☼ 5   ↕ 6ft (2m) ↔ 5ft (1.5m)

Elegant, spreading, layered branches carry
neat, pleated leaves and, in early summer,
lacecap flowerheads that are white when
they emerge and mature to pink.

**OTHER EVERGREEN
MEDIUM-SIZED SHRUBS**

Daphne odora
Ilex crenata
Kalmia latifolia cultivars
Rhododendron PJM hybrids

Philadelphus coronarius 'Variegatus'
MOCK ORANGE
☼ 4   ↕ 8ft (2.5m) ↔ 8ft (2.5m)

Striking, white-margined leaves are the
main attraction of this dense, bushy shrub.
Its richly fragrant flower clusters in late
spring and early summer are a bonus.

Paeonia delavayi
TREE PEONY
☼ ☼ 6   ↕ 6ft (2m) ↔ 5ft (1.5m)

Cup-shaped, dark crimson flowers, each
with a leafy bract beneath it, appear in
late spring on long stalks above bold,
deeply cut bright green leaves.

Pieris japonica
JAPANESE ANDROMEDA
☼ ☼ 5 PH   ↕ 6ft (2m) ↔ 6ft (2m)

This compact evergreen shrub has narrow,
leathery leaves, which are bronze when
young. Drooping tassels of white flowers
appear in late winter and early spring.

Viburnum sargentii
'Onondaga'
☼ ☼ 4   ↕ 8ft (2.5m) ↔ 5ft (1.5m)

The maplelike foliage of this vigorous
shrub is bronze when young and colors
richly in autumn. Its beautiful spring lacecap flowers are white, but pink in bud.

SHRUBS

115

Small Shrubs

THE VARIETY OF ATTRACTIVE small shrubs available to gardeners is exciting, if potentially bewildering. In large gardens, many of these can be planted in groups of three to five or more, but where space is more limited, any of the following will make an attractive and satisfying feature as a single plant, either alone or used as a centerpiece in a mixed border. They include some of the best small shrubs, and most are sun-loving.

Cytisus x *praecox* 'Warminster'
WARMINSTER BROOM
☼ 6　　　‡4ft (1.2m) ↔ 5ft (1.5m)

This is one of the most reliable of all small flowering shrubs. In late spring, its slender green branches are wreathed with small, scented, creamy yellow pea flowers.

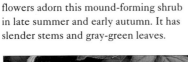

Caryopteris x *clandonensis*
'Arthur Simmonds'
☼ 6　　　‡30in (75cm) ↔ 30in (75cm)

Numerous clusters of small lavender-blue flowers adorn this mound-forming shrub in late summer and early autumn. It has slender stems and gray-green leaves.

Cistus x *aguilari* 'Maculatus'
SUN ROSE
☼ 9　　　‡4ft (1.2m) ↔ 4ft (1.2m)

Magnificent white flowers, each with dark red blotches and a yellow eye, appear in summer. Wavy-edged leaves, clammy to the touch, cover this bushy evergreen.

OTHER SMALL DECIDUOUS SHRUBS

Berberis thunbergii 'Aurea', see p.150
Caryopteris x *clandonensis* 'Longwood'
Daphne x *burkwoodii* 'Somerset'
Daphne mezereum
Deutzia gracilis 'Nikko'
Fothergilla gardenii, see p.157
Hydrangea macrophylla
　'All Summer Beauty'
Potentilla fruticosa 'Goldfinger'
Prunus glandulosa 'Sinensis'
Spiraea japonica

Ceratostigma willmottianum
CHINESE PLUMBAGO
☼ 7　　　‡3ft (1m) ↔ 3ft (1m)

This loosely domed shrub carries cobalt-blue flowers from late summer through to autumn, when its neat, pointed leaves turn red. Dies down in severe winters.

Cistus x *corbariensis*
SUN ROSE
☼ 8　　　‡30in (75cm) ↔ 4ft (1.2m)

A broad mound of wrinkled, wavy-edged leaves is obscured in summer by masses of white, yellow-eyed flowers, pink when in bud. Among the hardiest sun roses.

Deutzia gracilis
SLENDER DEUTZIA
☼ 5　　　‡3ft (1m) ↔ 3ft (1m)

The bright green leaves of this elegant shrub form a most attractive backdrop for its white flower clusters that last from late spring to early summer.

S H R U B S

116

Fuchsia 'Mrs. Popple'
FUCHSIA
☼ 8   ↕4ft (1.2m) ↔4ft (1.2m)

One of the hardiest fuchsias, this vigorous shrub has glossy foliage and a continuous supply of richly colored, pendent flowers from summer into autumn.

Philadelphus 'Manteau d'Hermine'
MOCK ORANGE
☼ 5   ↕30in (75cm) ↔5ft (1.5m)

Clusters of long-lasting, fragrant, double, creamy white flowers are borne in summer, covering this broad, low shrub of compact, bushy habit.

Potentilla 'Abbotswood'
SHRUBBY POTENTILLA
☼ 6   ↕30in (75cm) ↔4ft (1.2m)

In summer and early autumn, this low-domed bush is plastered with small white flowers, resembling miniature roses. Its deeply divided leaves are gray-green.

Hebe recurva
HEBE
☼ 9   ↕24in (60cm) ↔4ft (1.2m)

This low, dome-shaped evergreen hebe produces narrow blue-gray leaves and an abundance of white flowers, carried on small, slender spikes in summer.

OTHER SMALL EVERGREEN SHRUBS

Artemisia arborescens, see p.50
Aucuba japonica
Choisya 'Aztec Pearl', see p.144
Daphne retusa
Erica terminalis
Hedera helix 'Conglomerata'
Paxistima canbyi
Phlomis italica, see p.131
Pieris japonica 'Pygmaea'
Sarcococca hookeriana var. *humilis*
Skimmia japonica, see p.171

Rhododendron yakushimanum
YAK RHODODENDRON
☼ ☼ 6 ⬇   ↕3ft (1m) ↔5ft (1.5m)

This small rhododendron is popular and reliable, and forms a tight evergreen dome. Its trusses of pink flowers, in late spring and early summer, fade to white.

Salix hastata 'Wehrhahnii'
WILLOW
☼ 5   ↕3ft (1m) ↔5ft (1.5m)

This handsome, shrubby little willow is well worth growing for the silvery catkins that emerge in spring, before its leaves unfurl. Dislikes dry soils.

Phygelius x *rectus* 'Moonraker'
PHYGELIUS
☼ 8   ↕5ft (1.5m) ↔5ft (1.5m)

Long, upright spires of pendulous, tubular, creamy yellow flowers are held by this striking evergreen or semievergreen from summer into autumn. Of suckering habit.

S H R U B S

Shrubs for Groundcover

HE NUMBER OF SHRUBS that make good groundcovers is enormous. Some have far-reaching, trailing, or creeping stems that lie close to the soil surface, while others produce short ascending or arching branches that give a low, mounded effect. Yet more are of a suckering nature. To achieve good results as quickly as possible, groundcover shrubs should be planted in groups of three or five, or even more, depending on the area to be covered. Remove weeds before planting.

Euonymus fortunei 'Emerald 'n' Gold'
EVERGREEN EUONYMUS
☼ ☼ ☼ 5   ↕24in (60cm) ↔4ft (1.2m)

This adaptable, bright-foliaged evergreen forms dense hummocks of green shoots and gold-margined leaves, usually pink-tinted in winter. Climbs if supported.

Cornus canadensis
BUNCHBERRY
☼ ☼ 2 PH   ↕5in (13cm) ↔12in (30cm)

In late spring and early summer, the starry, white-bracted flowerheads of this carpeting perennial are borne above ruffs of oval leaves. Red berries follow.

OTHER EVERGREEN SHRUBS FOR GROUNDCOVER
Arctostaphylos uva-ursi 'Vancouver Jade'
Calluna vulgaris, many
Ceanothus thyrsiflorus var. *repens*
Iberis sempervirens
Leucothoe catesbaei
Mahonia repens
Paxistima canbyi
Santolina chamaecyparissus, see p.153
Sarcococca hookeriana var. *humilis*
Vaccinium vitis-idaea

Cotoneaster dammeri
BEARBERRY COTONEASTER
☼ ☼ 6   ↕3in (8cm) ↔6ft (2m)

This is one of the best evergreen ground-covering shrubs. Its densely leafy, trailing stems are studded with white flowers in summer and red berries in winter.

Euonymus fortunei 'Emerald Gaiety'
EVERGREEN EUONYMUS
☼ ☼ ☼ 5   ↕3ft (1m) ↔5ft (1.5m)

Tough, adaptable, and easy to grow, this shrub forms a dense, low cover of rounded leaves, margined white and marbled gray. Leaves are often pink-tinted in winter.

x *Halimiocistus sahucii*
SUN ROSE
☼ 8   ↕12in (30cm) ↔4ft (1.2m)

Crowded with narrow, dark green leaves, this dense, low, bushy evergreen is covered with small, roselike, yellow-eyed, white flowers in late spring and early summer.

S H R U B S

Hedera helix 'Glacier'
ENGLISH IVY
☼ ☼ ☀ 6   ↕4in (10cm) ↔10ft (3m)

One of the best variegated ivies suitable
for groundcover, this will climb if given
support. The evergreen silver-gray leaves
each have an irregular white margin.

Hedera helix 'Ivalace'
ENGLISH IVY
☼ ☼ ☀ 5   ↕4in (10cm) ↔5ft (1.5m)

This attractive groundcover forms dense
hummocks or patches of glossy dark green
leaves, which are shallowly lobed and
crinkled. Will climb with support.

Hypericum calycinum
ST. JOHN'S-WORT
☼ ☼ 6   ↕12in (30cm) ↔5ft (1.5m)

The creeping roots of this evergreen form
a close green carpet of leafy shoots, topped
by golden yellow flowers with red-tipped
stamens from summer into autumn.

Leptospermum rupestre
LEPTOSPERMUM
☼ 9   ↕3in (8cm) ↔6ft (2m)

This evergreen shrub will create a packed
carpet of tiny, deep green leaves, studded
in summer with small white flowers. Its
leaves turn bronze in winter.

**OTHER DECIDUOUS SHRUBS
FOR GROUNDCOVER**

Rhus aromatica
Rosa wichuraiana
Rubus calycinoides
Xanthorhiza simplicissima

Viburnum davidii
DAVID VIBURNUM
☼ ☼ 8   ↕3ft (1m) ↔5ft (1.5m)

Broad mounds of boldly veined evergreen
leaves need space. The white flowers are
small, and pollinated female plants bear
striking blue berries in autumn.

Vinca minor
CREEPING MYRTLE
☼ ☀ 5   ↕4in (10cm) ↔5ft (1.5m)

Long, slender, prostrate stems and paired,
glossy green leaves provide reliable groundcover. Charming blue, purple, or white
flowers open from spring into summer.

S
H
R
U
B
S

Small Shrub Roses for Limited Space

NUMEROUS SHRUB ROSES are medium to large in size and require considerable space in which to develop to their full potential. Fortunately, certain roses are of lesser stature and therefore suitable for planting where space is limited. Some of the following may need support to prevent their slender stems from flopping to the ground when in flower.

Rosa gallica var. *officinalis*
APOTHECARY'S ROSE
☼ 4   ↕ 3ft (1m) ↔ 3ft (1m)

Lush foliage and an abundant supply of scented, semidouble, deep pink flowers cover this spreading, low-branching species rose in summer. Hips are attractive.

Rosa x *centifolia* 'Cristata'
CRESTED MOSS ROSE
☼ 4   ↕ 5ft (1.5m) ↔ 4ft (1.2m)

Distinct green, mossy buds open to reveal richly scented pink blooms on nodding stalks in summer. The rather lax stems of this prickly bush may need support.

Rosa gallica 'Versicolor'
ROSA MUNDI GALLICA ROSE
☼ 4   ↕ 3ft (1m) ↔ 3ft (1m)

This well-known rose began as a mutation of *R. gallica* var. *officinalis*, and differs in its flowers, which are pale pink with crimson stripes. Prune to maintain its size.

OTHER SMALL SHRUB ROSES
Rosa 'Cecile Brunner'
Rosa 'Comte de Chambord'
Rosa 'Jacques Cartier'
Rosa 'Little White Pet'
Rosa 'Lutea Maxima'
Rosa 'Margo Koster'
Rosa 'Marie Pavie'
Rosa nitida
Rosa 'Perle d'Or'
Rosa 'Rose de Rescht'
Rosa 'The Fairy'

Rosa 'Buff Beauty'
HYBRID MUSK ROSE
☼ 6   ↕ 4ft (1.2m) ↔ 4ft (1.2m)

A popular and reliable rose with shining green foliage that is coppery brown when young. Deliciously scented, fully double flowers are freely borne in summer.

Rosa x *centifolia* 'Muscosa'
COMMON MOSS ROSE
☼ 4   ↕ 5ft (1.5m) ↔ 4ft (1.2m)

Coarse foliage provides a good backdrop for the richly scented pink flowers opening from mossy buds in summer. This loose-stemmed bush may need support.

Low-growing Roses for Groundcover

I N SUNNY SITUATIONS, low-spreading roses or those with trailing stems provide a useful and charming groundcover. They are particularly suited to steep banks, wall tops, or beneath plantings of other roses, especially those whose stems become unsightly with age. In recent years, a host of new, free-flowering cultivars have become available. Where space permits, you can achieve impressive displays with generous plantings, but in small gardens a single plant can give as much pleasure.

Rosa 'Grouse'
ROSE CULTIVAR

☼ 5   ↕ 18in (45cm) ↔ 10ft (3m)

In summer, this free-growing rose, with its long, trailing stems and shining foliage, produces a succession of small, fragrant, pale pink blooms.

Rosa 'Max Graf'
RUGOSA HYBRID

☼ 4   ↕ 18in (45cm) ↔ 10ft (3m)

Large, single flowers have an apple scent and are carried in summer. The shining, bright green foliage of this dense rose is carried on long, trailing stems.

Rosa 'Nozomi'
ROSE CULTIVAR

☼ 5   ↕ 18in (45cm) ↔ 1.2m (4ft)

This charming creeping rose has arching stems clothed with small, neat, dark green leaves, and bears single blush pink and white flowers in summer.

OTHER GROUNDCOVER ROSES
Rosa macrantha
Rosa nitida
Rosa 'Paulii'
Rosa 'Pheasant'
Rosa 'Pink Wave'
Rosa 'Red Cascade'
Rosa 'Sea Foam'
Rosa 'Snow Fairy'
Rosa 'The Fairy'
Rosa virginiana
Rosa 'William Baffin'

Rosa 'Partridge'
ROSE CULTIVAR

☼ 5   ↕ 18in (45cm) ↔ 10ft (3m)

The pure white flowers of this rose, borne in abundance throughout summer, are small and fragrant. It is similar in growth to *R.* 'Grouse', to which it is related.

MINIATURE ROSES
Rosa 'Black Jade'
Rosa 'Cupcake'
Rosa 'Dee Bennett'
Rosa 'Jean Kenneally'
Rosa 'Minnie Pearl'
Rosa 'New Beginning'
Rosa 'Pacesetter'
Rosa 'Party Girl'
Rosa 'Popcorn'
Rosa 'Rainbow's End'
Rosa 'Starina'

Rosa 'Seagull'
ROSE CULTIVAR

☼ 5   ↕ 24in (60cm) ↔ 12ft (4m)

A strong-growing climbing rose, good for groundcover where space allows. Large, branched clusters of fragrant, semidouble white flowers open in summer.

S H R U B S

Shrubs for Heavy Clay Soils

IF YOU HAVE A CLASSIC clay soil (one that is heavy and sticky when wet, shrinking and cracking when it is dry), then it is a good idea to try to improve it by careful drainage and by adding liberal and frequent amounts of very coarse sand, together with rough, especially fibrous, organic matter. Avoid working clay soil when it is wet. Despite the doom and gloom that is commonly associated with heavy clay, however, a large and diverse selection of shrubs can thrive in such soils.

Cytisus 'Killiney Red'
BROOM
☼ 6 PH⊽   ‡3ft (1m) ↔ 4ft (1.2m)

One of many brooms tolerant of clay soils, 'Killiney Red' is a dwarf, compact variety. Slender green shoots carry many flowers in late spring and early summer.

Berberis darwinii
DARWIN'S BARBERRY
☼ 7   ‡10ft (3m) ↔ 12ft (4m)

This large, mounded evergreen shrub is densely covered with small, dark green leaves. Clusters of orange-yellow flowers in spring are followed by black berries.

Escallonia 'Langleyensis'
ESCALLONIA
☼ 8   ‡6ft (2m) ↔ 6ft (2m)

Evergreen and wind-tolerant, this tried and tested shrub has arching stems, small, glossy leaves on weeping branches, and tiny bunches of pink summer flowers.

OTHER DECIDUOUS SHRUBS FOR HEAVY CLAY SOILS

Berberis thunbergii
Cotinus coggygria 'Royal Purple', see p.154
Cytisus x *praecox* 'Allgold', see p.128
Deutzia gracilis 'Nikko'
Forsythia x *intermedia* 'Lynwood', see p.136
Kerria japonica 'Pleniflora', see p.101
Lonicera fragrantissima
Magnolia 'Susan'
Rhododendron occidentale, see p.134
Ribes sanguineum 'White Icicle'
Sambucus nigra 'Guincho Purple', see p.155
Spiraea x *vanhouttei*, see p.135
Syringa vulgaris cultivars
Viburnum sargentii 'Onondaga' see p.115

Chaenomeles x *superba* 'Nicoline'
FLOWERING QUINCE
☼ ☼ 5   ‡3ft (1m) ↔ 5ft (1.5m)

The branches of this tough, reliable shrub are studded in spring with a profusion of large scarlet flowers. These are followed by small, yellow, applelike fruits.

Hydrangea arborescens 'Grandiflora'
HILLS OF SNOW HYDRANGEA
☼ ☼ 4   ‡5ft (1.5m) ↔ 6ft (2m)

Large heads of white flowers appear from summer through to early autumn. Broad, oval leaves clothe this tough and reliable, mounded shrub. It dislikes dry soils.

S H R U B S

Magnolia stellata 'Waterlily'
STAR MAGNOLIA
☼ 4   ↕ 10ft (3mm) ↔ 12ft (4m)

Eventually broader than it is high, this charming shrub is slow-growing. Fragrant, multipetaled blooms cover the branches in spring. Leaves turn yellow in autumn.

Neillia thibetica
NEILLIA
☼ 6   ↕ 8ft (2.5m) ↔ 8ft (2.5m)

The flowers of this strong-growing shrub are held in lax, tail-like spikes on arching branches amid its jagged, pointed leaves from late spring into early summer.

Philadelphus 'Virginal'
MOCK ORANGE
☼ 5   ↕ 10ft (3m) ↔ 8ft (2.5m)

A strong-growing shrub, this is deservedly one of the most popular, due to its great abundance of large, richly fragrant, double or semidouble white summer flowers.

Potentilla 'Elizabeth'
SHRUBBY POTENTILLA
☼ 2   ↕ 30in (75cm) ↔ 5ft (1.5m)

This broad, low mounding plant bears dense branches and small, deeply divided leaves. It is covered with bright yellow flowers from late spring to autumn.

Rhododendron 'Mrs. G.W. Leak'
RHODODENDRON
☼ ☼ 7   ↕ 12ft (4m) ↔ 12ft (4m)

This large evergreen shrub is particularly striking in late spring, when it is covered with bold trusses of pink, funnel-shaped flowers splashed brown and crimson.

OTHER EVERGREEN SHRUBS FOR HEAVY CLAY SOILS

Aucuba japonica
Berberis verruculosa
Choisya ternata, see p.158
Cotoneaster franchetii
Escallonia rubra 'Crimson Spire'
Mahonia bealei
Osmanthus x *burkwoodii*, see p.159
Pyracantha 'Mohave'
Skimmia japonica, see p.171
Viburnum davidii, see p.119

Spiraea japonica 'Anthony Waterer'
SPIREA
☼ 4   ↕ 4ft (1.2m) ↔ 4ft (1.2m)

Erect and compact, this is an extremely popular flowering shrub. It produces dark green, jaggedly toothed leaves, and flat crimson-pink flowerheads in summer.

Spiraea nipponica 'Snowmound'
SPIREA
☼ 4   ↕ 6ft (2m) ↔ 6ft (2m)

Tufts of white flowers are carried all along the upper sides of densely leafy, arching stems, making this a spectacular shrub at its peak in late spring.

Shrubs for Acid Soils

THE SHRUBS PREFERRING, if not demanding, acid soils are relatively few in number, but they encompass some of the loveliest, most popular shrubs. Rhododendrons, camellias, and heathers are well-known acid-lovers, but many other shrubs have similar requirements. Although they thrive in naturally acid soils, many of these plants will grow reasonably well in specially prepared beds, or in containers filled with acid soil mix.

S H R U B S

Daboecia cantabrica 'Bicolor'
DABOECIA
☼ 5 PH   ↕18in (45cm) ↔24in (60cm)

This low, bushy, evergreen shrub is dense and wiry, with nodding white, purple, or purple-striped flowers, held in loose spikes, from late spring into autumn.

Camellia x *williamsii* 'Donation'
CAMELLIA
☼ 7 PH   ↕10ft (3m) ↔6ft (2m)

One of the best camellias for general cultivation, this free-growing, upright evergreen carries an abundance of large flowers from late winter into spring.

Desfontainea spinosa
DESFONTAINEA
☼ 8 PH   ↕6ft (2m) ↔5ft (1.5m)

Tubular red flowers are borne from mid-summer to autumn in the leaf axils of this slow-growing evergreen. The leaves are small and hollylike. Dislikes dry soils.

Calluna vulgaris 'Annemarie'
HEATHER, LING
☼ 5 PH   ↕18in (45cm) ↔18in (45cm)

Reliable and free-flowering, this heather forms a compact bush. Long spires of double, light pink flowers rise above dark evergreen foliage in autumn.

Camellia japonica 'Adolphe Audusson'
CAMELLIA
☼ 7 PH   ↕10ft (3m) ↔8ft (2.5m)

This reliable camellia is a dense, bushy evergreen with glossy, dark green leaves. Large, deep red, gold-stamened flowers appear from late winter into spring.

Clethra delavayi
CLETHRA
☼ 7 PH   ↕12ft (4m) ↔10ft (3m)

Dense, horizontal spikes of fragrant white flowers, pink when in bud, give this shrub a most distinguished appearance when they open in summer. Dislikes dry soil.

Enkianthus cernuus var. *rubens*
ENKIANTHUS
☼ 6 PH   ↕8ft (2.5m) ↔6ft (2m)

Bunches of fringed, bell-shaped flowers hang beneath neat clusters of leaves in late spring. The leaves color richly in autumn. Dislikes dry soils.

Erica cinerea 'C.D. Eason'
BELL HEATHER
☼ 6 PH ♥   ↕12in (30cm) ↔24in (60cm)

From summer to autumn, this dense, low-growing evergreen is covered by crowded spikes of carmine pink, pitcher-shaped flowers. It has needlelike leaves.

Pieris 'Forest Flame'
PIERIS
☼ 7 PH ♥   ↕12ft (4m) ↔6ft (2m)

The leaves of this erect evergreen emerge crimson, and then lighten to pink and cream before turning glossy green. Its sprays of white flowers appear in spring.

Rhododendron 'May Day'
RHODODENDRON
☼ ☼ 7 PH ♥   ↕5ft (1.5m) ↔5ft (1.5m)

Excellent for all but the very coldest areas, this flat-topped or domed evergreen bears dark green leaves and is covered in spring with trusses of red trumpet flowers.

OTHER EVERGREEN SHRUBS FOR ACID SOIL

Arbutus unedo
Calluna vulgaris 'Blazeaway'
Crinodendron hookerianum, see p.132
Gardenia augusta
Gaultheria shallon
Grevillea juniperina f. *sulphurea*
Kalmia latifolia 'Ostbo Red'
Leptospermum scoparium 'Red Damask'
Rhododendron PJM hybrids
Rhododendron yakushimanum, see p.117

S H R U B S

Kalmia latifolia
MOUNTAIN LAUREL
☼ ☼ 5 PH ♥   ↕10ft (3m) ↔10ft (3m)

Free-flowering and impressive, this shrub, clad in cheerful glossy evergreen leaves, bears clusters of small pink flowers, darker when in bud, in early summer.

OTHER DECIDUOUS SHRUBS FOR ACID SOIL

Clethra alnifolia
Cyrilla racemiflora
Enkianthus campanulatus
Fothergilla gardenii, see p.157
Itea virginica
Rhododendron prunifolium
Rhododendron schlippenbachii
Vaccinium corymbosum, see p.135
Viburnum nudum
Zenobia pulverulenta

Rhododendron 'Hinomayo'
EVERGREEN AZALEA
☼ ☼ 6 PH ♥   ↕5ft (1.5m) ↔5ft (1.5m)

This dense, twiggy evergreen is crowded with small leaves and plastered in spring by little funnel-shaped pink flowers. It will not tolerate dry soils.

Rhododendron 'Narcissiflorum'
GHENT AZALEA
☼ 5 PH ♥   ↕6ft (2m) ↔6ft (2m)

A vigorous shrub that produces masses of pale yellow, darker-flushed flowers with a sweet scent in spring and early summer. Leaves often color bronze in autumn.

Shrubs for Alkaline Soils

FAR FROM BEING PROBLEMATIC, alkaline soils are suitable for a huge variety of shrubs, many of which actually thrive in the high pH and the warmer, free-draining conditions that prevail there. A number of these plants are also drought-tolerant, although this does not mean moisture is not essential. Such soils need to be given organic matter as well, in the form of a mulch. Sufficient water and enough organic matter improves the ability of most garden shrubs to grow well, and keeps leaves a healthy green.

Indigofera heterantha
INDIGO
☼ 7   ↕ 5ft (1.5m) ↔ 5½ft (1.7m)

This multistemmed shrub has arching branches clothed in fernlike leaves. Small, rich mauve-pink pea flowers are produced all through summer into autumn.

Buddleia davidii 'Dartmoor'
BUTTERFLY BUSH
☼ 6   ↕ 8ft (2.5m) ↔ 8ft (2.5m)

In late summer and autumn, distinctive flowerheads, popular with butterflies and bees, cover this vigorous shrub. Its arching branches carry long, pointed leaves.

Kolkwitzia amabilis 'Pink Cloud'
BEAUTY BUSH
☼ 5   ↕ 10ft (3m) ↔ 10ft (3m)

A vigorous shrub of mounded habit this has small, oval leaves, and masses of bell flowers in spring and early summer. Pale, bristly seed clusters follow.

Deutzia longifolia 'Veitchii'
DEUTZIA
☼ 7   ↕ 7ft (2.2m) ↔ 5½ft (1.7m)

One of the most reliable of all deutzias, this has arching branches, narrow leaves, and large clusters of star-shaped summer flowers that are rich, lilac-stained pink.

Hibiscus syriacus 'Red Heart'
ROSE OF SHARON
☼ 6   ↕ 7ft (2.2m) ↔ 7ft (2.2m)

The branches of this shrub slowly spread with age. Boldly lobed leaves unfurl late in the season. Large flowers are carried from late summer into autumn.

OTHER EVERGREEN SHRUBS
FOR ALKALINE SOIL

Berberis darwinii, see p.122
Choisya 'Aztec Pearl', see p.144
Escallonia 'Iveyi'
Itea ilicifolia, see p.99
Jasminum humile, see p.101
Mahonia x *media* 'Buckland', see p.167
Olearia macrodonta, see p.146
Osmanthus x *burkwoodii*, see p.159
Sarcococca hookeriana var. *digyna*,
  see p.167

Osmanthus delavayi
OSMANTHUS, FALSE HOLLY
☼ ☼ 8   ↕ 7ft (2.2m) ↔ 7ft (2.2m)

Mounded evergreen shrub with slender, arching stems packed with little, dark green leaves. In spring, clusters of small, sweet-smelling, tubular flowers appear.

Santolina pinnata subsp.
neapolitana 'Sulphurea'
☼ 7   ↕ 28in (70cm) ↔ 3ft (1m)

Long-stalked, button-shaped clusters of tiny flowers top narrow, feathery leaves in midsummer. This is a low, dome-shaped evergreen shrub of dense habit.

Weigela 'Looymansii Aurea'
WEIGELA
☼ 6   ↕ 5ft (1.5m) ↔ 3½ft (1.1m)

This shrub is principally grown for its golden foliage, which later becomes yellowish green. Funnel-shaped flowers open in late spring and early summer.

Philadelphus 'Boule d'Argent'
MOCK ORANGE
☼ 5   ↕ 5ft (1.5m) ↔ 5ft (1.5m)

One of several mock oranges suitable for small gardens, this has a bushy habit and arching branches. Striking clusters of lightly fragrant flowers appear in summer.

Spiraea canescens
SPIREA
☼ 7   ↕ 7ft (2.2m) ↔ 5½ft (1.7m)

The arching stems of this graceful shrub are covered for much of their length with clusters of tiny white summer flowers set above small gray-green leaves.

Xanthoceras sorbifolium
YELLOWHORN
☼ 5   ↕ 10ft (3m) ↔ 7ft (2.2m)

An uncommon, unusual shrub of upright growth, with much-divided leaves and erect flower spikes from late spring. It may produce large fruits after a hot summer.

> **OTHER DECIDUOUS SHRUBS FOR ALKALINE SOILS**
>
> *Abelia triflora*
> *Buddleia alternifolia* 'Argentea'
> *Chaenomeles speciosa* 'Moerloosei',
>   see p.100
> *Cotinus coggygria*
> *Dipelta floribunda*
> *Forsythia* x *intermedia* 'Lynwood',
>   see p.136
> *Hydrangea paniculata*
> *Rubus* 'Benenden', see p.165

Prunus tenella
DWARF RUSSIAN ALMOND
☼ 2   ↕ 28in (70cm) ↔ 4ft (1.2m)

This low, bushy shrub has many slender stems, narrow, glossy green leaves, and bright pink flowers crowding the branches in spring. 'Fire Hill' is a superb selection.

Syringa x *persica*
PERSIAN LILAC
☼ 3   ↕ 7ft (2.2m) ↔ 7ft (2.2m)

A reliable and justifiably popular lilac, this forms a large bush in time. Slender branches bear spectacular conical heads of fragrant flowers in late spring.

S H R U B S

Shrubs for Sandy Soils

NUMEROUS SHRUBS favor sandy soils because they provide well-drained soil conditions. In times of drought, however, sandy soils can turn to dust, and plants growing in them may require a great deal of irrigation. Such soils can, of course, be improved by changing their structure with the addition of liberal and regular amounts of moisture-retentive organic matter such as compost, but it is still a good idea to plant shrubs tolerant of drought and rapid drainage.

Cytisus x *praecox* 'Allgold'
BROOM
☼ 6   ↕6ft (2m) ↔6ft (2m)

The slender, arching shoots of this shrub form a compact mound. Its gray-green branchlets are crowded with small, long-lasting, yellow pea flowers in spring.

Ballota acetabulosa
BALLOTA
☼ 7   ↕24in (60cm) ↔30in (75cm)

This gray-green, woolly plant has erect stems with rounded leaves, and bears tiny, two-lipped pink flowers in summer. Prune back hard if damaged in cold winters.

Callistemon citrinus 'Splendens'
BOTTLEBRUSH
☼ 10   ↕6ft (2m) ↔6ft (2m)

Brilliant red, tightly packed, brushlike spikes adorn this evergreen in summer. It has many arching stems and branches of narrow, leathery, glossy green leaves.

OTHER SHRUBS FOR SANDY SOIL
Baccharis halimifolia
Ceanothus americanus
Hypericum prolificum
Kolkwitzia amabilis 'Pink Cloud' see p.126
Myrica pensylvanica
Nerium oleander
Prunus maritima
Rosa carolina
Robinia hispida, see p.99
Santolina chamaecyparissus, see p.153

Brachyglottis monroi
SHRUBBY SENECIO
☼ 9   ↕3ft (1m) ↔5ft (1.5m)

Low-domed and compact, this evergreen shrub is crowded with small, wavy-edged, dark green, white-backed leaves. It carries yellow daisy flowers in summer.

Cistus x *purpureus*
SUN ROSE
☼ 9   ↕3ft (1m) ↔3ft (1m)

In early summer, this rounded, bushy evergreen carries single, roselike flowers. Narrow gray-green leaves are a perfect foil for its deep purplish pink blooms.

Dorycnium hirsutum
DORYCNIUM
☼ 7   ↕24in (60cm) ↔24in (60cm)

This small, mounded shrub is entirely covered with silvery gray down. Clusters of little white pea flowers in summer are followed by attractive reddish seed pods.

SHRUBS

Grevillea 'Canberra Gem'
GREVILLEA
☼ 9   ↕ 6ft (2m) ↔ 6ft (2m)

One of the hardiest grevilleas, 'Canberra Gem' forms an evergreen mound of green, needlelike leaves. Loose flower clusters are borne from late winter into spring.

Hibiscus syriacus 'Woodbridge'
ROSE OF SHARON
☼ 6   ↕ 8ft (2.5m) ↔ 10ft (3m)

Slow-growing and late-leafing, this shrub is upright at first, spreading as it matures. Beautiful, saucer-shaped flowers are produced in summer and autumn.

Lavatera 'Barnsley'
TREE MALLOW
☼ 7   ↕ 6ft (2m) ↔ 6ft (2m)

All through summer, this semievergreen carries a succession of lovely, pale blush pink, almost white, red-eyed flowers. Its lobed leaves are sage green and downy.

Lespedeza thunbergii
LESPEDEZA
☼ 6   ↕ 5ft (1.5m) ↔ 8ft (2.5m)

This is one of the best autumn-flowering shrubs. Its long, arching stems become weighed down with large sprays of purple pea flowers. May require support.

Potentilla fruticosa var. *mandshurica* 'Manchu'
☼ 2   ↕ 18in (45cm) ↔ 24in (60cm)

Twiggy branches, clothed with silver gray leaves, form a low mound. The bush is densely packed with small, single white flowers from late spring into early autumn.

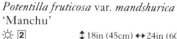

Romneya coulteri
CALIFORNIA POPPY
☼ 8   ↕ 6ft (2m) ↔ 6ft (2m)

This strong-growing plant has blue-gray stems and deeply cut foliage. Large, fragrant white poppy flowers with golden stamens appear in late summer.

Shrubs for Dry, Sunny Sites

A GREAT MANY SHRUBS thrive in situations that are sunny and relatively dry; if your winters are mild, then the choice is both immense and exciting. Where winter temperatures are not as favorable, make use of any shelter available, be it a backing wall or protection provided by more hardy plants nearby. Many of the shrubs thriving in dry, sunny situations hail from regions such as the Mediterranean, where sun, heat, and stony, well-drained soils often go hand in hand.

Euphorbia characias subsp. *wulfenii*
SHRUBBY EUPHORBIA
☼ 7   ↕ 3ft (1m) ↔ 3ft (1m)

This evergreen produces erect, biennial stems with gray-green leaves the first year, followed next spring by large heads of little yellow-green, cup-shaped flowers.

Cistus x *cyprius*
SUN ROSE
☼ 7   ↕ 6ft (2m) ↔ 5ft (1.5m)

Large white flowers with yellow stamens and red blotches appear in early summer. Both the shoots and leaves of this vigorous evergreen are sticky to the touch.

OTHER SHRUBS FOR DRY SUN
Artemisia 'Powis Castle', see p.72
Caragana arborescens
Carpenteria californica, see p.158
Caryopteris incana
Fremontodendron 'California Glory', see p.99
Lavandula angustifolia 'Hidcote', see p.164
Potentilla fruticosa
Xanthoceras sorbifolium, see p.127
Zauschneria californica

Erythrina crista-galli
CORAL TREE
☼ 9   ↕ 6ft (2m) ↔ 6ft (2m)

Eye-catching spikes of waxy coral-red flowers open in late summer. The prickly shoots bear leaves, each composed of three leaflets. Dies back in cold winters.

Euryops pectinatus
EURYOPS
☼ 9   ↕ 3ft (1m) ↔ 3ft (1m)

An evergreen mound of deeply cut gray-green leaves is topped with long-stalked, bright yellow, daisylike flowers, from late winter through to early summer.

Grindelia chiloensis
GRINDELIA

☼ 9   ↕ 30in (75cm) ↔ 24in (60cm)

Reminiscent of a yellow aster, this shrub is evergreen and bears long-stalked, bright yellow daisy flowers from late winter into early summer. It is sticky to the touch.

Hibiscus syriacus 'Blue Bird'
ROSE OF SHARON

☼ 6   ↕ 8ft (2.5m) ↔ 6ft (2m)

Erect at first, this late-leafing shrub spreads with age and carries a wealth of large trumpet-shaped, lilac-blue flowers in late summer and autumn.

Olearia stellulata
DAISY BUSH

☼ 9   ↕ 5ft (1.5m) ↔ 5ft (1.5m)

During late spring, the stems and narrow, wavy-edged leaves of this dense evergreen are almost completely obscured by masses of white, daisylike flowers.

Phlomis fruticosa
JERUSALEM SAGE

☼ 7   ↕ 3ft (1m) ↔ 3ft (1m)

This low, mound-forming evergreen is worth growing exclusively for its downy, aromatic, gray-green leaves; golden flowers during summer are an added bonus.

Phlomis italica
PHLOMIS

☼ 9   ↕ 3ft (1m) ↔ 24in (60cm)

The stems and leaves of this low, upright evergreen are covered with gray-green, woolly hairs. Whorls of two-lipped summer flowers are a lovely shade of lilac-pink.

Sophora davidii
SOPHORA

☼ 6   ↕ 5ft (1.5m) ↔ 6ft (2m)

Loose-stemmed when young, this shrub becomes dense and spiny with age. Bluish white pea flowers are produced among its small, deeply divided leaves in summer.

Fabiana imbricata 'Violacea'
FABIANA

☼ 9   ↕ 8ft (2.5m) ↔ 6ft (2m)

The stems of this upright to vase-shaped evergreen are clothed with tiny, heathlike leaves and crowded in early summer with pale violet, tubular flowers.

SHRUBS

131

Shrubs Tolerant of Shade

YOU MAY BE SURPRISED at the range of shrubs suitable for growing in shade. Many are woodlanders in the wild, preferring to grow where they are not directly exposed to the sun's rays. This does not mean they can survive without any light – all green-leaved plants need light to photosynthesize. Some, however, are more tolerant of lower light levels than others, and it is these that are most successful when planted in the shade of deciduous trees, or that cast by buildings.

Euonymus fortunei 'Sarcoxie'
EVERGREEN EUONYMUS
☼ ☀ 5   ↕ 5ft (1.5m) ↔ 5ft (1.5m)

Strong-growing and bushy, this upright evergreen shrub has leathery, dark green, glossy-topped leaves. In autumn, creamy white capsules encase orange seeds.

Euonymus fortunei   'Vegetus'
EVERGREEN EUONYMUS
☼ ☀ 5   ↕ 12in (30cm) ↔ 6ft (2m)

The presence of both creeping and erect stems enable this tough, bushy evergreen to form extensive patches. Its green leaves and pinkish seed capsules are numerous.

Crinodendron hookerianum
LANTERN TREE
☼ ☀ 9 PH   ↕ 10ft (3m) ↔ 6ft (2m)

From late spring through to early summer, the branches of this handsome evergreen are strung with beautiful red flowers that resemble lanterns. Dislikes dry soils.

OTHER DECIDUOUS SHRUBS
TOLERANT OF SHADE

Berberis thunbergii, see p.156
Cornus canadensis, see p.118
Euonymus alatus, see p.157
Euonymus obovatus
Hydrangea macrophylla
Hypericum androsaemum
Kerria japonica
Rhodotypos scandens, see p.135
Rubus odoratus
Symphoricarpos x *chenaultii* 'Hancock'

Daphne laureola var. *philippi*
SPURGE LAUREL
☼ ☀ ☀ 7   ↕ 12in (30cm) ↔ 2ft (60cm)

A dwarf variety of a woodland evergreen, this is just as effective when grown in full sun. Crowded light green flower clusters emerge in late winter and early spring.

Hydrangea macrophylla 'Veitchii'
LACECAP HYDRANGEA
☼ ☀ 6   ↕ 5ft (1.5m) ↔ 8ft (2.5m)

Broader than it is high, this bold-foliaged bush carries heads of tiny flowers, each surrounded by a ring of larger florets, from mid- to late summer. Dislikes dry soils.

S H R U B S

Hydrangea serrata 'Bluebird'
LACECAP HYDRANGEA
☼ ☀ 6   ↕ 4ft (1.2m) ↔ 5ft (1.5m)

The pointed leaves of this dense, bushy shrub often color well in autumn. Violet-blue, lacecap flowers in summer have pale marginal florets. Dislikes dry soils.

Pachysandra terminalis
JAPANESE SPURGE
☼ ☀ 4   ↕ 4in (10cm) ↔ 8in (20cm)

This evergreen, suckering shrublet likes moist soils and makes a superb ground-cover for shade. Its dark green leaves back little white flower spikes in spring.

Skimmia japonica 'Fructu-albo'
SKIMMIA
☼ ☀ 7   ↕ 30in (75cm) ↔ 30in (75cm)

This spring-flowering cultivar will produce an abundance of white berries if you plant a male variety of this dense, low evergreen nearby to effect pollination.

Lonicera pileata
SHRUBBY HONEYSUCKLE
☼ ☀ 6   ↕ 24in (60cm) ↔ 6ft (2m)

Its low and wide-spreading habit makes this an excellent evergreen groundcover. Tiny, inconspicuous, late spring flowers are occasionally followed by violet berries.

Prunus laurocerasus 'Otto Luyken'
CHERRY LAUREL
☼ ☀ 6   ↕ 3ft (1m) ↔ 6ft (2m)

The branches of this low evergreen shrub are clothed with narrow, glossy, leathery leaves. Erect spikes of white flowers in late spring are followed by black fruits.

Mahonia nervosa
CASCADES MAHONIA
☼ ☀ 6 PH   ↕ 24in (60cm) ↔ 3ft (1m)

This evergreen, suckering shrub produces short, erect stems with handsome leaves that turn red or purplish in winter. Spikes of yellow flowers appear in early summer.

OTHER EVERGREEN SHRUBS
TOLERANT OF SHADE

Aucuba japonica
x *Fatshedera lizei*, see p.144
Fatsia japonica, see p.111
Ilex crenata
Osmanthus heterophyllus
Rhododendron catawbiense
Rubus tricolor
Ruscus hypoglossum
Sarcococca hookeriana var. *humilis*
Viburnum davidii, see p.119

Vinca major 'Variegata'
VARIEGATED LARGE PERIWINKLE
☼ ☀ 7   ↕ 12in (30cm) ↔ 5ft (1.5m)

Striking, variegated leaves are margined creamy white and form a superb ground-cover that is rampant if unchecked. Blue flowers last from spring to autumn.

S H R U B S

133

Shrubs Tolerant of Wet Soil or Streambanks

PERMANENTLY MOIST SOILS, or sites that occasionally flood, are not ideal planting spots. This makes shrubs tolerant of wet soil valuable to gardeners faced with damp or boggy areas. Where practical and desirable, you can modify such soils by draining, but if you decide to leave them alone, the following plants can generally be relied upon to thrive.

Aronia arbutifolia
RED CHOKEBERRY
☼ ☼ 5 ↕ 10ft (3m) ↔ 6ft (2m)

This vigorous shrub forms clumps of erect stems that eventually arch widely. Small white spring flowers are followed by red berries. Its leaves turn red in autumn.

Clethra alnifolia
SWEET PEPPERBUSH
☼ ☼ 4 PH ↕ 6ft (2m) ↔ 5ft (1.5m)

Spikes of small, sweetly scented white flowers are produced in late summer. The toothed leaves of this upright, frequently suckering shrub give yellow autumn tints.

Lindera benzoin
SPICEBUSH
☼ 5 PH ↕ 10ft (3m) ↔ 10ft (3m)

The bright green foliage of this free-growing shrub is aromatic and turns clear yellow in autumn. Clusters of small, greenish yellow flowers appear in spring.

OTHER SHRUBS TOLERANT OF WET SOIL OR STREAMBANKS

Amelanchier canadensis
Aronia melanocarpa
Calycanthus floridus
Cephalanthus occidentalis
Cornus alba 'Elegantissima', see p.148
Cornus stolonifera 'Flaviramea', see p.168
Dirca palustris
Hamamelis vernalis
Ilex glabra
Ilex verticillata
Myrica cerifera
Photinia villosa, see p.228
Rhododendron vaseyi
Rosa carolina
Sorbaria aitchisonii
Viburnum opulus 'Xanthocarpum'
Viburnum sieboldii

Myrica gale
SWEET GALE, BOG MYRTLE
☼ 4 PH ↕ 3ft (1m) ↔ 3ft (1m)

Catkins crowd this small, aromatic shrub in spring, before its blue-green leaves unfurl. Fruiting spikes, seen here, follow. Tolerant of extremely boggy conditions.

Physocarpus opulifolius 'Dart's Gold'
NINEBARK
☼ 2 ↕ 6ft (2m) ↔ 6ft (2m)

Golden yellow leaves, carried from spring and all through summer, eclipse the late spring flowers of this tough and adaptable shrub. The bark on older stems peels.

Rhododendron occidentale
WESTERN AZALEA
☼ 6 PH ↕ 6ft (2m) ↔ 6ft (2m)

Bold clusters of fragrant, funnel-shaped flowers appear in early summer, and vary from white to pink or pale yellow. Glossy green leaves color richly in autumn.

SHRUBS

Rhodotypos scandens
JETBEAD
☼ ☼ 5   ↕ 6ft (2m) ↔ 6ft (2m)

Pure white flowers, borne from late spring
through summer, are followed by small,
shining black fruits. This vigorous shrub
has toothed, conspicuously veined leaves.

**SHRUBBY WILLOWS TOLERANT
OF WET SOIL OR STREAMBANKS**

Salix acutifolia
Salix discolor
Salix elaeagnos
Salix exigua, see p.153
Salix gracilistyla 'Melanostachys'
Salix irrorata
Salix japonica
Salix purpurea 'Nana'
Salix triandra
Salix udensis 'Sekka'

Spiraea x *vanhouttei*
BRIDAL WREATH
☼ 4   ↕ 5ft (1.5m) ↔ 5ft (1.5m)

The arching stems of this strong-growing
shrub form a dense mound. Clusters of
white flowers are carried all along the
upper sides of its branches in summer.

Salix daphnoides
VIOLET WILLOW
☼ 5   ↕ 20ft (6m) ↔ 20ft (6m)

This vigorous shrub is grown for its pale
violet winter shoots. Male forms such as
'Aglaia' have attractive catkins in spring,
silver at first, then turning to yellow.

Vaccinium corymbosum
HIGHBUSH BLUEBERRY
☼ ☼ 4 PH   ↕ 5ft (1.5m) ↔ 5ft (1.5m)

Clusters of small flowers in late spring are
white or pale pink in color, and followed
by edible black berries. In autumn, the
leaves of this bushy shrub turn crimson.

Viburnum opulus
CRANBERRY BUSH
☼ ☼ 4   ↕ 12ft (4m) ↔ 12ft (4m)

White lacecap flowerheads opening in
summer give way to clusters of glistening
red berries. The leaves of this vigorous
shrub are orange, purple, or red in autumn.

S H R U B S

135

Shrubs Tolerant of Air Pollution

OTHER EVERGREEN SHRUBS
TOLERANT OF AIR POLLUTION

Aucuba japonica
Camellia japonica 'Adolphe Audusson',
  see p.124
Cotoneaster sternianus, see p.162
Elaeagnus x *ebbingei* 'Gilt Edge',
  see p.149
Euonymus fortunei 'Emerald Gaiety',
  see p.118
Sarcococca hookeriana var. *digyna*,
  see p.167

THE DAYS WHEN INDUSTRIAL AIR POLLUTION was commonplace in manufacturing towns and cities are thankfully now ended. Pollution, however, remains a problem, particularly from vehicle exhausts, hence the value of shrubs showing some degree of tolerance. The following are among the most successful.

Brachyglottis 'Sunshine'
SHRUBBY SENECIO
☼ 9 — ↕ 3ft (1m) ↔ 5ft (1.5m)

Of all flowering shrubs, this is one of the most reliably tolerant, with its striking gray-green foliage, silvery when young, and bright yellow summer flowers.

Forsythia x *intermedia* 'Lynwood'
FORSYTHIA
☼ ☼ 5 — ↕ 10ft (3m) ↔ 8ft (2.5m)

Spectacular in flower, and thus deservedly popular. The branches of this robust shrub are wreathed with masses of rich yellow bell-shaped, starlike flowers in spring.

Buddleia davidii 'Royal Red'
BUTTERFLY BUSH
☼ 6 — ↕ 12ft (4m) ↔ 12ft (4m)

The arching branches of this vigorous shrub produce silvery leaves that become green in summer, when its fragrant flower spikes appear, lasting into autumn.

Hypericum 'Hidcote'
SHRUBBY HYPERICUM
☼ ☼ 6 — ↕ 4ft (1.2m) ↔ 5ft (1.5m)

From summer into autumn, this vigorous evergreen or semievergreen shrub carries a long succession of large, golden yellow flowers amid neat, dark green foliage.

Mahonia aquifolium 'Smaragd'
OREGON GRAPEHOLLY
☼ ☼ 5 — ↕ 30in (75cm) ↔ 5ft (1.5m)

This low-growing, spreading evergreen bears glossy green, spine-toothed leaves, bronze when young. Bright yellow flower clusters are produced in spring.

SHRUBS

Skimmia x *confusa* 'Kew Green'
SKIMMIA
☼ ☼ ☼ 7   ↕30in (75cm) ↔4ft (1.2m)

Deep green, aromatic leaves are topped in spring by dense, conical heads of fragrant, creamy white flowers. An excellent and adaptable, mounded evergreen shrub.

Olearia x *haastii*
DAISY BUSH
☼ 8   ↕6ft (2m) ↔6ft (2m)

Crowded heads of fragrant, white, daisy-like flowers cover this tough, reliable, compact evergreen in summer. Its small oval leaves have white-felted undersides.

> **OTHER DECIDUOUS SHRUBS TOLERANT OF AIR POLLUTION**
>
> *Amelanchier lamarckii*, see p.222
> *Buddleia davidii*, many
> *Colutea* x *media* 'Copper Beauty'
> *Lonicera ledebourii*
> *Sambucus nigra* 'Guincho Purple', see p.155
> *Sorbaria aitchisonii*
> *Spartium junceum*, see p.139
> *Viburnum opulus*, see p.135
> *Weigela florida* 'Variegata', see p.149

Rhododendron 'Susan'
RHODODENDRON
☼ 6 PH   ↕10ft (3m) ↔10ft (3m)

Compact, bushy, and quite vigorous, this evergreen bears rounded flower trusses in spring. The flowers, with dark margins and purple spots, fade to near white.

Syringa vulgaris 'Mme. Lemoine'
LILAC
☼ 4   ↕12ft (4m) ↔10ft (3m)

Spectacular, crowded heads of fragrant white flowers are produced in late spring and early summer. Upright when young, it spreads with age.

Philadelphus 'Beauclerk'
MOCK ORANGE
☼ 5   ↕8ft (2.5m) ↔6ft (2m)

This lovely shrub is well worth growing for its abundance of large, broad-petaled white flowers, carried from early to mid-summer. The blooms are fragrant.

Ribes sanguineum 'Pulborough Scarlet'
FLOWERING CURRANT
☼ 6   ↕8ft (2.5m) ↔6ft (2m)

Fairly upright when young and spreading as it matures, this vigorous shrub's aromatic leaves are preceded, or accompanied, by pendent red flower clusters in spring.

Tamarix tetrandra
TAMARISK
☼ 6   ↕12ft (4m) ↔12ft (4m)

The dark shoots of this loose-stemmed shrub are clothed with scalelike green leaves. In late spring and early summer, crowded plumes of tiny flowers appear.

Shrubs Tolerant of Coastal Exposure

CONTRARY TO POPULAR BELIEF, a great number of shrubs can be grown in gardens near the sea. Some are more than happy to take the full blast of coastal winds and even salt spray. Others, however, while tolerant to a degree, prefer some shelter to thrive. Those listed here are among the most reliable for seaside gardens.

S H R U B S

Escallonia 'Apple Blossom'
ESCALLONIA
☼ 8   ↕ 6ft (2m) ↔ 6ft (2m)

Shining, dark green foliage clothes this dense evergreen shrub. Clusters of pink and white flowers the color of apple blossoms adorn it in summer.

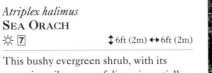

Atriplex halimus
SEA ORACH
☼ 7   ↕ 6ft (2m) ↔ 6ft (2m)

This bushy evergreen shrub, with its attractive, silvery gray foliage, is partially deciduous in cold areas. It is excellent as a specimen or as an informal hedge.

Bupleurum fruticosum
SHRUBBY HARE'S-EAR
☼ 7   ↕ 6ft (2m) ↔ 6ft (2m)

A bushy evergreen shrub, mainly grown for its shining, dark bluish green leaves. It produces tiny yellowish flowerheads from summer into autumn.

OTHER DECIDUOUS SHRUBS TOLERANT OF COASTAL EXPOSURE

Baccharis halimifolia
Elaeagnus angustifolia
Halimodendron halimifolium
Hippophaë rhamnoides, see p.214
Hydrangea macrophylla 'Ayesha'
Lycium barbarum
Myrica pensylvanica
Rosa 'Harison's Yellow'
Rosa rugosa, see p.141
Tamarix ramosissima

Buddleia globosa
GLOBE BUTTERFLY BUSH
☼ 7   ↕ 10ft (3m) ↔ 10ft (3m)

When in flower in summer, the tiny, tight, globular orange-yellow heads make this shrub stand out. Robust, with bold leaves, it is semievergreen in mild areas.

Colutea arborescens
BLADDER SENNA
☼ 6   ↕ 8ft (2.5m) ↔ 8ft (2.5m)

A vigorous shrub of open habit, this has small, much-divided leaves. The clusters of yellow pea flowers in summer are replaced by inflated seed capsules.

Fuchsia magellanica
HARDY FUCHSIA
☼ 7   ↕ 6ft (2m) ↔ 6ft (2m)

Dense, leafy mounds make this ideal as a specimen plant or an informal hedge. Its lanternlike flowers hang freely from the shoots from midsummer into autumn.

Hebe x *franciscana* 'Blue Gem'
HEBE
☼ 9   ↕ 24in (60cm) ↔ 4ft (1.2m)

This evergreen shrub makes an excellent
specimen in mild-winter areas. Its short
violet flower spikes are produced from
summer to early winter.

Hydrangea macrophylla
'Lanarth White'
☼ ☼ 7   ↕ 5ft (1.5m) ↔ 6ft (2m)

In summer, long-lasting, domed heads of
dark blue, fertile flowers and starry white,
sterile florets cover this reliable, compact,
mounded shrub. Leaves are light green.

Olearia nummulariifolia
DAISY BUSH
☼ 9   ↕ 6ft (2m) ↔ 6ft (2m)

Stiff shoots crowded with tiny, leathery
evergreen leaves characterize this rounded
shrub. Small, fragrant flowers open near
the ends of the branches in summer.

Spartium junceum
SPANISH BROOM
☼ 8   ↕ 8ft (2.5m) ↔ 8ft (2.5m)

Spanish Broom is a vigorous shrub with
smooth, dark green, almost leafless shoots,
and sprays of fragrant yellow pea flowers
lasting from early summer into autumn.

**OTHER EVERGREEN SHRUBS
TOLERANT OF COASTAL EXPOSURE**

Arctostaphylos uva-ursi
Ilex glabra
Nerium oleander
Ruscus aculeatus, see p.171

Lupinus arboreus
TREE LUPINE
☼ 8   ↕ 3ft (1m) ↔ 3ft (1m)

This vigorous, mounded semievergreen,
with the fingered leaves that are typical of
lupines, bears numerous tapered spikes of
fragrant yellow flowers in early summer.

Tamarix ramosissima
TAMARISK
☼ 3   ↕ 12ft (4m) ↔ 12ft (4m)

Openly branched and vigorous, this shrub
has feathery blue-green foliage on long
branches, and plumes of tiny pink flowers
from late summer into early autumn.

S
H
R
U
B
S

139

Shrubs for Screening or Hedges

SHRUBS SUITABLE FOR HEDGING can be pruned or clipped annually for a formal effect, or allowed to develop a more natural appearance. Those of stronger growth and ultimately large habit are useful for screening to hide intrusive views, filter noise, or lessen the effect of wind. Sizes given refer to the average ultimate size of a single plant without pruning.

OTHER SHRUBS FOR SMALL HEDGES

Berberis thunbergii 'Atropurpurea Nana', see p.154
Buxus sempervirens 'Suffruticosa', see p.170
Ilex crenata 'Convexa'
Lavandula angustifolia 'Hidcote', see p.164
Myrtus communis var. *tarentina*
Santolina chamaecyparissus, see p.153
Teucrium x *lucidrys*

Berberis x *stenophylla*
BARBERRY
☼ 7   ↕ 8ft (2.5m) ↔ 8ft (2.5m)

Useful as an informal hedge, this tough, adaptable evergreen has slender arching stems, narrow dark green leaves, and tiny golden yellow flowers in spring.

Buxus sempervirens 'Handsworthensis'
HANDSWORTH BOXWOOD
☼ ☼ 6   ↕ 10ft (3m) ↔ 10ft (3m)

This evergreen is upright, densely leafy, and strong-growing, making it reliable as a formal hedge or screen. Its leathery deep green leaves are rounded or oblong.

Cotoneaster lacteus
COTONEASTER
☼ 7   ↕ 12ft (4m) ↔ 10ft (3m)

One of the best evergreens for a formal hedge or an informal screen, this bears veined leaves, white summer flowers, and red berries from autumn into winter.

OTHER EVERGREEN SHRUBS FOR SCREENING OR HEDGES

Berberis julianae
Camellia, many
Elaeagnus pungens
Euonymus kiautschovicus
Ilex cornuta 'Burfordii'
Ilex glabra
Osmanthus heterophyllus
Pittosporum, many
Rhaphiolepis indica
Viburnum tinus 'Eve Price', see p.167

Cotoneaster simonsii
COTONEASTER
☼ 6   ↕ 8ft (2.5m) ↔ 6ft (2m)

Shiny deciduous or semievergreen leaves cover this vigorous shrub, ideal as a formal hedge. White flowers open in summer, and red berries ripen in autumn.

Elaeagnus x ebbingei
ELAEAGNUS

☼ 6   ↕12ft (4m) ↔12ft (4m)

In autumn, small, fragrant, silvery white flowers crowd the branches among shining green leaves. This vigorous evergreen is suitable for formal and informal screens.

Griselinia littoralis
BROADLEAF

☼ 9   ↕20ft (6m) ↔15ft (5m)

This vigorous evergreen shrub, with bright green leaves, is excellent grown alone or mixed, as it is here, with *Prunus cerasifera* 'Nigra'. Well-suited to seaside gardens.

Prunus laurocerasus 'Rotundifolia'
CHERRY LAUREL

☼ ☼ ☼ 6   ↕10ft (3m) ↔6ft (2m)

Cherry Laurel is an excellent choice for formal hedging, with its striking, glossy green evergreen leaves and upright growth. Can also be grown informally.

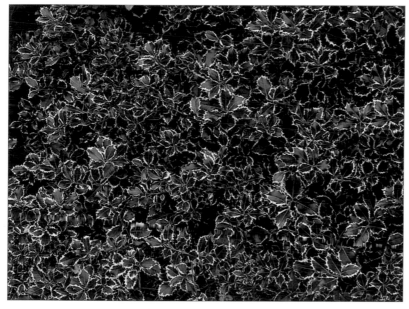

Prunus lusitanica
PORTUGAL LAUREL

☼ ☼ 8   ↕20ft (6m) ↔20ft (6m)

Particularly impressive in spring, when it produces white flower tassels, this bushy evergreen shrub carries shining, slender, pointed green leaves on red stalks.

Ilex aquifolium 'Argentea-marginata'
SILVER ENGLISH HOLLY

☼ 6   ↕25ft (8m) ↔12ft (4m)

One of the best formal hedges or screens, this shrub or tree has cream-margined, prickly-toothed, evergreen leaves, and red fruits when pollinated by a male holly.

OTHER DECIDUOUS SHRUBS FOR SCREENING OR HEDGES

Berberis thunbergii 'Atropurpurea'
Chaenomeles, many
Elaeagnus angustifolia
Forsythia x intermedia 'Lynwood', see p.136
Hibiscus syriacus 'Blue Bird', see p.131
Poncirus trifoliata
Potentilla, many
Rhamnus frangula 'Columnaris'
Viburnum prunifolium

Fuchsia magellanica 'Riccartonii'
FUCHSIA

☼ 7   ↕6ft (2m) ↔6ft (2m)

Superb as an informal hedge, particularly in coastal areas, this vigorous shrub soon forms a dense bush, strung with lanternlike flowers in late summer.

Rosa rugosa
RUGOSA ROSE

☼ 3   ↕5ft (1.5m) ↔5ft (1.5m)

This species rose is popular as an informal hedge, with its large, wrinkled leaves and magenta flowers borne from summer into autumn, followed by tomato-like hips.

Shrubs for Rock Gardens, Raised Beds, and Screes

NUMEROUS SHRUBS NEAT IN HABIT, and attractive in flower, foliage, and fruit are prevented by their small size from being used in a mixed border, unless it is well away from the domination of larger, stronger-growing neighbors. Such shrubs are ideal for planting in rock gardens or raised beds where their special, smaller charms can better be appreciated.

Genista lydia
GENISTA
☼ 6   ↕ 22in (55cm) ↔ 30in (75cm)

This shrub is a superb sight in late spring and early summer, when it is covered with clusters of tiny pea flowers. Ideal for a dry wall top, where its stems can tumble.

OTHER ROCK GARDEN SHRUBS
Anthyllis hermanniae
Berberis x *stenophylla* 'Corallina Compacta'
Convolvulus cneorum, see p.152
Crassula sarcocaulis
Daphne collina
Helichrysum selago
Hypericum olympicum 'Citrinum'
Penstemon pinifolius
Sorbus poteriifolia
Teucrium polium

Acer palmatum 'Corallinum'
JAPANESE MAPLE
☼ ☼ 6   ↕ 30in (75cm) ↔ 18in (45cm)

A striking, slow-growing, compact shrub, capable of twice the above size in moist, rich, well-drained soils. Grown mainly for its brilliant coral pink stems in spring.

Daphne retusa
DAPHNE
☼ ☼ 6   ↕ 28in (70cm) ↔ 28in (70cm)

A domed shrub with leathery evergreen leaves, this bears fragrant flowers (purple when in bud) in clusters from late spring, followed by bright red berries.

Berberis empetrifolia
BARBERRY
☼ 7 PH   ↕ 12in (30cm) ↔ 18in (45cm)

The stems of this dwarf evergreen are wiry and prickly, and its branches clothed with small, narrow, spine-tipped leaves. Tiny golden flowers appear in late spring.

Euryops acraeus
EURYOPS
☼ 9   ↕ 12in (30cm) ↔ 12in (30cm)

Distinctive shrub, forming a small mound of narrow silvery leaves, above which late spring flowers rise on thin, downy stalks. Thrives in sun and well-drained soils.

Hebe cupressoides 'Boughton Dome'
HEBE
☼ 8   ↕ 12in (30cm) ↔ 18in (45cm)

This attractive evergreen mound of tiny, dark gray-green leaves resembles a dwarf juniper and produces clusters of white summer flowers. Needs good drainage.

SHRUBS

Helianthemum 'Fire Dragon'
ROCK ROSE
☼ 6   ↕ 11in (28cm) ↔ 22in (55cm)

This evergreen carpet-forming shrub has narrow gray-green leaves and is covered with brilliant orange-scarlet flowers from late spring, continuing into summer.

Penstemon serrulatus
BEARDTONGUE
☼ 5   ↕ 24in (60cm) ↔ 12in (30cm)

A loose semievergreen shrub, this forms clumps of dark green foliage, and erect stems that bear branched heads of tubular blue to purple flowers in summer.

Punica granatum var. *nana*
DWARF POMEGRANATE
☼ 8   ↕ 24in (60cm) ↔ 24in (60cm)

The glossy leaves of this charming little pomegranate turn gold in autumn. Funnel-shaped flowers appear in early autumn. Appreciates warmth and good drainage.

Linum arboreum
TREE FLAX
☼ 10   ↕ 11in (28cm) ↔ 12in (30cm)

Clusters of bright yellow flowers appear throughout summer, whenever the sun shines. This low, dome-shaped evergreen needs warmth and good drainage.

Parahebe cataractae
PARAHEBE
☼ 9   ↕ 12in (30cm) ↔ 12in (30cm)

This choice, reliable plant will form loose mounds of evergreen leaves and, in late summer and early autumn, sprays of small flowers with crimson and white centers.

OTHER CARPETING SHRUBS

Cistus salviifolius 'Avalanche'
Cytisus purpureus 'Atropurpureus'
Genista sagittalis
Helianthemum apenninum 'Roseum'
Hypericum empetrifolium var. *oliganthum*

Salix reticulata
NETTED WILLOW
☼ 1   ↕ 1½in (4cm) ↔ 12in (30cm)

Carpets of prostrate stems are clothed in oval leaves that are pale beneath and net-veined above. Male plants have pretty spring catkins. Best in moist soils.

Shrubs for Containers

JUST ABOUT ANY SHRUB can be planted in a container, although some are more suitable than others. Generally, large and vigorous shrubs are best avoided unless you prune them regularly. Pots and tubs are particularly useful on patios, terraces, and in courtyards, or for growing tender shrubs that are kept under shelter in cold weather. For those who garden on a particular soil type and who wish to grow a plant unsuited to it, containers provide a practical solution to this problem.

Felicia amelloides 'Santa Anita'
BLUE DAISY
☼ 10   ↕ 12in (30cm) ↔ 12in (30cm)

Long-stalked, yellow-eyed, blue daisylike flowers rise above a bushy mound of oval evergreen leaves, from late spring through to autumn.

OTHER TENDER SHRUBS FOR CONTAINERS
Abutilon pictum 'Thompsonii'
Brugmansia x *candida* 'Charles Grimaldi'
Cestrum nocturnum
Nerium oleander

Aloysia triphylla
LEMON VERBENA
☼ 8   ↕ 6ft (2m) ↔ 6ft (2m)

Mainly grown for its deliciously lemon-scented leaves, this slender-stemmed bush produces flimsy flower spikes in summer. Prune in late winter to control size.

Choisya 'Aztec Pearl'
CHOISYA
☼ ☼ 8   ↕ 4ft (1.2m) ↔ 4ft (1.2m)

The fingered leaves of this free-growing evergreen are aromatic. Its fragrant white flower clusters, pink in bud, occur in late spring, and again in late summer.

Cestrum elegans
CESTRUM
☼ 10   ↕ 10ft (3m) ↔ 6ft (2m)

The arching stems and leafy branches of this vigorous evergreen shrub bow beneath its freely produced clusters of tubular red flowers from spring through summer.

x *Fatshedera lizei*
FATSHEDERA
☼ ☼ 7   ↕ 6ft (2m) ↔ 6ft (2m)

This handsome evergreen shrub forms a loose mound of boldly lobed, shining, dark green leaves. Loose heads of small cream flowers are carried in autumn.

Fuchsia 'Celia Smedley'
FUCHSIA
☼ 9   ↕ 5ft (1.5m) ↔ 3ft (1m)

Vigorous and upright, this is one of the more hardy fuchsias. Pendulous, pinkish white and red flowers with greenish white tubes open throughout summer.

Fuchsia 'Thalia'
FUCHSIA
☼ 10 ↕ 3ft (1m) ↔ 3ft (1m)

Deservedly popular, this erect shrub bears
drooping clusters of long, slender flowers
carried in summer above dark reddish
green, velvety leaves.

Lantana camara
LANTANA
☼ 10 ↕ 5ft (1.5m) ↔ 5ft (1.5m)

This prickly-stemmed, summer-flowering
evergreen is rampant in hot climates, but
easily controlled by tip-pruning. Several
colors, changing with age, are available.

OTHER HARDY SHRUBS
FOR CONTAINERS

Berberis thunbergii 'Atropurpurea Nana',
 see p.154
Deutzia gracilis, see p.116
Deutzia scabra 'Variegata'
Euonymus japonicus 'Microphyllus'
Mahonia aquifolium, see p.163
Prunus laurocerasus 'Otto Luyken',
 see p.133
Skimmia japonica, see p.171
Spiraea japonica 'Goldflame',
 see p.151
Syringa microphylla 'Superba', see p.115

Prostanthera rotundifolia
ROUND-LEAVED MINT BUSH
☼ 9 ↕ 5ft (1.5m) ↔ 5ft (1.5m)

When they are bruised, the tiny leaves of
this dense, rounded evergreen are sweetly
aromatic. Masses of bell-shaped flowers
open from spring into early summer.

Mimulus aurantiacus
SHRUBBY MIMULUS
☼ 9 ↕ 24in (60cm) ↔ 3ft (1m)

A succession of two-lipped orange-yellow
flowers are borne from late spring through
to autumn. The narrow evergreen leaves
of this low bush are sticky to the touch.

Pieris japonica 'Little Heath'
JAPANESE ANDROMEDA
☼ ☼ 5 ↕ 4ft (1.2m) ↔ 3ft (1m)

A choice, compact evergreen, this pieris is
grown mainly for its small, slender, white-
margined leaves, which are red when they
emerge in spring. Slow-growing.

Rhododendron 'Homebush'
KNAPHILL AZALEA
☼ ☼ 6 ↕ 5ft (1.5m) ↔ 5ft (1.5m)

This charming, relatively compact shrub
is popular on account of its tight, rounded
heads of trumpet-shaped flowers that are
produced in late spring.

Evergreen Shrubs

WHERE WINTER TEMPERATURES are not low enough to severely inhibit their growth, shrubs having evergreen foliage provide some of the most worthwhile ornamental subjects for the garden. They come in an impressive range of shapes, sizes, textures, and colors, adding variety as well as permanence to the mixed bed or border. Most have flowers and sometimes fruit as a bonus. Some evergreen shrubs are so distinguished that they are ideal as courtyard or lawn specimens, while others with a low spreading habit make effective groundcover in sun or shade. Less hardy evergreens are usually more successful when grown in the shelter of other shrubs or a wall.

Elaeagnus pungens 'Maculata'
THORNY ELAEAGNUS
☼ **6-7** ↕ 8ft (2.5m) ↔ 10ft (3m)

Robust and dense with its brown-scaly branchlets, this shrub has gold-splashed green leaves. Clusters of tiny, scented, creamy white flowers appear in autumn.

Aucuba japonica 'Rozannie'
AUCUBA
☼ ☼ **6-7** ↕ 30in (75cm) ↔ 30in (75cm)

The tiny female flowers of this compact dwarf shrub appear in spring and produce red fruits when pollinated. This cultivar is excellent in a bed or in a container.

Buxus sempervirens 'Vardar Valley'
BOXWOOD
☼ ☼ **5** ↕ 30in (75cm) ↔ 4ft (1.2m)

This valuable cultivar of Boxwood has a low, wide-spreading habit. With its glossy, densely packed leathery leaves, it is superb for groundcover in most soils.

Daphne odora 'Aureo-marginata'
WINTER DAPHNE
☼ **7** ↕ 3½ft (1.1m) ↔ 4ft (1.2m)

For a warm, sheltered corner, this is a most reliable evergreen. Sweetly scented flowers are borne from winter into spring, and its leaves have narrow yellow margins.

Olearia macrodonta
NEW ZEALAND HOLLY
☼ ☼ **9** ↕ 11ft (3.5m) ↔ 11ft (3.5m)

This sturdy shrub has attractive, pale brown, ultimately shaggy, bark and holly-like leaves. Fragrant, daisylike white flowerheads appear in early summer.

OTHER EVERGREEN SHRUBS

Berberis julianae
Camellia japonica
Choisya ternata, see p.158
Euonymus kiautschovicus
Ilex crenata
Ilex x meserveae
Kalmia latifolia, see p.125
Pyracantha coccinea
Rhaphiolepis umbellata
Rhododendron PJM hybrids
Skimmia japonica

S H R U B S

Ozothamnus rosmarinifolius
OZOTHAMNUS
☼ 9   ↕ 6ft (2m) ↔ 5ft (1.5m)

The erect stems of this vigorous shrub are crowded with threadlike leaves. Its tiny scented flowers are borne in early summer. Needs a warm, well-drained site.

Pittosporum tenuifolium
'Irene Paterson'
☼ 9   ↕ 8ft (2.5m) ↔ 3½ft (1.1m)

A broadly columnar shrub, this has thin black stems and small, wavy green leaves, marbled white when mature, pink-tinted in winter. Excellent for containers.

Prunus lusitanica subsp. *azorica*
PORTUGAL LAUREL
☼ ☼ 8   ↕ 20ft (6m) ↔ 20ft (6m)

This vigorous form of the Portugal Laurel is densely branched with light green leaves, red at first. Shining, dark purple fruits follow fragrant summer flowers.

EVERGREEN GROUNDCOVER SHRUBS

Arctostaphylos uva-ursi 'Vancouver Jade'
Ceanothus gloriosus
Ceanothus thyrsiflorus var. *repens*
Gaultheria shallon
Hypericum calycinum, see p.119
Mahonia nervosa, see p.133
Rubus tricolor
Sarcococca hookeriana var. *humilis*
Vaccinium vitis-idaea
Viburnum davidii, see p.119

Vaccinium glaucoalbum
VACCINIUM
☼ 7 PH   ↕ 24in (60cm) ↔ 30in (75cm)

Handsome and compact, this low-growing shrub has leathery green leaves. Drooping clusters of pink-tinted white spring flowers are followed by blue-black berries.

Prunus laurocerasus 'Zabeliana'
CHERRY LAUREL
☼ ☼ 5-6   ↕ 32in (80cm) ↔ 7ft (2.2m)

A tough, wide-spreading form of the Cherry Laurel, with narrow, glossy leaves. Flower spikes in late spring are followed by red fruits, ripening to shiny black.

Rhododendron 'Dora Amateis'
RHODODENDRON
☼ ☼ 5 PH   ↕ 2ft (60cm) ↔ 2ft (60cm)

This free-flowering dwarf rhododendron of compact habit has glossy foliage, and terminal trusses of funnel-shaped, pink-tinged white flowers in late spring.

Viburnum x *pragense*
VIBURNUM
☼ 6   ↕ 8ft (2.5m) ↔ 8ft (2.5m)

The narrow green leaves of this vigorous shrub are boldly veined on top. Creamy white flowers, pink-tinged when in bud, are produced in domed heads in spring.

Variegated-leaved Shrubs

VARIEGATION COMES in a number of forms. Generally a green leaf has a white or yellow margin; occasionally, a white or yellow leaf has a green margin. There are, however, a host of shrubs with green, gray, or purple leaves that are spotted, blotched, or streaked a lighter shade. Two-color variegation may be joined by paler or darker shades of the dominant colors. The bolder the variegation, the more dramatic the effect when planted with foliage of one color.

Buxus sempervirens 'Elegantissima'
VARIEGATED BOXWOOD
☼ 6 ↕ 5½ft (1.7m) ↔ 3½ft (1.1m)

Neat and slow-growing, this is arguably the best variegated form of Boxwood. The bush is dome-shaped, with small evergreen, white-margined leaves.

Cornus alba 'Elegantissima'
SILVER-VARIEGATED DOGWOOD
☼ 2 ↕ 7ft (2.2m) ↔ 7ft (2.2m)

A reliable variegated dogwood that bears white-margined gray-green leaves on reddish shoots. Prune hard in late winter for brighter stems and larger leaves.

Buddleia davidii 'Harlequin'
BUTTERFLY BUSH
☼ 6 ↕ 8ft (2.5m) ↔ 8ft (2.5m)

A vigorous and attractive shrub, this has arching stems and creamy white-margined leaves. Large, dense spikes of red-purple flowers occur from summer into autumn.

OTHER DECIDUOUS
VARIEGATED SHRUBS

Berberis thunbergii 'Rose Glow'
Cornus alba 'Spaethii'
Daphne x *burkwoodii* 'Carol Mackie'
Fuchsia magellanica 'Sharpitor'
Hypericum x *moserianum* 'Tricolor'
Ligustrum sinense 'Variegatum'
Lonicera nitida 'Silver Beauty'
Sambucus nigra 'Pulverulenta'
Stachyurus chinensis 'Magpie'
Weigela praecox 'Variegata'

Cornus mas 'Variegata'
VARIEGATED CORNELIAN CHERRY
☼ ☼ 5 ↕ 12ft (4m) ↔ 12ft (4m)

This dense, bushy shrub has leaves with bold white margins. Small clusters of tiny yellow flowers stud the twigs in late winter, before the leaves unfurl.

Aucuba japonica 'Crotonifolia'
SPOTTED AUCUBA
☼ ☼ 6-7 ↕ 6ft (2m) ↔ 5½ft (1.7m)

The jade green shoots of this spectacular, dense, bushy shrub develop into shiny, leathery green leaves, blotched yellow. This is a most reliable evergreen.

Cotoneaster horizontalis 'Variegatus'
VARIEGATED COTONEASTER
☼ 6   ↕18in (45cm) ↔4ft (1.2m)

Also known as *C. atropurpureus* 'Variegata', the low, wide-spreading stems are densely clothed with tiny, cream-margined leaves. These are tinted red in autumn.

Ilex aquifolium 'Ferox Argentea'
SILVER HEDGEHOG HOLLY
☼ ☀ 6-7   ↕12ft (4m) ↔5ft (1.5m)

An attractive, bushy evergreen holly, with small, prickly leaves that have creamy white margins. This is a male form, useful as a pollinator for berrying hollies.

Rhamnus alaternus 'Argenteovariegata'
VARIEGATED BUCKTHORN
☼ 7   ↕8ft (2.5m) ↔5½ft (1.7m)

A handsome, bushy evergreen, this has small, glossy gray-green leaves, margined creamy white. Discreet yellow flowers will produce red summer berries.

Viburnum tinus 'Variegatum'
VARIEGATED LAURUSTINUS
☼ ☀ 7   ↕8ft (2.5m) ↔6ft (2m)

The leaves of this mounded or conical evergreen shrub are boldly and irregularly margined. Red-budded, fragrant white flowers occur from autumn through winter.

Elaeagnus x ebbingei 'Gilt Edge'
ELAEAGNUS
☼ 7   ↕8ft (2.5m) ↔8ft (2.5m)

This robust evergreen has brown, scaly stems and shining green leaves with golden yellow margins. Its small, sweetly fragrant flowers appear in autumn.

OTHER EVERGREEN VARIEGATED SHRUBS

Coronilla valentina subsp. *glauca* 'Variegata'
Euonymus fortunei 'Silver Queen', see p.100
Euonymus japonicus 'Latifolius Albomarginatus'
Pieris japonica 'Little Heath', see p.145
Pittosporum 'Garnettii'
Prunus laurocerasus 'Marbled White', see p.163

Osmanthus heterophyllus 'Variegatus'
VARIEGATED FALSE HOLLY
☼ ☀ 7   ↕7ft (2.2m) ↔4ft (1.2m)

This evergreen bush of relatively slow growth has small, white-margined, holly-like leaves. Clusters of little, sweetly scented white flowers occur in autumn.

Weigela florida 'Variegata'
VARIEGATED WEIGELA
☼ 6   ↕5ft (1.5m) ↔5ft (1.5m)

One of the most popular and easily grown variegated shrubs, with distinctly edged leaves that provide a perfect foil for pink flowers in late spring and early summer.

S H R U B S

Shrubs with Golden or Yellow Leaves

THERE IS NOTHING like a bright splash of yellow or gold foliage to bring a most welcome touch of warmth to the garden, especially in the depths of winter. An abundance of shrubs, both evergreen and deciduous, have leaves in varying shades of yellow. Careful use of these can create striking contrasts with green- or purple-leaved plants.

SHRUBS

Berberis thunbergii 'Aurea'
GOLDEN JAPANESE BARBERRY
☼ 5   ↕ 30in (75cm) ↔ 30in (75cm)

Dense, compact mounding plants with small, rounded, vivid yellow leaves that turn yellow-green. May scorch in full sun except in cool summers.

Cornus alba 'Aurea'
GOLDEN-LEAVED DOGWOOD
☼ ☼ 2   ↕ 10ft (3m) ↔ 10ft (3m)

This vigorous dogwood forms a sizeable mound of dark red branches, clothed all through summer and into autumn with broad leaves of a lovely soft yellow color.

Erica arborea 'Albert's Gold'
TREE HEATH
☼ 4   ↕ 6ft (2m) ↔ 6ft (2m)

Tiny, crowded golden leaves cover twiggy branches, creating plumes of golden yellow throughout the year. Masses of honey-scented white flowers appear in spring.

Calluna vulgaris 'Gold Haze'
HEATHER, LING
☼ 5   ↕ 20in (50cm) ↔ 18in (45cm)

One of many similar heathers 'Gold Haze' has tightly arranged foliage of a golden hue, brighter in winter. White flowers are produced in late summer.

Choisya ternata 'Sundance'
MEXICAN ORANGE-BLOSSOM
☼ ☼ 8   ↕ 5ft (1.5m) ↔ 6ft (2m)

The bright yellow, aromatic leaves of this evergreen, mounded shrub fade with age. Fragrant white flowers are produced in late spring. Dislikes cold winds.

Fuchsia 'Genii'
FUCHSIA
☼ ☼ 9   ↕ 4½ft (1.4m) ↔ 30in (75cm)

This small, colorful, upright shrub has red shoots and bright lime yellow foliage. It carries small, pendulous violet and red flowers from summer into autumn.

Ligustrum 'Vicaryi'
GOLDEN PRIVET
☀ ☀ 5   ↕ 10ft (3m) ↔ 10ft (3m)

This is a vigorous semievergreen shrub of dense, bushy habit. The dusty-scented white flowers and bright yellow leaves are carried throughout the summer.

OTHER DECIDUOUS SHRUBS WITH GOLDEN OR YELLOW LEAVES

Acer palmatum 'Aureum'
Acer shirasawanum 'Aureum'
Caryopteris x *clandonensis*
 'Worcester Gold'
Cornus mas 'Aurea'
Fuchsia 'Golden Marinka'
Physocarpus opulifolius 'Dart's Gold',
 see p.134
Ptelea trifoliata 'Aurea', see p.219
Ribes alpinum 'Aureum'
Rubus cockburnianus 'Golden Vale'
Rubus parviflorus 'Sunshine Spreader'
Sambucus nigra 'Aurea', see p.171
Sambucus racemosa 'Plumosa Aurea'
Spiraea japonica 'Limemound'
Viburnum lantana 'Aurea'
Weigela 'Looymansii Aurea', see p.127
Weigela 'Rubidor'

Sambucus racemosa 'Sutherland Gold'
☀ 4   ↕ 10ft (3m) ↔ 10ft (3m)

The large, deeply divided yellow leaves of this vigorous golden elder do not readily scorch. Clusters of yellow flowers, borne in spring, are followed by red berries.

Lonicera nitida 'Baggesen's Gold'
BAGGESEN'S GOLD HONEYSUCKLE
☀ 7   ↕ 15ft (5m) ↔ 15ft (5m)

Attractive, tiny yellow leaves crowd the slender, arching shoots of this dense, bushy evergreen. Capable of greater height when trained against   a wall.

Ribes sanguineum 'Brocklebankii'
GOLDEN FLOWERING CURRANT
☀ 6   ↕ 3ft (1m) ↔ 4ft (1.2m)

Although clusters of pink flowers decorate this bushy shrub in spring, the aromatic golden yellow leaves, liable to scorch in full sun, are its main attraction.

OTHER EVERGREEN SHRUBS WITH GOLDEN OR YELLOW LEAVES

Aucuba japonica 'Sulphurea'
Calluna vulgaris 'Beoley Gold'
Erica erigena 'Golden Lady'
Erica vagans 'Valerie Proudley'
Escallonia laevis 'Gold Brian'
Escallonia laevis 'Gold Ellen'
Euonymus japonicus 'Ovatus Aureus'
Ilex x *attenuata* 'Sunny Foster'
Ilex crenata 'Golden Gem'
Ligustrum ovalifolium 'Aureum'

Spiraea japonica 'Goldflame'
GOLDFLAME SPIREA
☀ 4   ↕ 30in (75cm) ↔ 3ft (1m)

Leaves on a low, dense mound of twiggy branches emerge orange-red, then turn to golden yellow, and finally to green. Small summer flowerheads are rose pink.

Philadelphus coronarius 'Aureus'
GOLDEN MOCK ORANGE
☀ 5   ↕ 8ft (2.5m) ↔ 5ft (1.5m)

The yellow spring leaves of this shrub fade to greenish in late summer, and can scorch in full sun. Creamy white, fragrant flowers are produced in late spring.

Viburnum opulus 'Aureum'
GOLDEN SNOWBALL BUSH
☀ 4   ↕ 8ft (2.5m) ↔ 6ft (2m)

Bright yellow, maplelike leaves are red-bronze when young. Its white flowerheads appear in summer, followed by red berries in autumn. Leaves scorch in hot sun.

S H R U B S

Shrubs with Blue-gray or Silver Leaves

THE SILVERY FLASH of sunlight catching blue-gray leaves shifting in a breeze is a pleasing sight in any garden. Silver-foliaged shrubs can also be grown for their softening effect near leaves of a darker or brighter hue. The blue-gray or silvery color may be due to a silky or woolly coating of hairs, silvery scales, or a white, powdery bloom.

SHRUBS

Convolvulus cneorum
CONVOLVULUS
☼ 8   ↕ 30in (75cm) ↔ 3ft (1m)

Silky, silvery leaves and stems make this one of the loveliest dwarf evergreen shrubs. White, yellow-throated flowers cover it from late spring to late summer.

Berberis dictyophylla
BARBERRY
☼ 6   ↕ 6ft (2m) ↔ 6ft (2m)

This graceful shrub has striking stems and leaves with a whitish bloom. Light yellow summer flowers give way to berries that, with the leaves, turn scarlet in autumn.

Calluna vulgaris 'Silver Queen'
HEATHER, LING
☼ 5 PH ⬇   ↕ 16in (40cm) ↔ 18in (45cm)

Although it produces mauve-pink flower spikes in late summer and early autumn, this dwarf evergreen is popular mainly for its silver-gray, downy foliage.

Hebe pimeleoides 'Quicksilver'
HEBE
☼ 9   ↕ 10in (25cm) ↔ 24in (60cm)

The dark, wiry stems and branches of this low, spreading evergreen shrub bear small silver-blue leaves, and short spikes of pale lilac flowers in summer.

OTHER EVERGREEN SHRUBS WITH BLUE-GRAY OR SILVER LEAVES

Acacia baileyana
Andromeda polifolia
Artemisia 'Huntington'
Artemisia 'Powis Castle', see p.72
Ballota pseudodictamnus
Brachyglottis 'Sunshine', see p.136
Dendromecon rigida
Elaeagnus macrophylla
Euryops acraeus, see p.142
Hebe pinguifolia 'Pagei'
Lavandula angustifolia 'Hidcote', see p.164
Rhododendron campanulatum subsp. *aeruginosum*
Rhododendron cinnabarinum Concatenans Group
Teucrium fruticans
Yucca glauca

Cistus
'Peggy Sammons'
SUN ROSE
☼ 8   ↕ 3ft (1m) ↔ 3ft (1m)

The pale pink flowers of this lovely, bushy evergreen are freely produced in summer, and resemble small, single roses. Gray-green leaves and stems are downy.

OTHER DECIDUOUS SHRUBS WITH BLUE-GRAY OR SILVER LEAVES

Buddleia alternifolia 'Argentea'
Buddleia 'Lochinch', see p.158
Dorycnium hirsutum, see p.128
Elaeagnus angustifolia
Hippophae rhamnoides, see p.214
Romneya coulteri, see p.129
Rosa fedtschenkoana
Salix elaeagnos
Salvia officinalis, see p.165
Shepherdia argentea

Helichrysum italicum
CURRY PLANT
☼ 9 ↕ 24in (60cm) ↔ 3ft (1m)

Threadlike leaves crowd the erect stems
of this low, aromatic evergreen subshrub.
Its leaves and stems are silvery gray and
downy, and summer flowers are yellow.

Leptospermum lanigerum
LEPTOSPERMUM
☼ 9 ↕ 10ft (3m) ↔ 6ft (2m)

The reddish shoots of this evergreen bush
are clothed in narrow gray or silvery gray
leaves. Its small white flowers are freely
produced in early summer.

Perovskia atriplicifolia 'Blue Spire'
RUSSIAN SAGE
☼ 5 ↕ 4ft (1.2m) ↔ 4ft (1.2m)

Spires of small violet-blue flowers open in
late summer and autumn, from gray-white
upright stems. These are all clothed with
deeply cut gray-green leaves.

Rosa glauca
REDLEAF ROSE
☼ 3 ↕ 6ft (2m) ↔ 6ft (2m)

Borne on reddish violet stems, the leaves
of this rose are glaucous purple in sun and
mauve-tinted gray-green in shade. Late
spring flowers are a bonus.

Salix exigua
COYOTE WILLOW
☼ 4 ↕ 12ft (4m) ↔ 5ft (1.5m)

This tall, upright shrub has long, flexuous
stems, each clothed with beautiful leaves,
narrow, silvery, and silky, ever shifting and
shimmering in the slightest breeze.

Santolina chamaecyparissus
LAVENDER COTTON
☼ 6 ↕ 30in (75cm) ↔ 3ft (1m)

Narrow, aromatic, woolly whitish leaves
crowd this evergreen shrub, forming a low,
dense dome. Long-stalked, buttonlike
yellow flowerheads occur in summer.

S H R U B S

Shrubs with Purple, Red, or Bronze Leaves

PURPLE OR REDDISH foliage in spring or summer can be extremely useful in the garden, providing that it is not overused. These relatively somber colors are particularly effective when contrasted with silver or gray foliage; even more dramatic effects can be achieved when they are placed alongside plants with yellow or gold foliage.

S H R U B S

Acer palmatum 'Garnet'
JAPANESE MAPLE
☼ 5   ↕12ft (4m) ↔12ft (4m)

This strong-growing shrub, with an open, spreading habit, has slender, dark shoots clothed in large, deep garnet red leaves with finely cut lobes. Dislikes dry soils.

Berberis thunbergii 'Red Chief'
JAPANESE BARBERRY
☼ 5   ↕1.2m (4ft) ↔1.2m (4ft)

'Red Chief' is a vigorous, upright or vase-shaped shrub, spreading as it matures. It has bright red, arching shoots and narrow, glossy-topped, red-purple leaves.

Corylus maxima 'Purpurea'
PURPLE-LEAF FILBERT
☼ 5   ↕20ft (6m) ↔20ft (6m)

Vase-shaped at first, spreading later, this popular form of filbert is planted for its large, deep purple leaves. Purplish catkins drape branches in late winter.

Acer palmatum 'Red Pygmy'
JAPANESE MAPLE
☼ 5   ↕5ft (1.5m) ↔4ft (1.2m)

The dark purple leaves of this densely branched, slow-growing shrub turn green with age. Leaves on mature plants differ from the juvenile leaves shown here.

Berberis thunbergii 'Atropurpurea Nana'
JAPANESE BARBERRY
☼ 5   ↕24in (60cm) ↔24in (60cm)

This dwarf, dome-shaped shrub of dense, twiggy habit has small, rounded, reddish purple leaves and is particularly suitable for growing in a rock garden.

Cotinus coggygria 'Royal Purple'
SMOKE TREE
☼ 5   ↕↔4m (12ft)

One of the most striking shrubs for foliage, this will form a dense mound of rounded, deep red-purple leaves. Plumes of tiny, smoky pink flowers appear in summer.

Hebe 'Amy'
HEBE
☼ 9   ↕ 3ft (1m) ↔ 3ft (1m)

The glossy, dark coppery purple leaves of this small, rounded evergreen shrub turn green in time. Rich violet-purple flowers are borne in short spikes in summer.

OTHER EVERGREEN SHRUBS WITH PURPLE, RED, OR BRONZE LEAVES

Leucothoe 'Scarletta'
Nandina domestica 'Nana Purpurea'
Photinia serrulata
Pieris formosa var. *forrestii*

Pittosporum tenuifolium 'Tom Thumb'
PITTOSPORUM
☼ 9   ↕ 24in (60cm) ↔ 24in (60cm)

The dark shoots of this dome-shaped dwarf evergreen shrub are crowded with shining, crinkly-edged leaves of a deep reddish purple, which emerge green.

OTHER DECIDUOUS SHRUBS WITH PURPLE, RED, OR BRONZE LEAVES

Acer palmatum 'Bloodgood'
Hibiscus acetosella 'Red Shield'
Itea virginica 'Henry's Garnet'
Weigela florida 'Minuet'

Prunus cerasifera 'Hessei'
PURPLE-LEAF PLUM
☼ 5   ↕ 12ft (4m) ↔ 12ft (4m)

In spring, snow white blossoms precede the leaves, which emerge green and then turn bronze-purple with cream or pink variegation. Bushy form of the cherry plum.

Prunus x *cistena*
PURPLE-LEAF SAND CHERRY
☼ 2   ↕ 5ft (1.5m) ↔ 5ft (1.5m)

Purple-leaf Sand Cherry is a small, erect shrub with glossy leaves, red at first, maturing to deep reddish purple. Small blush white flowers appear in spring.

Prunus spinosa 'Purpurea'
PURPLE-LEAF SLOE
☼ 5   ↕ 12ft (4m) ↔ 12ft (4m)

This is a dense, bushy shrub or small tree, with spiny branches and bright red leaves that change to a deep reddish purple. Small, pale pink flowers open in spring.

Sambucus nigra 'Guincho Purple'
PURPLE-LEAF ELDER
☼ 6   ↕ 12ft (4m) ↔ 12ft (4m)

The deeply divided leaves of this vigorous shrub are green at first, maturing to dark purple, then red in autumn. Its pink-budded summer flowers open white.

Shrubs with Colorful Foliage in Autumn

Given FAVORABLE CONDITIONS, many deciduous shrubs will produce colorful tints before their leaves are shed in autumn; those here have been chosen for their quality and reliability. The impact of a group of shrubs in autumn color is spectacular, but even a single well-selected and sited shrub can provide eye-catching effects in a small garden.

Cotinus coggygria 'Flame'
SMOKE BUSH

☀ 5   ↕12ft (4m) ↔12ft (4m)

Strong-growing and bushy, this shrub has clouds of purplish pink summer flowers. Its bold leaves turn fiery orange and red in autumn. The sap may cause a rash.

OTHER SHRUBS WITH COLORFUL FOLIAGE IN AUTUMN

Aronia arbutifolia, see p.134
Chionanthus virginicus, see p.110
Enkianthus perulatus
Itea virginica
Lindera benzoin
Rhododendron schlippenbachii
Rhus copallina
Spiraea prunifolia
Vaccinium corymbosum, see p.135
Viburnum dentatum

Berberis thunbergii
JAPANESE BARBERRY

☀ 5   ↕5ft (1.4m) ↔5ft (1.4m)

Arching, thorny branches are clothed with small leaves, orange and red in autumn. Small yellow flowers are produced in spring, and scarlet berries follow in autumn.

Acer palmatum var. *heptalobum*
JAPANESE MAPLE

☀ ☀ 5   ↕20ft (6m) ↔20ft (6m)

Most Japanese maples are worth growing for their impressive autumn tints. The large, seven-lobed green leaves of this one turn red or orange-red. Dislikes dry soils.

Callicarpa japonica
BEAUTYBERRY

☀ 5   ↕4½ft (1.4m) ↔4½ft (1.4m)

The leaves of this shrub turn yellowish to purplish or pinkish lavender in autumn. When planted in groups, violet berries are usually produced at the same time.

Disanthus cercidifolius
DISANTHUS

☀ 6 PH   ↕10ft (3m) ↔10ft (3m)

This spreading shrub is grown principally for its rounded blue-green leaves. During autumn, they turn a rich wine purple, then crimson and orange. Dislikes dry soils.

SHRUBS

Ribes odoratum
CLOVE CURRANT
☼ ☀ 5   ↕ 6ft (2m) ↔ 5ft (1.5m)

This open-habited shrub has upright stems
loosely clothed with lobed and rounded
leaves that turn red and purple in autumn.
Golden spring flowers are clove-scented.

S H R U B S

Euonymus alatus
BURNING BUSH
☼ ☀ 4   ↕ 6ft (2m) ↔ 10ft (3m)

This spectacular shrub turns brilliant
shades of pink and crimson in autumn.
The green twigs have curious corky-
winged projections along their length.

Fothergilla gardenii
FOTHERGILLA
☼ ☀ 5 PH ▼   ↕ 3ft (1m) ↔ 3ft (1m)

Although the small white flowerheads in
spring are pretty enough, autumn leaves in
brilliant orange, red, and purple are surely
this plant's most impressive feature.

Hamamelis vernalis 'Sandra'
VERNAL WITCH HAZEL
☼ ☀ 5 PH ▼   ↕ 10ft (3m) ↔ 10ft (3m)

Young purple leaves mature green, then
become yellow, orange, red, and purple in
autumn. Tiny, crowded, spidery, scented
yellow flowers follow in late winter.

**EVERGREEN SHRUBS WITH
COLORFUL FOLIAGE IN WINTER**

Calluna vulgaris 'Blazeaway'
Eurya japonica 'Winter Wine'
Mahonia aquifolium, see p.163
Nandina domestica 'Firepower'

157

Shrubs with Fragrant Flowers

W HEN PRESENTED with a lovely flower, most people will
instinctively take a sniff, assuming that a pleasing scent
accompanies a beautiful blossom. Sadly, this is not always the
case. Numerous shrubs do have fragrant flowers, though, and
these include some whose fragrance is far more noticeable or
appealing than the appearance of the flower itself.

S H R U B S

Coronilla valentina subsp. *glauca*
CORONILLA
☼ 8   ↕ 4½ft (1.4m) ↔ 4½ft (1.4m)

The leaves of this bushy evergreen are
blue-green and fleshy. Clusters of small
yellow pea flowers continue from winter
into early summer.

Acacia dealbata
MIMOSA, SILVER WATTLE
☼ 10 PH ▽   ↕ 20ft (6m) ↔ 20ft (6m)

Popular with florists, this fast-growing
evergreen has feathery blue-green leaves
and plumes of bright yellow flowerheads from winter into spring.

Carpenteria californica
CARPENTERIA
☼ 8   ↕ 6ft (2m) ↔ 6ft (2m)

The evergreen leaves of this bushy shrub
are leathery and dark green, and the bark
is papery and peeling. Its summer flowers
are white with yellow centers.

Daphne x *burkwoodii* 'Somerset'
DAPHNE
☼ 5   ↕ 4ft (1.2m) ↔ 4ft (1.2m)

This narrow-leaved, bushy shrub is one of
the best daphnes for general cultivation.
In late spring, it is plastered with clusters
of small, starry pink and white flowers.

Buddleia 'Lochinch'
BUTTERFLY BUSH
☼ 6-7   ↕ 10ft (3m) ↔ 10ft (3m)

This vigorous shrub, with softly hairy,
pointed, gray-green leaves, bears tapered
plumes of tubular, orange-eyed, lilac-blue
flowers from summer into autumn.

Choisya ternata
MEXICAN ORANGE-BLOSSOM
☼ ☼ 8   ↕ 6ft (2m) ↔ 6ft (2m)

This good-looking evergreen forms a dense
mound of glossy, aromatic leaves. White
flowers are freely borne in late spring and
again, less abundantly, in autumn.

**OTHER HARDY SHRUBS WITH
FRAGRANT FLOWERS**

Buxus microphylla
Calycanthus floridus
Chimonanthus praecox, see p.166
Chionanthus virginicus, see p.110
Clethra alnifolia, see p.134
Daphne cneorum
Elaeagnus multiflora
Fothergilla gardenii, see p.157
Hamamelis, many
Lavandula, many
Lonicera fragrantissima
Philadelphus, many
Rhododendron arborescens
Rhododendron 'Narcissiflorum', see p.125
Ribes odoratum, see p.157
Rosa, many
Sarcococca hookeriana var. *humilis*
Viburnum carlesii

Erica arborea var. *alpina*
TREE HEATH
☼ 7 PH ❄   ↕ 6ft (2m) ↔ 6ft (2m)

Bright green, needlelike evergreen leaves
crowd this dense, compact, upright shrub.
Plumes of tiny, honey-scented flowers are
produced in spring.

Osmanthus x *burkwoodii*
OSMANTHUS
☼ 7   ↕ 10ft (3m) ↔ 10ft (3m)

This strong-growing, compact evergreen
shrub is densely packed with small, dark
green, leathery leaves, and carries masses
of small white flowers in spring.

**OTHER LESS-HARDY SHRUBS
WITH FRAGRANT FLOWERS**

Brunfelsia pauciflora
Buddleia asiatica
Citrus, many
Clerodendron trichotomum, see p.110
Cytisus battandieri, see p.98
Daphne odora 'Aureo-marginata',
  see p.146
Edgeworthia chrysantha
Elaeagnus pungens 'Maculata',
  see p.146
Euphorbia mellifera
Gardenia augusta
Hoheria lyalii
Itea ilicifolia, see p.99
Michelia figo
Myrtus communis
Osmanthus fragrans
Pittosporum tobira

Rhododendron luteum
YELLOW AZALEA
☼ 6 PH ❄   ↕ 8ft (2.5m) ↔ 8ft (2.5m)

Rounded trusses of funnel-shaped flowers
in spring are a lovely yellow color. Rich
green leaves turn to shades of crimson,
purple, and orange in autumn.

Syringa 'Mme. Antoine Buchner'
FRENCH HYBRID LILAC
☼ 4   ↕ 12ft (4m) ↔ 12ft (4m)

Upright at first, this bushy shrub spreads
with maturity. Pink-mauve flowers, in
magnificent crowded heads, are purple-
red in bud and open in midspring.

Viburnum x *carlcephalum*
VIBURNUM
☼ 5   ↕ 10ft (3m) ↔ 10ft (3m)

This vigorous, bushy shrub bears white
flowers, pink in bud, in rounded and
crowded heads in spring. Its dark green
leaves sometimes color richly in autumn.

S H R U B S

Shrubs with Aromatic Leaves

G ARDENERS ARE NORMALLY aware of fragrance in flowers, but the aroma of foliage is all too often neglected. The leaves of many shrubs are aromatic, but for most the scent is subtle and detectable only when leaves are bruised. Some, such as the gummy leaves of cistus, are more obvious when it is hot and sunny.

SHRUBS

Rosmarinus officinalis 'Prostratus'
CREEPING ROSEMARY
☼ 8 ⇕ 6in (15cm) ↔ indefinite

Ideal for a wall top, this forms carpets of densely packed stems, clothed in narrow evergreen leaves. Pale blue flowers appear in late spring and early summer.

Cistus ladanifer
GUM CISTUS
☼ 8 ⇕ 4ft (1.2m) ↔ 4ft (1.2m)

The narrow, willowlike, dark green leaves of this evergreen shrub are coated, like the branches, in a sticky, aromatic gum. Large white flowers appear in summer.

Elsholtzia stauntonii
MINT BUSH
☼ 5 ⇕ 5ft (1.5m) ↔ 5ft (1.5m)

This bushy subshrub has sharply toothed leaves that smell of mint when bruised. Dense spikes of mauve flowers are carried in late summer and early autumn.

Salvia microphylla var. *neurepia*
LITTLELEAF SAGE
☼ 7 ⇕ 4ft (1.2m) ↔ 3ft (1m)

The slender, upright stems of this bushy shrub are clothed with apple green leaves. Spikes of brilliant scarlet flowers are borne from summer into early autumn.

OTHER DECIDUOUS SHRUBS WITH AROMATIC LEAVES

Aloysia triphylla, see p.144
Artemisia abrotanum
Comptonia peregrina
Myrica pensylvanica

Prostanthera cuneata
PROSTANTHERA
☼ 9 ⇕ 3ft (1m) ↔ 4½ft (1.4m)

The branches of this shrub are crowded with tiny, glossy, dark green leaves that smell of wintergreen. It produces masses of white flowers in spring.

OTHER EVERGREEN SHRUBS WITH AROMATIC LEAVES

Buxus sempervirens
Choisya ternata, see p.158
Eucalyptus, several
Helichrysum italicum, see p.153
Illicium anisatum, see p.100
Laurus nobilis
Lavandula 'Hidcote Giant'
Myrtus communis
Santolina chamaecyparissus, see p.153
Thymus vulgaris, see p.165

Shrubs with Ornamental Fruit

MOST SHRUBS with ornamental fruit, especially the many kinds that bear edible berries, bring a welcome touch of color to the garden and provide birds and small animals with a useful source of food. Many fruit freely, but some need to be planted in groups to ensure pollination, while others require a male to pollinate a group of berry-bearing females.

Ilex x *meserveae* 'Blue Princess'
BLUE HOLLY
☼ ☀ 5   ↕ 10ft (3m) ↔ 4ft (1.2m)

This is a dense, upright evergreen with spiny, purple-tinged leaves. Red berries are freely borne if its spring flowers are pollinated by those of a male form.

Callicarpa bodinieri var. *giraldii*
BEAUTYBERRY
☼ 7   ↕ 7ft (2.2m) ↔ 6ft (2m)

Clusters of small, bright mauve or pale violet berries are borne in autumn, when the leaves are mauve-tinted. Plant several together for good pollination.

Euonymus hamiltonianus var. *sieboldianus* 'Red Elf'
☼ ☀ 5   ↕ 10ft (3m) ↔ 10ft (3m)

Upright at first, this strong-growing shrub spreads with age. It is grown mainly for the clusters of deep pink capsules that split to reveal orange seeds in autumn.

OTHER SHRUBS WITH ORNAMENTAL FRUIT

Ilex verticillata
Pyracantha coccinea
Symplocos paniculata
Viburnum dilatatum
Viburnum opulus 'Xanthocarpum'

SHRUBS

Cotoneaster frigidus 'Fructuluteo'
TREE COTONEASTER
☼ ☀ 7   ↕ 20ft (6m) ↔ 20ft (6m)

This large, strong-growing shrub or small, multistemmed tree has bold foliage, white flowers in summer, and bunches of long-lasting yellow berries in autumn.

Gaultheria mucronata 'Wintertime'
PERNETTYA
☼ 7 PH   ↕ 3ft (1m) ↔ 4ft (1.2m)

If you include a male plant in a group for good pollination, this suckering evergreen will bear white berries from autumn into winter. Forms dense clumps in time.

Viburnum wrightii 'Hessei'
VIBURNUM
☼ ☀ 5   ↕ 3ft (1m) ↔ 3ft (1m)

Heads of small white flowers are produced in early summer, and form bunches of red berries in autumn. The broad, veined leaves often color richly in autumn.

Shrubs that Provide Berries for Birds

MANY WOULD SAY A GARDEN is incomplete without the presence of birds, be they residents or just regular visitors. Songbirds are particularly desirable. In spring and summer there is plenty of food to attract them, but in autumn and winter it can be scarce. Entice birds to visit by planting some shrubs that produce reliable crops of berries.

Ilex aquifolium 'J.C. van Tol'
VAN TOL'S ENGLISH HOLLY
☼ ☼ 6   ↕ 20ft (6m) ↔ 12ft (4m)

This extremely useful holly carries few-spined leaves and red berries that crowd the purple shoots in winter. It will fruit even when no male plant is present.

> **OTHER LARGE SHRUBS THAT PROVIDE BERRIES FOR BIRDS**
>
> *Amelanchier* x *grandiflora*
> *Aralia spinosa*
> *Aronia arbutifolia*
> *Berberis koreana*
> *Cornus mas*, see p.166
> *Cornus racemosa*
> *Cotoneaster multiflorus*
> *Elaeagnus multiflora*
> *Photinia villosa*, see p.228
> *Rosa*, many
> *Rubus spectabilis*
> *Sambucus canadensis*
> *Sambucus racemosa*
> *Viburnum opulus*, see p.135

Cotoneaster 'Cornubia'
COTONEASTER
☼ ☼ 7   ↕ 20ft (6m) ↔ 20ft (6m)

This strong-growing semievergreen shrub has clusters of tiny white flowers in early summer, and ample bunches of large red berries from autumn into early winter.

Cotoneaster sternianus
COTONEASTER
☼ ☼ 6   ↕ 10ft (3m) ↔ 10ft (3m)

The branches of this evergreen or semi-evergreen shrub are clothed with small gray-green leaves, and covered in autumn with clusters of orange-red berries.

Crataegus x *schraderiana*
HAWTHORN
☼ ☼ 6   ↕ 15ft (5m) ↔ 15ft (5m)

Masses of white flowers cover this large shrub or small tree in late spring or early summer. The blooms are followed by drooping clusters of dark purple-red berries.

Leycesteria formosa
HIMALAYAN HONEYSUCKLE
☼ ☼ 7   ↕ 6ft (2m) ↔ 5ft (1.5m)

An upright shrub (or subshrub in colder climates), this carries drooping clusters of white flowers with claret-colored bracts in summer. Reddish purple berries follow.

Lonicera xylosteum
EUROPEAN FLY HONEYSUCKLE
☀ ☀ 4   ↕ 10ft (3m) ↔ 10ft (3m)

Strong-growing and bushy, this shrub has
spreading or arching branches and bears
creamy white flowers in spring or early
summer, followed by red berries.

Sambucus nigra
ELDERBERRY
☀ ☀ 6   ↕ 20ft (6m) ↔ 20ft (6m)

This European elderberry produces
flattened heads of fragrant, creamy white
flowers in early summer, followed by its
heavy bunches of tiny black berries.

Mahonia aquifolium
OREGON GRAPE
☀ ☀ ☀ 5   ↕ 3ft (1m) ↔ 5ft (1.5m)

The glossy green leaves of this dense, low
evergreen shrub are prickly. Its bloomy
blue-black berries are preceded in spring
by crowded yellow flower clusters.

**OTHER SMALL SHRUBS THAT
PROVIDE BERRIES FOR BIRDS**

Aronia melanocarpa
Berberis thunbergii
Cotoneaster apiculatus
Cotoneaster horizontalis
Daphne mezereum
Gaultheria mucronata
Gaultheria shallon
Hedera helix 'Arborescens', see p.164
Mahonia nervosa, see p.133
Malus sargentii 'Tina'
Myrica pensylvanica
Ribes odoratum, see p.157
Rosa nitida
Vaccinium corymbosum, see p.135
Vaccinium parviflorum
Vaccinium vitis-idaea 'Koralle'
Viburnum acerifolium
Viburnum nudum

Prunus laurocerasus 'Marbled White'
VARIEGATED CHERRY LAUREL
☀ ☀ 6-7   ↕ 15ft (5m) ↔ 15ft (5m)

Dense and compact, this bright-foliaged
evergreen has green- and cream-marbled
leaves. White flower spikes in late spring
are followed by shining black fruits.

Viburnum opulus 'Compactum'
COMPACT SNOWBALL BUSH
☀ ☀ 4   ↕ 5ft (1.5m) ↔ 5ft (1.5m)

The maplelike leaves of this dense shrub
color richly in autumn, when its bunches
of bright red berries appear. Lacecap
heads of white flowers open in spring.

S H R U B S

Shrubs Attractive to Butterflies

FLOWERING SHRUBS that appeal to butterflies offer a bonus that few gardeners would wish to ignore. Many are also sweetly scented. The nectar of their flowers is attractive to butterflies, as well as to a host of other beneficial insects, including hoverflies and bees. All these industrious creatures help make the garden a more interesting and lively place.

Buddleia davidii 'Peace'
BUTTERFLY BUSH
☼ 6   ↕12ft (4m) ↔ 12ft (4m)

Buddleias come in many colors and are among the most popular plants with bees and butterflies. 'Peace' has fragrant white flower spikes from summer into autumn.

Calluna vulgaris 'Anthony Davis'
HEATHER, LING
☼ 5 PH   ↕18in (45cm) ↔ 20in (50cm)

This fine, bushy heather is crowded with gray-green evergreen foliage. Long sprays of white flowers are produced from late summer into early autumn.

Escallonia 'Donard Seedling'
ESCALLONIA
☼ 8   ↕3m (10ft) ↔ 3m (10ft)

A favorite in milder climates, this shrub has arching stems, each densely clothed in glossy evergreen leaves. Masses of pale pink buds open white or blush in summer.

Hebe albicans
HEBE
☼ 9   ↕24in (60cm) ↔ 3ft (1m)

In summer, spikes crowded with white flowers grow from the upper leaf axils of this dwarf, mounded, compact hebe. Its evergreen leaves are blue-green.

Hedera helix 'Arborescens'
TREE IVY
☼ ☼ ☼ 6   ↕4½ft (1.4m) ↔ 6ft (2m)

This ivy forms a dense evergreen mound of glossy leaves. Heads of brownish green flowers in autumn are a veritable honey pot for late-flying insects.

Lavandula angustifolia 'Hidcote'
LAVENDER
☼ 6   ↕24in (60cm) ↔ 30in (75cm)

In summer, long-stalked spikes with small, fragrant violet flowers rise above the narrow gray-green leaves of this aromatic evergreen. A deservedly popular plant.

Pyracantha 'Watereri'
FIRETHORN
☼ ☀ 7   ↕ 8ft (2.5m) ↔ 8ft (2.5m)

The spreading branches of this vigorous evergreen bear narrow, glossy, dark green leaves. White flower clusters occur in early summer, and red berries in autumn.

Rubus 'Benenden'
FLOWERING RASPBERRY
☼ 5   ↕ 10ft (3m) ↔ 10ft (3m)

The strong, upright stems of this shrub are arching and eventually wide-spreading. Lovely flowers, like small white roses, are borne in late spring and early summer.

OTHER SMALL SHRUBS ATTRACTIVE TO BUTTERFLIES

Caryopteris x *clandonensis* 'Arthur Simmonds', see p.116
Lavandula stoechas
Salvia greggii

Ligustrum quihoui
PRIVET
☼ ☀ 6   ↕ 8ft (2.5m) ↔ 8ft (2.5m)

A most elegant privet, this has slender, arching branches, glossy evergreen leaves, and branched, conical heads of tiny white flowers from late summer into autumn.

Salvia officinalis
COMMON SAGE
☼ 6   ↕ 24in (60cm) ↔ 3ft (1m)

Sage is a popular culinary herb. It forms a mound of semievergreen, aromatic gray-green leaves, and produces spikes of two-lipped purple-blue flowers in late spring.

Syringa x *hyacinthiflora* 'Esther Staley'
EARLY LILAC
☼ 3   ↕ 12ft (4m) ↔ 10ft (3m)

Upright at first, and spreading later, this is a strong-growing, bushy shrub. Striking, dense heads of fragrant lilac-pink flowers appear in spring.

OTHER LARGE SHRUBS ATTRACTIVE TO BUTTERFLIES

Abelia x *grandiflora*
Amorpha canescens
Aralia spinosa
Buddleia 'Lochinch', see p.158
Ceanothus americanus
Clerodendrum bungei, see p.114
Clethra alnifolia, see p.134
Ligustrum sinense, see p.110
Syringa microphylla 'Superba', see p.115
Vitex agnus-castus

Thymus vulgaris
COMMON THYME
☼ 6   ↕ 12in (30cm) ↔ 10in (25cm)

Most often used in the herb garden, this dwarf subshrub has narrow, aromatic, gray-green leaves with slender spikes of pale purplish pink flowers all through summer.

Late-winter-flowering Shrubs

FLOWERING SHRUBS are at no time more welcome and more valued than during the late winter months. This is partly due to their being few in number and, having fewer rivals, they command our full attention, particularly when planted where their flowers are easily seen against a darker background such as a wall or an evergreen hedge.

Daphne bholua 'Jacqueline Postill'
DAPHNE
☀ ☀ 9   ↕ 6ft (2m) ↔ 5ft (1.5m)

Best in a sheltered position, this vigorous, upright evergreen bears clusters of richly fragrant flowers that bloom over a long period. Dislikes dry soils.

Erica carnea 'Springwood White'
WINTER HEATH
☀ ☀ 3   ↕ 6in (15cm) ↔ 18in (45cm)

This reliable, scented evergreen shrublet forms a good, low groundcover with its dense, needlelike foliage. Spikes of small white bellflowers continue into spring.

Cornus mas
CORNELIAN CHERRY
☀ ☀ 5   ↕ 15ft (5m) ↔ 15ft (5m)

The twigs of this broad, rounded shrub or small tree are studded with little clusters of tiny yellow flowers. These twigs are also useful for cutting to display inside.

OTHER LATE-WINTER-FLOWERING SHRUBS

Abeliophyllum distichum
Daphne odora 'Aureo-marginata', see p.146
Garrya elliptica, see p.100
Hamamelis mollis 'Pallida'
Lonicera fragrantissima
Rhododendron dauricum
Skimmia japonica, see p.171
Stachyurus praecox
Viburnum farreri

Chimonanthus praecox 'Grandiflorus'
WINTERSWEET
☀ 6   ↕ 8ft (2.5m) ↔ 10ft (3m)

This large, slow-growing, spreading shrub is justly famous for its deliciously fragrant, small, cup-shaped flowers. These are pale yellow with a purple heart.

Hamamelis x *intermedia* 'Jelena'
WITCH HAZEL
☀ ☀ 5 PH   ↕ 12ft (4m) ↔ 12ft (4m)

In autumn, the large, softly hairy leaves turn orange-red and scarlet, and in winter, spidery orange flowers densely crowd the bare twigs. Dislikes dry soils.

Sycopsis sinensis
SYCOPSIS
☼ ☀ 8   ↕ 15ft (5m) ↔ 12ft (4m)

This uncommon, erect evergreen shrub carries glossy, dark green, pointed leaves and produces compact clusters of tiny flowers. Grows best in a sheltered site.

SHRUBS

Mahonia x *media* 'Buckland'
MAHONIA
☼ ☀ 8   ↕ 10ft (3m) ↔ 10ft (3m)

Erect at first, this big and bold evergreen spreads with age. Long, cylindrical spikes of tiny, fragrant yellow flowers are borne above divided, prickle-toothed leaves.

Viburnum x *bodnantense* 'Dawn'
WINTER-FLOWERING VIBURNUM
☼ ☀ 6   ↕ 10ft (3m) ↔ 8ft (2.5m)

From autumn all through to spring, the leafless twigs of this reliable shrub are studded with clusters of strongly fragrant pink flowers, darker in bud.

Lonicera x *purpusii* 'Winter Beauty'
WINTER HONEYSUCKLE
☼ ☀ 5   ↕ 6ft (2m) ↔ 12ft (4m)

Vigorous, and with a spreading habit, this honeysuckle is mainly grown for its small, sweetly fragrant white flowers. These are carried over a very long period.

Sarcococca hookeriana var. *digyna*
CHRISTMAS BOX, SWEET BOX
☼ ☀ ☀ 6   ↕ 4ft (1.2m) ↔ 3ft (1m)

This suckering evergreen in time forms dense clumps of upright shoots. Clusters of tiny, sweetly scented white flowers are carried in the axils of its narrow leaves.

Viburnum tinus 'Eve Price'
LAURUSTINUS
☼ ☀ 9   ↕ 8ft (2.5m) ↔ 8ft (2.5m)

Heads of reddish buds open into many white flowers with a subtle fragrance from autumn onward. Neat and rounded, this shrub has glossy, dark evergreen leaves.

Shrubs with Ornamental Twigs in Winter

ORNAMENTAL FEATURES that enliven a garden in winter are most welcome. In addition to the indisputable attraction of winter flowers and evergreen foliage, the stems and twigs of many plants offer surprisingly decorative colors and forms. The dramatic effect of some, such as dogwood and willow, can be improved by hard pruning.

SHRUBS

Cornus stolonifera 'Flaviramea'
GOLDEN-TWIGGED DOGWOOD

☼ ☀ 2   ↕ 6ft (2m) ↔ 10ft (3m)

The greenish yellow winter shoots of this vigorous suckering and layering shrub are brighter if regularly pruned and if in full sun. Leaves turn yellow in autumn.

Cornus alba 'Sibirica'
TATARIAN DOGWOOD

☼ ☀ 2   ↕ 6ft (2m) ↔ 6ft (2m)

This is among the best in cultivation for colored stems. It produces red winter shoots, and large summer leaves when pruned. These give rich autumn tints.

Corylus avellana 'Contorta'
HARRY LAUDER'S WALKING STICK

☼ ☀ 5   ↕ 15ft (5m) ↔ 15ft (5m)

In late winter, charming lamb's-tail catkins enliven the coiled and twisted shoots of this strong-growing shrub.

SHRUBS WITH ORNAMENTAL BARK FOR WINTER EFFECT

Abelia triflora
Clethra barbinervis
Deutzia scabra
Dipelta floribunda
Euonymus alatus, see p.157
Physocarpus opulifolius
Prunus tomentosa
Rhododendron barbatum
Rhododendron thomsonii
Rosa sericea f. *pteracantha*

Cornus sanguinea 'Winter Beauty'
REDTWIG DOGWOOD

☼ ☀ 4   ↕ 5ft (1.5m) ↔ 6ft (2m)

With regular pruning, this shrub produces winter stems that are a fiery orange-yellow at the base, shading to pink and red at the tips. Leaves turn golden yellow in autumn.

OTHER COLORED-STEMMED SHRUBS FOR WINTER EFFECT

Cornus alba 'Kesselringii'
Cornus sericea 'Silver and Gold'
Hydrangea macrophylla 'Nigra'
Kerria japonica 'Pleniflora', see p.101
Leycesteria formosa, see p.162
Rubus biflorus
Rubus thibetanus, see p.169
Salix alba var. *vitellina* 'Britzensis'
Salix irrorata
Stephanandra tanakae

Shrubs with Spines or Thorny Branches

F OR MANY GARDENERS, shrubs whose stems or branches are spiny or thorny have a positive security value because they can deter prowlers and uninvited individuals. Others find they are at best a nuisance, and at worst a danger. Whatever your attitude to plants that happen to be hostile to the touch, they undeniably include some very fine ornamental shrubs.

Rubus thibetanus
WHITE-STEMMED BRAMBLE
☼ ☼ 7 　　　　 ↕ 8ft (2.5m) ↔ 10ft (3m)

Clumps of thorny, bloomy white, purple-barked winter stems become clothed with prettily divided, fernlike, silvery-hairy leaves. Small summer flowers are pink.

OTHER SHRUBS WITH SPINES OR THORNY BRANCHES
Berberis koreana
Chaenomeles, most
Poncirus trifoliata
Pyracantha 'Mohave'
Robinia hispida
Rosa roxburghii
Rosa soulieana, see p.113
Rubus cockburnianus
Rubus ulmifolius 'Bellidiflorus'
Ulex europaeus 'Flore Pleno'

Berberis 'Goldilocks'
BARBERRY
☼ ☼ 8 　　　　 ↕ 12ft (4m) ↔ 12ft (4m)

The stems and arching branches of this bushy evergreen are viciously spiny. It has shiny, dark green, prickle-toothed leaves, and golden yellow flowers in spring.

Pyracantha 'Orange Glow'
FIRETHORN
☼ ☼ 6 ❋ 　　　 ↕ 12ft (4m) ↔ 12ft (4m)

This vigorous evergreen shrub has spiny branches, glossy green oblong leaves, clusters of white flowers in summer, and orange berries in autumn and winter.

Rosa eglanteria
SWEET BRIAR, EGLANTINE
☼ 4 　　　　　 ↕ 8ft (2.5m) ↔ 8ft (2.5m)

The arching, thorny stems of this vigorous shrub are clothed in apple-scented leaves. It produces single pink flowers in summer, and small red hips in autumn.

Zanthoxylum piperitum
JAPAN PEPPER
☼ ☼ 6 　　　　 ↕ 8ft (2.5m) ↔ 8ft (2.5m)

The erect, ascending, spiny stems of this bushy shrub bear aromatic, glossy green leaves that become yellow in autumn. Red fruits in autumn contain peppery seeds.

169

Rabbitproof Shrubs

SHRUBS THAT RABBITS IGNORE are surely all worthy of consideration, particularly by gardeners in rural areas. It may be the taste of the leaves and shoots, or their texture, that is unpalatable to rabbits, but whatever it is, such plants are extremely valuable where these creatures are a problem. It may be assumed that most other forms of the shrubs featured here, as well as their immediate relatives, are also rabbitproof.

Hypericum kouytchense
SHRUBBY HYPERICUM
☼ 7 ‡ 30in (75cm) ↔ 4ft (1.2m)

From summer into autumn, the arching stems of this mounded semievergreen carry numerous yellow flowers. These are followed by bronze-red seed capsules.

Aucuba japonica
AUCUBA
☼ ☼ ☼ 7 ‡ 8ft (2.5m) ↔ 6ft (2m)

Long, pointed, glossy, dark green leaves cover this dense evergreen. Female plants produce red berries when pollinated by a male. Several forms exist, some variegated.

Fuchsia 'Tom Thumb'
FUCHSIA
☼ 8 ‡ 20in (50cm) ↔ 20in (50cm)

Dwarf and upright, this neat fuchsia has small, glossy green leaves and showers of charming, pendent red and purple flowers, through summer and into early autumn.

Kalmia angustifolia f. *rubra*
RED SHEEP LAUREL
☼ 2 PH ‡ 18in (45cm) ↔ 3ft (1m)

Red Sheep Laurel forms a low, bushy mound of narrow evergreen leaves. Clusters of small, deep red flowers are produced in early summer. Dislikes dry soils.

Buxus sempervirens 'Suffruticosa'
EDGING BOXWOOD
☼ 6 ‡ 30in (75cm) ↔ 30in (75cm)

All forms of boxwood are unpalatable to rabbits. This dense and compact cultivar has long been used as a low, evergreen edging to borders, as well as in parterres.

Gaultheria mucronata 'Mulberry Wine'
PERNETTYA
☼ 7 PH ‡ 3ft (1m) ↔ 3ft (1m)

This low evergreen with pointed, leathery leaves on wiry branches spreads in time. When pollinated by a male, large berries are borne from autumn through winter.

Rhododendron 'Strawberry Ice'
EXBURY AZALEA
☼ 6 PH ‡ 8ft (2.5m) ↔ 8ft (2.5m)

Showy clusters of yellow-throated, pale pink trumpet flowers are carried in spring. The leaves of this bushy azalea may color attractively before they fall in autumn.

Sambucus nigra   'Aurea'
GOLDEN ELDER
☼ 6   ↕ 12ft (4m) ↔ 4m (12ft)

This large, bushy shrub has golden yellow leaves, and bears flattened heads of tiny, fragrant white flowers in summer. Shining black berries follow in autumn.

Rosa 'Rosy Cushion'
SHRUB ROSE
☼ 5-6   ↕ 3ft (1m) ↔ 4ft (1.2m)

Glossy green foliage offsets clusters of scented pink flowers with white centers throughout summer. A strong-growing rose, this is low, dense, and spreading.

DEERPROOF SHRUBS

Berberis thunbergii, see p.156
Buddleia davidii
Buxus sempervirens
Cornus alba
Euonymus alatus, see p.157
Lindera benzoin, see p.134
Pieris japonica, see p.115
Poncirus trifoliata
Robinia hispida, see p.99
Viburnum sargentii
Weigela florida

Rosmarinus officinalis
ROSEMARY
☼ 7   ↕ 5ft (1.5m) ↔ 5ft (1.5m)

Rosemary is a popular, aromatic evergreen bush. Small, purplish blue flowers clothe the branches all through summer, along with its narrow gray-green leaves.

Ruscus aculeatus
BUTCHER'S BROOM
☼ ☼ 7   ↕ 30in (75cm) ↔ 3ft (1m)

Tough and adaptable, this evergreen shrub forms clumps of erect stems, crowded with spine-tipped leaves. If pollinated, the female plants produce long-lasting fruits.

Skimmia japonica
SKIMMIA
☼ ☼ 7   ↕ 4ft (1.2m) ↔ 4ft (1.2m)

This bushy mound of aromatic evergreen leaves is dotted with white flower clusters in spring and, if both sexes are present, female plants then produce red berries.

OTHER RABBITPROOF SHRUBS

Ceanothus thyrsiflorus var. *repens*
Cornus sanguinea
Cotoneaster horizontalis
Daphne tangutica
Euonymus alatus
Poncirus trifoliata
Prunus laurocerasus 'Otto Luyken', see p.133
Spiraea japonica 'Anthony Waterer', see p.123
Vinca minor

CONIFERS

ALL CONIFERS ARE EITHER trees or shrubs but, as is usual, I have chosen to treat them separately. They comprise a distinct and primitive group of woody plants and add an individual element to the garden. All but a few are evergreen. The deciduous kinds, specified in the descriptions, offer the interesting feature of autumn color.

△ Tsuga heterophylla

△ DOMED SPECIMEN Chamaecyparis pisifera *'Filifera Aurea' makes an ideal golden yellow specimen for a larger lawn.*

THE BEAUTY OF CONIFERS

- Large conifers are linchpins, giving a feeling of permanence to a garden.
- Offer a wonderfully wide selection of shapes, colors, and textures.
- Contribute evergreen foliage effects, especially valuable in winter.
- Deciduous foliage changes seasonally.
- Dwarf and slow-growing conifers are ideal for rock gardens, patios, screes.
- Provide shelter in the garden when used as screens, hedges, windbreaks.

Conifers are extremely versatile due to their great variety in size, form, color, and texture. You can use them for countless effects and situations. Many are of such noble proportions and elegance of form that they can make magnificent specimens for important positions.

DECORATIVE FOLIAGE

Conifer foliage tends to be either small and scalelike, as in cypress and *Thuja*, or long and needlelike, as in pine, spruce, and cedar. Junipers have needlelike or scale-like leaves and, in some cases, both. Yew has narrow, strap-shaped leaves, and many conifer cultivars have lovely mossy or soft, feathery juvenile foliage. Add to this all the shades of blue, green, and yellow,

as well as the interesting variegations, and it is obvious why conifers occupy such a special place among garden plants. Deciduous conifers, such as larch, *Metasequoia*, and *Ginkgo*, brighten autumn with a final flash of gold or yellow before their leaves fall.

TOO BIG, TOO SOON

As with broad-leaved trees, consider the vigor, ultimate height and shape, and intended purpose of your chosen conifer. Some species used as hedging, for instance, grow rapidly and require regular pruning to achieve the best results. Do not plant fast-growing hedges if you cannot maintain them – there are numerous small- to medium-sized conifers for limited space.

△ WINTER APPEAL *The rich reddish brown bark of deciduous* Metasequoia glyptostroboides *is impressive.*

◁ CONIFERS AND HEATHERS *This is an excellent example of the use of conifers with late-winter-flowering ericas.*

▷ COLOR AND TEXTURE *Just a few well-chosen conifers combine to create a colorful and extremely showy feature.*

Large Conifers

SOME OF THE MOST SPECTACULAR large trees in the world are conifers. Given the evergreen nature of all but a small minority, they bring a sense of permanence and continuity to the large garden or estate. Most conifers are comparatively long-lived. They generally thrive best on deep, moist, but well-drained soils, although they are remarkably adaptable to most sites. A handful are tolerant of wet sites, but few will survive in completely waterlogged conditions.

Cryptomeria japonica
JAPANESE RED CEDAR
☼ ☼ 6   ↕ 70ft (20m) ↔ 22ft (7m)

The narrow leaves of this columnar to conical tree are arranged spirally on the shoots. Fibrous bark is reddish brown, and its small green cones mature to brown.

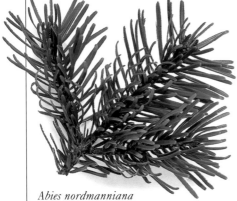

Abies nordmanniana
NORDMANN FIR
☼ ☼ 5   ↕ 80ft (25m) ↔ 28ft (9m)

The spreading branches of this columnar to conical fir are packed with slender green leaves. Erect, greenish brown cones appear in summer on the upper branches.

Cedrus libani
CEDAR OF LEBANON
☼ 6   ↕ 78ft (24m) ↔ 50ft (15m)

This conifer is a familiar sight in parks. Conical when young, it later assumes the typical flat-topped and tiered cedar habit. Sharp leaves are green to blue-green.

Ginkgo biloba
GINKGO, MAIDENHAIR TREE
☼ ☼ 4   ↕ 70ft (20m) ↔ 22ft (7m)

This distinctive deciduous conifer has an ancient pedigree. Conical when young with rising branches, it later spreads. Fan-shaped leaves turn yellow in autumn.

Araucaria araucana
MONKEY PUZZLE, CHILE PINE
☼ 7   ↕ 60ft (18m) ↔ 40ft (12m)

When young, this tree is conical, and has whorled branches to ground level. Finally, it is mop-headed with a tall stem. Broad, sharp leaves densely clothe the branches.

OTHER LARGE COLUMNAR OR CONICAL CONIFERS

Abies concolor
Abies grandis
Abies magnifica
Araucaria heterophylla
Calocedrus decurrens
Cedrus libani
  subsp. *atlantica* 'Fastigiata'
Chamaecyparis lawsoniana 'Wisselii',
  see p.178
x *Cupressocyparis leylandii* 'Naylor's Blue'
Cupressus sempervirens
Juniperus virginiana 'Canaertii'
Metasequoia glyptostroboides, see p.182
Picea omorika
Picea orientalis
Pinus strobus 'Fastigiata'
Taxodium ascendens 'Nutans', see p.181
Taxodium distichum

Sequoia sempervirens
REDWOOD, COAST REDWOOD
☼ ☼ **8**   ↕ 100ft (30m) ↔ 25ft (8m)

Conical when it is young, this distinctive conifer becomes columnar later. It has rich red, fibrous, spongy bark, and its branches are clothed with lush, yewlike foliage.

Picea abies
NORWAY SPRUCE
☼ ☼ **2**   ↕ 80ft (25m) ↔ 22ft (7m)

Norway Spruce, a traditional Christmas tree, is conical at first, but broadens and spreads with age. Its layered branches are closely packed with dark green needles.

OTHER LARGE CONIFERS OF ULTIMATELY SPREADING HABIT

Cedrus libani subsp. *atlantica* f. *glauca*,
  see p.193
Cupressus macrocarpa, see p.184
Larix decidua
Larix x *eurolepis*
Larix kaempferi
Larix x *pendula*
Picea sitchensis
Pinus ayacahuite
Pinus x *holfordiana*
Pinus nigra, see p.187
Pinus radiata, see p.187
Pinus strobus, see p.182
Pinus sylvestris
Pinus wallichiana
Pseudotsuga menziesii
Tsuga canadensis, see p.181
Tsuga heterophylla, see p.183

Pinus jeffreyi
JEFFREY PINE
☼ **5**   ↕ 70ft (20m) ↔ 28ft (9m)

This robust, distinguished pine is conical or rounded at first, then broad-columnar later. Its fissured bark is dark gray-brown, and its long needles are blue-green.

Sequoiadendron giganteum
GIANT SEQUOIA, GIANT REDWOOD
☼ **6**   ↕ 100ft (30m) ↔ 35ft (11m)

Renowned worldwide for its longevity, this species will form a tall column of down-curved branches clothed with blue-green foliage. Bark is reddish brown.

Wide-spreading and Vase-shaped Conifers

CONIFERS WITH ASCENDING or wide-spreading branches, ultimately wider than they are high, are numerous. They make excellent single specimens where a severe or formal line, such as the straight edge of a long border, needs to be broken or softened. Alternatively, consider them as a feature in a lawn, where their full spread can be admired.

Cupressus macrocarpa 'Gold Spread'
MONTEREY CYPRESS
☼ 7   ↕ 3ft (1m) ↔ 8ft (2.5m)

This ornamental form of the Monterey Cypress is low and compact. Horizontal or slightly ascending branches are densely crowded with bright yellow foliage.

Juniperus x *media* 'Blue and Gold'
JUNIPER
☼ 4   ↕ 5ft (1.5m) ↔ 5ft (1.5m)

The stems crowding the base of this choice juniper are packed with intense blue-gray foliage, scattered with sprays of creamy yellow. Whole shoots can be creamy yellow.

Juniperus x *media* 'Pfitzeriana Glauca'
JUNIPER
☼ 4   ↕ 6ft (2m) ↔ 12ft (4m)

'Pfitzeriana Glauca' is a strong-growing juniper of dense habit, whose ascending and spreading stems are densely crowded with prickly blue-gray foliage.

Juniperus davurica
'Expansa Variegata'
☼ 5   ↕ 30in (75cm) ↔ 6ft (2m)

Low and wide-spreading, this vigorous juniper has virtually horizontal branches crowded with prickly, bluish green foliage, interspersed with creamy white sprays.

Juniperus x *media* 'Pfitzeriana Aurea'
GOLDEN PFITZER JUNIPER
☼ 4   ↕ 6ft (2m) ↔ 12ft (4m)

The terminal shoots and closely packed foliage of this strong-growing juniper are suffused golden yellow in summer, and become yellowish green in winter.

Juniperus x *media* 'Plumosa Aurea'
JUNIPER
☼ 4   ↕ 5ft (1.5m) ↔ 6ft (2m)

The many stems of this compact juniper are crowded with plumelike sprays, each crammed with yellow, scalelike foliage that turns bronze-gold in winter.

Cephalotaxus harringtonia
  'Duke Gardens'
Cephalotaxus harringtonia 'Prostrata'
Chamaecyparis lawsoniana
  'Tamariscifolia'
Picea abies 'Tabuliformis'
Picea bicolor 'Howell's Dwarf'
Pinus strobus 'Prostrata'
Taxus baccata 'Repandens'
Torreya californica 'Spreadeagle'

Juniperus virginiana 'Grey Owl'
EASTERN RED CEDAR
☼ 3   ↕ 8ft (2.5m) ↔ 12ft (4m)

A handsome and strong-growing juniper,
this has ascending branches densely
clothed with soft, silvery gray foliage. A
most effective, and ultimately large, shrub.

Juniperus squamata 'Blue Carpet'
SINGLESEED JUNIPER
☼ 5   ↕ 12in (30cm) ↔ 6ft (2m)

The wide-spreading stems of this vigorous
juniper form a large, low carpet of prickly
glaucous blue foliage. It is one of the most
effective plants of its kind.

OTHER WIDE-SPREADING JUNIPERS

Juniperus chinensis 'Kaizuka'
Juniperus chinensis 'Maney'
Juniperus chinensis 'Mint Julep'
Juniperus × *media* 'Blaauw'
Juniperus × *media* 'Gold Coast'
Juniperus × *media* 'Hetzii'
Juniperus × *media* 'Old Gold'
Juniperus × *media* 'Pfitzeriana'
Juniperus × *media* 'Sulphur Spray'
Juniperus virginiana 'Blue Cloud'

C O N I F E R S

Juniperus sabina var. *tamariscifolia*
SAVIN JUNIPER
☼ 4   ↕ 3ft (1m) ↔ 6ft (2m)

This effective and low-growing form of
the Savin Juniper produces close-packed
layers of spreading branches, each densely
clothed in bright green, prickly leaves.

**OTHER WEEPING, WIDE-
SPREADING CONIFERS**

Cedrus deodora 'Pendula'
Cedrus libani subsp. *atlantica*
  'Glauca Pendula'
Larix kaempferi 'Pendula'

Taxus baccata 'Dovastonii Aurea'
ENGLISH YEW
☼ ☀ 6   ↕ 15ft (5m) ↔ 20ft (6m)

This elegant shrub or small tree has tiers
of horizontal branches and long, sweeping
branchlets. Leaves on golden shoots have
bright yellow margins. Non-fruiting.

Columnar or Narrowly Conical Conifers

S LENDER OR NARROW CROWNS are great assets in conifers, because they can be planted in restricted spaces. Their generally compact nature means that they very rarely, if ever, need to be pruned. Their strong, vertical lines make them ideal for breaking or lifting otherwise low plantings. They also provide a striking focal point.

Austrocedrus chilensis
CHILEAN CEDAR
☼ 9   ↕ 40ft (12m) ↔ 10ft (3m)

The short, ascending branches of this uncommon, dense conifer are clothed in feathery sprays of green or blue-green, scalelike foliage. Small terminal cones.

OTHER COLUMNAR CONIFERS

Calocedrus decurrens
Cupressus sempervirens
  'Swane's Golden', see p.192
Juniperus chinensis 'Aurea'
Juniperus communis 'Compressa'
Juniperus virginiana 'Glauca'
Sequoiadendron giganteum 'Glaucum'
Taxus baccata 'Standishii'
Taxus x *media* 'Flushing'
Thuja occidentalis 'Holmstrup'
Thuja occidentalis 'Spiralis'

OTHER COLUMNAR CYPRESSES

Chamaecyparis lawsoniana
  'Alumii Magnificent'
C. lawsoniana 'Blom'
C. lawsoniana 'Columnaris'
C. lawsoniana 'Fraseri'
C. lawsoniana 'Grayswood Pillar'
C. lawsoniana 'Green Pillar', see p.186
C. lawsoniana 'Hillieri'
C. lawsoniana 'Kilmacurragh'
C. lawsoniana 'Pottenii'
C. lawsoniana 'Winston Churchill'

Chamaecyparis lawsoniana 'Wisselii'
LAWSON CYPRESS
☼ 6   ↕ 50ft (15m) ↔ 10ft (3m)

A distinctive form of Lawson cypress, this has erect, close-packed branches and blue-green foliage in three-dimensional sprays. Tiny cones in spring are brick red.

Cupressus sempervirens
ITALIAN CYPRESS
☼ 8   ↕ 50ft (15m) ↔ 10ft (3m)

The gray-green, scalelike leaves that form this characteristic narrow column are held in erect sprays. Fairly large, shiny gray-brown cones ripen in their second year.

Juniperus chinensis 'Keteleeri'
CHINESE JUNIPER
☼ 4   ↕ 50ft (15m) ↔ 15ft (5m)

This columnar to narrowly conical tree of dense, compact habit has closely packed sprays of gray-green, scalelike foliage. Excellent and reliable for formal planting.

CONIFERS

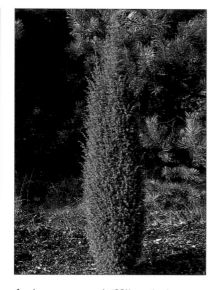

Juniperus communis 'Hibernica'
IRISH JUNIPER
☼ 4   ↕12ft (4m) ↔ 20in (50cm)

This juniper forms a dense, slender column composed of crowded, needlelike leaves. Each of these has a fine silver line on its inside face.

Pinus omorika
SERBIAN SPRUCE
☼ ☼ 4   ↕60ft (18m) ↔ 15ft (5m)

The downswept branches of this spirelike spruce arch at their tips and are crowded with narrow, dark green leaves. Clusters of long purple cones mature to brown.

Taxus baccata 'Fastigiata Robusta'
ENGLISH YEW
☼ ☼ 6   ↕30ft (10m) ↔ 5ft (1.5m)

In habit, this yew is erect, columnar, and eventually cigar-shaped, with ascending, close-packed branches. Narrow, dark green leaves are arranged all around the shoots.

Juniperus scopulorum 'Skyrocket'
ROCKY MOUNTAIN JUNIPER
☼ 4   ↕25ft (8m) ↔ 30in (75cm)

One of the narrowest of all conifers, this is a tall, slender, columnar juniper with a compact habit. Crowded sprays of blue-gray, scalelike foliage pack the branches.

Pinus sylvestris 'Fastigiata'
SCOTS PINE
☼ 2   ↕20ft (6m) ↔ 3ft (1m)

This is a columnar form of the Scots pine. The bark is reddish brown and its erect, close-packed branches are clothed with blue-green needles. Dislikes exposed sites.

Thuja occidentalis 'Smaragd'
AMERICAN ARBORVITAE
☼ ☼ 2   ↕8ft (2.5m) ↔ 30in (75cm)

The branches of this dense, narrowly conical conifer are clothed with flattened sprays of rich green foliage, which has a pleasant "fruity" scent when bruised.

C O N I F E R S

Medium-sized Conifers

A WIDE SELECTION of conifers exists in the height range of 20–50ft (6–15m), including many wild species that have both botanical interest and ornamental merit. Even more abundant are the numerous cultivars of conifers such as the Lawson Cypress, Hinoki Cypress, and Arborvitae (*Thuja* species). Any of these is worth considering in all but very small gardens. Most are rather hardy, but those that are less so will grow happily in milder areas or in a sheltered site.

Cupressus cashmeriana
KASHMIR CYPRESS
☼ ☀ [9] ↕ 40ft (12m) ↔ 18ft (5.5m)

This beautiful conical tree, which spreads with age, is perfect for a sheltered site. Its bloomy blue-green foliage is carried in elegant, drooping sprays. Dislikes dry soils.

Abies koreana
KOREAN FIR
☼ ☀ [5] ↕ 30ft (10m) ↔ 15ft (5m)

The ascending or spreading branches of this broad, conical tree are densely clothed with dark green, silvery-backed needles. Even small plants bear violet-blue cones.

Chamaecyparis obtusa
'Tetragona Aurea'
☼ [5] ↕ 30ft (10m) ↔ 15ft (5m)

Easily recognized and popular, this Hinoki cypress is bushy when young but becomes loosely conical. Mosslike sprays of yellow foliage clothe its angular branches.

OTHER MEDIUM-SIZED CONIFERS

Chamaecyparis nootkatensis 'Pendula'
Cupressus arizonica 'Pyramidalis'
Juniperus chinensis 'Aurea'
Picea glauca
Pinus bungeana
Pinus parviflora
Pinus sylvestris 'Aurea', see p.192
Pseudolarix amabilis
Sciadopitys verticillata
Thuja occidentalis 'Spiralis'
Tsuga mertensiana

Chamaecyparis obtusa 'Crippsii'
HINOKI CYPRESS
☼ [5] ↕ 30ft (10m) ↔ 15ft (5m)

This popular, colorful, loosely conical conifer has bright golden, aromatic foliage borne in large, flattened sprays. Rounded cones are brown. Dislikes dry soils.

Cunninghamia lanceolata
CHINA FIR
☼ ☀ [6] ↕ 43ft (13m) ↔ 15ft (5m)

The branches of this columnar tree are all lined with two rows of narrow, glossy green leaves that are silvery beneath, and sharp. Does not like exposed sites or dry soils.

Fitzroya cupressoides
PATAGONIAN CYPRESS
☀ [7] ↕ 30ft (10m) ↔ 15ft (5m)

Columnar when young, this bushy, juniper-like tree becomes more lax in habit with age. It has peeling, reddish brown bark and sprays of white-banded, scalelike leaves.

Taxodium ascendens 'Nutans'
POND CYPRESS
☼ 5   ↕ 50ft (15m) ↔ 15ft (5m)

Pond Cypress is a deciduous, columnar
tree. Its ascending branches are crowded
above with slender sprays of bright green
foliage. Ideal in deep or moist soils.

Pinus aristata
BRISTLECONE PINE
☼ 4   ↕ 25ft (8m) ↔ 15ft (5m)

Suitable for any but the smallest gardens,
this slow-growing, dense, bushy pine has
branches crowded with dark blue-green,
white-flecked needles. Cones are whiskery.

Picea breweriana
BREWER SPRUCE
☼ ☼ 5   ↕ 40ft (12m) ↔ 20ft (6m)

This is one of the most distinctive of the
spruces. Its spreading branches support
long, pendulous branchlets clothed with
narrow leaves. Cylindrical brown cones.

Podocarpus salignus
PODOCARPUS
☼ 9   ↕ 30ft (10m) ↔ 20ft (6m)

A most attractive columnar tree (broadly
conical later), this podocarpus has stringy,
reddish brown bark and narrow, shiny,
willowlike leaves. Dislikes dry soils.

Tsuga canadensis
EASTERN HEMLOCK
☼ ☼ 3   ↕ 50ft (15m) ↔ 30ft (10m)

This multistemmed tree has pendent or
arching sprays of small, dark green, silver-
backed leaves. Cones are freely borne and
ripen to brown. Dislikes dry soils.

C O N I F E R S

181

Conifers for Heavy Clay Soil

Many conifers will grow in heavy clay soil, providing that it is not permanently waterlogged. They encompass an extremely wide selection of sizes and shapes, and have foliage of great variety, both in color and texture. These are easy to grow and are evergreen unless specified deciduous.

Cryptomeria japonica
'Elegans Compacta'
☼ 6   ↕ 10ft (3m) ↔ 6ft (2m)

This is a dense, billowy, bushy form of Japanese Red Cedar. The fresh green foliage is soft to touch and turns a rich reddish bronze color in winter.

Metasequoia glyptostroboides
DAWN REDWOOD
☼ ☼ 5   ↕ 70ft (20m) ↔ 15ft (5m)

The feathery leaves of this magnificent deciduous conifer turn tawny pink in autumn. An ancient and vigorous tree, it is narrowly conical to almost columnar.

Pinus leucodermis
BOSNIAN PINE
☼ 5   ↕ 60ft (18m) ↔ 28ft (9m)

A handsome tree of dense, conical habit, this pine broadens as it ages. Its special features include rich green needles, white hairy buds, and cobalt blue cones.

Pinus mugo 'Mops'
MOUNTAIN PINE
☼ 2   ↕ 3ft (1m) ↔ 4ft (1.2m)

This dwarf mountain pine in time forms a compact mound of dark green needles. Slow-growing, it is ideal for a large rock garden or a big pot.

Pinus peuce
MACEDONIAN PINE
☼ 5   ↕ 60ft (18m) ↔ 20ft (6m)

Worth growing where space is available, this impressive pine has densely crowded gray-green needles and pendent, rounded and curved, resin-flecked cones.

**OTHER EVERGREEN CONIFERS
FOR HEAVY CLAY SOIL**

Abies koreana, see p.150
Chamaecyparis nootkatensis 'Pendula'
Chamaecyparis obtusa
Picea abies, see p.175
Picea glauca var. *albertiana* 'Conica',
   see p.189
Pinus coulteri
Pinus ponderosa
Saxegothaea conspicua
Thuja occidentalis

Pinus strobus
WHITE PINE
☼ 3   ↕ 70ft (20m) ↔ 28ft (9m)

A well-known conical pine, this broadens with age. Open branches bear slender gray-green needles and pendulous cones. Will not tolerate air pollution.

Pinus thunbergii
JAPANESE BLACK PINE
☼ 5   ↕ 43ft (13m) ↔ 25ft (8m)

Its dark green needles and hairy silvery
buds distinguish this easy-to-grow pine.
Conical when young and broadening with
age, this makes an excellent coastal tree.

Taxodium distichum
BALDCYPRESS
☼ 4   ↕ 70ft (20m) ↔ 28ft (9m)

This attractive deciduous, conical conifer
is excellent for a damp site. It has fibrous,
reddish brown bark and feathery green
leaves that turn gold in autumn.

Thuja koraiensis
KOREAN ARBORVITAE
☼ 6   ↕ 22ft (7m) ↔ 10ft (3m)

Loose and slow-growing, this columnar
conifer has broad sprays of bright green,
scaly foliage, silver-white beneath. When
bruised, the foliage smells of almonds.

OTHER DECIDUOUS CONIFERS FOR HEAVY CLAY SOILS
Ginkgo biloba, see p.174
Larix decidua
Larix kaempferi
Taxodium ascendens

Taxus baccata 'Aurea'
GOLDEN ENGLISH YEW
☼ ☀ 6   ↕ 15ft (5m) ↔ 10ft (3m)

The leaves of this striking golden form of
the English Yew become green in their
second year. Trim it annually to obtain a
neat, rounded habit, as seen here.

Tsuga heterophylla
WESTERN HEMLOCK
☼ ☀ 6   ↕ 70ft (20m) ↔ 30ft (10m)

Slender branches, crowded with green,
silver-backed needles and drooping at
the tips, form graceful layers. This fast-
growing conical conifer has small cones.

Conifers for Dry, Sunny Sites

MANY CONIFERS ARE NATIVE to warm, dry regions of the world, and a good number of these are readily available for planting in gardens where warm, dry summers are a regular feature. Some are vigorous, and soon create shade; others are slow-growing. All are evergreen, and best planted when small to give them the best chance of establishing.

CONIFERS

Pinus cembroides
MEXICAN PINYON
☼ 4 ↕ 20ft (6m) ↔ 15ft (5m)

This unusual and attractive, slow-growing pine is bushy and conical when young, becoming rounded with age. Stout, stiff gray-green needles crowd its branches.

OTHER PINES FOR DRY, SUNNY SITES
Pinus aristata, see p.181
Pinus armandii
Pinus bungeana
Pinus contorta
Pinus coulteri
Pinus edulis
Pinus monophylla
Pinus pinaster
Pinus sylvestris
Pinus yunnanensis

Cedrus deodara
DEODAR CEDAR
☼ 7 ↕ 80ft (25m) ↔ 40ft (12m)

A handsome, vigorous conifer, this has long, drooping branches when young, and ultimately assumes a typical flat-topped cedar shape with layered branches.

Juniperus drupacea
SYRIAN JUNIPER
☼ 7 ↕ 40ft (12m) ↔ 5ft (1.5m)

Distinctive and easily recognized, this juniper of close columnar habit is superb as a specimen in the lawn or in a border. It has bright green, needlelike leaves.

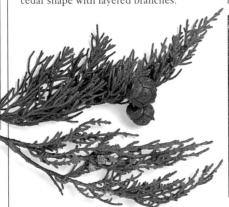

Cupressus macrocarpa
MONTEREY CYPRESS
☼ 8 ↕ 70ft (20m) ↔ 76ft (22m)

This popular, fast-growing conifer, with its sprays of feathery green foliage, is often grown in coastal areas as a screen. When young it is columnar, but spreads with age.

Juniperus rigida
TEMPLE JUNIPER
☼ 5 ↕ 25ft (8m) ↔ 15ft (5m)

Loosely branched and often sprawling, this tree or large bush has drooping sprays of needlelike green leaves that become bronze in winter, and peeling bark.

Pinus halepensis
ALEPPO PINE
☼ 9 ↕ 46ft (14m) ↔ 20ft (6m)

Excellent on sandy soils, this pine rounds with age. Needles on juvenile trees are blue-green; they are bright green on older trees. Egg-shaped cones are glossy orange.

Pinus muricata
BISHOP PINE
☼ 7   ↕60ft (18m) ↔ 28ft (9m)

This tough and adaptable, fast-growing pine is columnar at first, broadening and often becoming flat-topped later. It is very good on poor, or acid, sandy soils.

Pinus pinea
STONE PINE, UMBRELLA PINE
☼ 8   ↕40ft (12m) ↔ 30ft (10m)

Conical when young, Stone Pine gradually develops its characteristic head of packed, radiating branches. Mature trees have dark green foliage; juveniles have blue-green.

Pinus virginiana
SCRUB PINE, VIRGINIA PINE
☼ 5 PH   ↕46ft (14m) ↔ 28ft (9m)

Loose and often untidy, this is a pine with densely crowded gray to yellow-gray needles on pinkish white shoots. It bears small, prickly orange-brown winter cones.

Taxus cuspidata
JAPANESE YEW
☼ ☼ ☼ 4   ↕15ft (5m) ↔ 15ft (5m)

This multibranched shrub opens out and spreads with age. Yellowish green leaves, sometimes red-brown in winter, clothe its branches. Female plants bear red fruits.

Torreya californica
CALIFORNIA NUTMEG
☼ 6   ↕60ft (18m) ↔ 25ft (8m)

An impressive, upright conifer, this has whorled branches and long, narrow, spine-tipped leaves. If pollinated, female trees produce pendent, olivelike fruits.

OTHER CONIFERS FOR DRY, SUNNY SITES

Abies concolor
Cedrus libani subsp. *atlantica* f. *glauca*, see p.193
x *Cupressocyparis leylandii*, see p.186
Cupressus glabra 'Pyramidalis'
Cupressus sempervirens
Juniperus chinensis 'Mountbatten'
Juniperus communis 'Berkshire'
Juniperus conferta 'Blue Pacific'
Juniperus horizontalis 'Blue Chip'
Juniperus x *media* 'Pfitzeriana Compacta'
Juniperus squamata 'Blue Star', see p.189
Juniperus virginiana 'Canaertii'
Picea glauca var. *albertiana* 'Conica', see p.189
Picea pungens 'Koster', see p.193

185

Conifers for Hedges, Windbreaks, or Screening

CONIFERS ARE SUPERB subjects for hedging and screens –
most are evergreen and provide an attractive permanent
effect once established. The filtering effect on winds, and
subsequent benefit to plants they are sheltering, has also
long been recognized. Most conifers used for formal hedges or
screening are ultimately big and need regular trimming.

OTHER CONIFERS FOR HEDGES
AND SCREENING

Chamaecyparis lawsoniana cultivars
Chamaecyparis obtusa 'Crippsii',
  see p.180
x *Cupressocyparis leylandii*
  'Naylor's Blue'
Juniperus chinensis 'Mountbatten'
Juniperus chinensis 'Spartan'
Thuja occidentalis 'Techny'
Thuja plicata 'Atrovirens'
Tsuga canadensis, see p.181

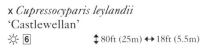

Chamaecyparis 'Green Hedger'
LAWSON CYPRESS
☼ 6   ↕ 50ft (15m) ↔ 20ft (6m)

Well clothed down to its base with sprays
of rich green foliage, this is one of the best
cypresses for screening. It is conical as a
single specimen. Dislikes dry soils.

Chamaecyparis lawsoniana
'Green Pillar'
☼ 6   ↕ 50ft (15m) ↔ 10ft (3m)

Good for screens or hedges, this columnar
cypress is moderately sized and requires
little clipping. Its vertical sprays of green
foliage are gold-tinged in early spring.

x *Cupressocyparis leylandii*
LEYLAND CYPRESS
☼ 6   ↕ 78ft (24m) ↔ 18ft (5.5m)

One of the fastest growing of all conifers –
too fast for many gardens – this is ideal as
a temporary screen or tall hedge. Its foliage
is dark green or gray-green.

x *Cupressocyparis leylandii*
'Castlewellan'
☼ 6   ↕ 80ft (25m) ↔ 18ft (5.5m)

Commonly planted as a hedge or screen,
this evergreen grows rapidly but can be
cut back hard. Densely packed bronze-
yellow foliage is golden on young plants.

Picea asperata
CHINESE SPRUCE
☼ 5   ↕ 50ft (15m) ↔ 30ft (10m)

The yellow-brown shoots of this tough,
conical spruce are all crowded with blue-
gray, needlelike foliage. Adaptable to
most soils, it makes a useful windbreak.

CONIFERS

Pinus nigra
AUSTRIAN PINE
☼ 4   ↕ 80ft (25m) ↔ 70ft (20m)

This tough, rugged, ultimately large tree is excellent as a windbreak for exposed sites. It has a domed crown and spreading branches. Dislikes dry soils.

Taxus baccata
ENGLISH YEW
☼ ☼ ☀ 6   ↕ 40ft (12m) ↔ 30ft (10m)

Yews, with their narrow, blackish green leaves, are popular for hedging. Regular clipping will encourage a dense habit, which is particularly effective in topiary.

Taxus x *media* 'Hicksii'
HICK'S YEW
☼ ☼ ☀ 5   ↕ 20ft (6m) ↔ 6ft (2m)

Tough, adaptable, and slow-growing, this yew is very good for screening or hedging. Columnar when young, it matures to vase-shaped. Bears red fruit if pollinated.

OTHER CONIFERS FOR WINDBREAKS

Abies concolor
Cupressus macrocarpa, see p.184
Juniperus virginiana
Picea abies
Picea nordmanniana
Picea sitchensis
Pinus cembra
Pinus leucodermis, see p.182
Pinus strobus
Pinus sylvestris
Pseudotsuga menziesii

Pinus radiata
MONTEREY PINE
☼ 7 PH   ↕ 80ft (25m) ↔ 70ft (20m)

An impressive large pine for shelter on exposed sites (except in cold inland areas), this has bold bunches of green needles, and attractive male cones in spring.

CONIFERS FOR SMALL HEDGES

Cryptomeria japonica 'Elegans Nana'
Juniperus communis 'Berkshire'
Thuja occidentalis 'Globosa'
Thuja orientalis 'Conspicua'
Thujopsis dolabrata 'Nana'

Thuja plicata
WESTERN RED CEDAR
☼ ☼ 5   ↕ 80ft (25m) ↔ 25ft (8m)

This handsome conical conifer makes a first-rate hedge or screen, with its close-packed sprays of glossy, scalelike foliage that smells of pineapple when bruised.

CONIFERS

187

Slow-growing or Dwarf Conifers

SLOW-GROWING CONIFERS, or those with a naturally dwarf habit, are ideal for small gardens, rock gardens, raised beds, or containers. Most are mutations of a normal-sized tree and are propagated by grafting onto seedling stock. Few other hardy woody plants offer such a wide range of shape, form, and color throughout the year.

Chamaecyparis lawsoniana 'Gnome'
LAWSON CYPRESS
☼ 6-7   ↕12in (30cm) ↔12in (30cm)

Dense, slow-growing form of the Lawson Cypress, this has flat sprays of scalelike foliage. Occasional tufts of coarse growth should be cut away to maintain shape.

Abies balsamea 'Nana'
BALSAM FIR
☼ 3   ↕20in (50cm) ↔30in (75cm)

This low, domed form of the Balsam Fir is dense and compact. The short, spreading, glossy green leaves have two grayish bands beneath and crowd the branchlets.

Abies nordmanniana
'Golden Spreader'
☼ 5   ↕18in (45cm) ↔4ft (1.2m)

This form of the Caucasian Fir is low-spreading and flat-topped. The crowded leaves are yellow above, yellowish white beneath, and golden yellow in winter.

OTHER DWARF CONIFERS OF ROUNDED OR DOMED HABIT

Chamaecyparis obtusa 'Caespitosa'
Picea abies 'Gregoryana'
Pinus mugo 'Gnome'
Pinus strobus 'Minima'
Pinus sylvestris 'Beuvronensis'
Thuja occidentalis 'Sunkist'
Thuja occidentalis 'Tiny Tim'
Thuja orientalis 'Meldensis'
Thujopsis dolobrata 'Nana'
Tsuga canadensis 'Jeddeloh'

Abies concolor 'Glauca Compacta'
WHITE FIR
☼ 4   ↕3½ft (1.1m) ↔4½ft (1.3m)

Ideal for larger rock gardens, this is a handsome, compact form of the White Fir. Its habit is irregular, with branches of narrow, spreading, grayish blue leaves.

Cedrus libani 'Sargentii'
CEDAR OF LEBANON
☼ 6   ↕30in (75cm) ↔8ft (2.5m)

A splendid, low-domed cedar. The long, weeping branches are covered with needle-like blue-green leaves. Tie the main stem upright to a stake to give height.

Chamaecyparis obtusa 'Nana Aurea'
HINOKI CYPRESS
☼ 5   ↕4½ft (1.3m) ↔26in (65cm)

An excellent golden dwarf conifer for general cultivation, this slow-growing, conical form of the Hinoki Cypress has fan-shaped sprays of scalelike foliage.

Juniperus squamata 'Blue Star'
DWARF JUNIPER
☀ 5 ↕ 18in (45cm) ↔ 20in (50cm)

The branches of this slow-growing juniper
of squat habit are densely crowded with
needlelike, silvery blue leaves. A most
satisfactory blue-gray dwarf conifer.

Picea pungens 'Montgomery'
BLUE COLORADO SPRUCE
☀ 2 ↕ 3½ft (1.1m) ↔ 3½ft (1.1m)

This reliable, dome-shaped form of the
Colorado Spruce is ideal for larger rock
gardens or as a specimen. Sharp-pointed
grayish needles crowd its branches.

Pinus leucodermis 'Schmidtii'
BOSNIAN PINE
☀ 5 ↕ 3ft (1m) ↔ 30in (75cm)

A slow-growing form of the Bosnian Pine
that forms a globular or conical bush, this
is compact in habit. Its short branches are
crowded with needlelike green leaves.

Picea glauca var. *albertiana* 'Conica'
DWARF ALBERTA SPRUCE
☀ 2 ↕ 6ft (2m) ↔ 36in (90cm)

This popular form of the White Spruce
retains its tight, conical habit if stray side
shoots are removed. Needlelike green
leaves crowd the branchlets.

**OTHER DWARF CONIFERS OF
COLUMNAR OR CONICAL HABIT**

Abies lasiocarpa 'Compacta'
Chamaecyparis lawsoniana
  'Ellwood's Gold'
x *Cupressocyparis leylandii* 'Hyde Hall'
Juniperus communis 'Compressa'
Juniperus communis 'Sentinel'
Picea abies 'Remontii'
Picea glauca var. *albertiana* 'Laurin'
Pinus parviflora 'Negishi'
Thuja plicata 'Rogersii'

OTHER SLOW OR DWARF CONIFERS

Chamaecyparis obtusa 'Rigid Dwarf'
Cryptomeria japonica 'Vilmoriniana'
Pinus densiflora 'Umbraculifera'
Thuja orientalis 'Elegantissima'
Tsuga canadensis 'Horstmann'

Thuja plicata 'Stoneham Gold'
WESTERN RED CEDAR
☀ 6 ↕ 5½ft (1.7m) ↔ 30in (75cm)

A choice form of the Western Red Cedar,
developing a conical habit. The aromatic,
scalelike leaves are borne in flat sprays
and become darker as they mature.

C O N I F E R S

189

Conifers for Groundcover

L OW-GROWING conifers are among the most effective groundcovers for the garden. Their evergreen leaves form a dense, carpetlike cover, and come in a variety of shades, including bright green, blue-green, and gray-green. Many were developed from mutations found on taller-growing conifers and are grafted or grown from cuttings.

Picea abies 'Reflexa'
NORWAY SPRUCE
☼ 2   ↕18in (45cm) ↔15ft (5m)

The branches of this unusual, irregular, low-growing form of the Norway Spruce are long, prostrate, and crowded with needlelike leaves that form a dense mat.

Juniperus communis 'Green Carpet'
COMMON JUNIPER
☼ 3   ↕5in (12cm) ↔4ft (1.2m)

This prostrate juniper makes an excellent groundcover and blends well with others of its kind. Its branches are crowded with prickly, needlelike, bright green leaves.

Juniperus procumbens 'Nana'
CREEPING JUNIPER
☼ 5   ↕12in (30cm) ↔6ft (2m)

Slightly raised mats or carpets are formed by the tightly packed, prostrate branches of this dwarf juniper. Bristly blue-green leaves crowd its shoots.

OTHER CONIFERS FOR GROUNDCOVER

Cephalotaxus harringtonia 'Prostrata'
Juniperus conferta 'Blue Pacific'
Juniperus conferta 'Emerald Sea'
Juniperus horizontalis 'Blue Chip'
Juniperus horizontalis 'Wiltonii'
Juniperus squamata 'Blue Carpet'
   see p.177
Picea pungens 'Procumbens'
Taxus baccata
   'Repandens'

Juniperus horizontalis 'Plumosa'
CREEPING JUNIPER
☼ 4   ↕6in (15cm) ↔6ft (2m)

Seen here next to *J. horizontalis* 'Glauca', with which it combines well, this reliable groundcover has sprays of gray-green foliage that turn bronze-purple in winter.

Microbiota decussata
MICROBIOTA
☼ ☼ ☼ 3   ↕12in (30cm) ↔6ft (2m)

The arching, spraylike branches of this low-growing, wide-spreading conifer are densely clothed with bright green, scale-like leaves, which turn bronze in winter.

Taxus baccata
'Repandens Aurea'
☼ ☼ 6   ↕18in (45cm) ↔6ft (2m)

Short, overlapping branchlets, crowded with yellow-margined leaves, dark green in shade, fill the long branches of this low-spreading form of the English Yew.

CONIFERS

Variegated Conifers

THE VARIEGATION IN CONIFERS usually takes the form of white or yellow sprays scattered in otherwise green foliage. Occasionally, however, the additional color is banded, such as in *Thuja plicata* 'Zebrina' *(see right)*, or the overall effect may appear speckled. These variegations may not appeal to all gardeners, but they can provide a pleasing contrast to greens, especially in winter. Such conifers also make interesting single specimens for the lawn.

Thuja plicata 'Zebrina'
WESTERN RED CEDAR

☼ 5   ↕70ft (20m) ↔ 40ft (12m)

A striking conical conifer, this is easily recognized by the dark green sprays of pineapple-scented foliage, boldly banded cream-yellow, and its reddish, fibrous bark.

OTHER VARIEGATED CONIFERS

Chamaecyparis lawsoniana
  'Fletcher's White'
Chamaecyparis obtusa 'Mariesii'
Chamaecyparis pisifera 'Snow'
x *Cupressocyparis leylandii* 'Silver Dust'
Juniperus chinensis 'Gold Star'
Pinus densiflora 'Oculus-draconis'
Pinus thunbergii 'Oculus-draconis'
Taxus baccata 'Fastigiata Aurea'
Thuja occidentalis 'Elegantissima'
Tsuga canadensis 'Gentsch White Tip'

Calocedrus decurrens 'Aureovariegata'
INCENSE CEDAR

☼ 6   ↕40ft (12m) ↔ 10ft (3m)

The short, spreading branches of this slow-growing cedar are covered by sprays of aromatic green foliage, interspersed with yellow sprigs.

x *Cupressocyparis leylandii* 'Harlequin'
VARIEGATED LEYLAND CYPRESS

☼ 6   ↕70ft (20m) ↔ 20ft (6m)

This variegated cultivar is just as easy and vigorous as the species, but its packed, plumelike, gray-green foliage is relieved by scattered, creamy white sprays.

Chamaecyparis nootkatensis 'Variegata'
VARIEGATED NOOTKA CYPRESS

☼ 5   ↕50ft (15m) ↔ 20ft (6m)

Pendulous sprays of pungent green foliage are coarse to the touch and interspersed with creamy white sprays. Nootka Cypress is loosely conical and dislikes dry soils.

Juniperus chinensis
'Kaizuka Variegata'

☼ 4   ↕10ft (3m) ↔ 6ft (2m)

The protruding branches of this distinctly angular, slow-growing juniper are crowded with bright green, almost mossy foliage, marked with patches of creamy white.

Thujopsis dolabrata 'Variegata'
VARIEGATED HIBA

☼ 6   ↕30ft (10m) ↔ 20ft (6m)

Broad, flattened sprays of aromatic green foliage have silvery marks beneath, and random sprays are splashed creamy white. It is slow-growing, and dislikes dry soils.

Conifers with Golden or Yellow Foliage

A WIDE VARIETY of conifers with golden or yellow foliage is available for both the large or small garden. In some cases, only the growing tips show yellow; in others, the entire foliage retains this cheerful color throughout the year, adding a warm glow to the garden during the drab winter months. All those illustrated here are reliable.

OTHER MEDIUM-SIZED TO LARGE CONIFERS WITH GOLDEN FOLIAGE

Cedrus deodara 'Aurea'
Chamaecyparis lawsoniana 'Lutea'
Chamaecyparis obtusa 'Crippsii', see p.180
Juniperus chinensis 'Aurea'
Picea abies 'Aurea'
Picea orientalis 'Skylands'
Thuja occidentalis 'Europe Gold'
Thuja plicata 'Aurea'
Thuja plicata 'Irish Gold'

Chamaecyparis pisifera 'Filifera Aurea'
SAWARA CYPRESS
☀ 5   ↕ 40ft (12m) ↔ 15ft (5m)

This dense, conical or mounded conifer produces numerous long, threadlike branches clothed with tiny, bright yellow leaves. It only slowly increases in size.

Cupressus sempervirens 'Swane's Golden'
☀ 8   ↕ 30ft (10m) ↔ 24in (60cm)

For very small gardens, this is probably the best conifer of its shape and color. It forms a tall, slender column of golden-tinged foliage in dense, crowded sprays.

Pinus sylvestris 'Aurea'
GOLDEN SCOTS PINE
☀ 2   ↕ 40ft (12m) ↔ 15ft (5m)

The normally blue-green needles of this slow-growing, broad, columnar tree turn a rich yellow from winter into spring. The colder the winter, the richer the color.

Cupressus macrocarpa 'Goldcrest'
MONTEREY CYPRESS
☀ 7   ↕ 30ft (10m) ↔ 10ft (3m)

One of the best of its color, this is a vigorous, columnar or slender, conical tree. It is dense and compact, with crowded, plumelike foliage. Avoid clipping.

OTHER SMALL OR SLOW-GROWING CONIFERS WITH GOLDEN FOLIAGE

Cedrus deodara 'Golden Horizon'
Cryptomeria japonica 'Sekkan-sugi'
Cupressus macrocarpa 'Gold Spread'
Juniperus communis 'Gold Cone'
Pinus sylvestris 'Moseri'
Thuja occidentalis 'Golden Globe'
Thuja occidentalis 'Rheingold'
Thuja occidentalis 'Trompenburg'
Thuja orientalis 'Aureus Nanus'
Thuja plicata 'Stoneham Gold', see p.189

Thuja plicata 'Collyer's Gold'
WESTERN RED CEDAR
☀ 6   ↕ 6ft (2m) ↔ 3ft (1m)

This is a slow-growing conifer of compact, dense, dome-shaped or conical habit. Its crowded sprays of foliage emerge a rich golden yellow, then turn light green.

Conifers with Blue-gray or Silver foliage

WHEN SEEN AGAINST a darker background, blue-gray or silvery conifers have a striking effect in the garden. The Blue Atlas Cedar and the Blue Colorado Spruce are perhaps the two most well known in general cultivation but, happily, there are many others of similar effect and equal merit, some suitable for small gardens. All shown here are evergreen.

Picea glauca 'Coerulea'
WHITE SPRUCE
☼ 2   ↕ 43ft (13m) ↔ 20ft (6m)

This vigorous, conical spruce has branches that are ascending at first, and spread with age. They are crowded with short blue-gray to silver needles. Dislikes dry soils.

OTHER CONIFERS WITH BLUE-GRAY OR SILVER FOLIAGE

Abies pinsapo 'Glauca'
Chamaecyparis lawsoniana 'Pelt's Blue'
Cupressus glabra 'Pyramidalis'
Juniperus chinensis 'Ames'
Juniprus scopulorum 'Blue Heaven'
Picea pungens 'Fat Albert'
Pinus koraiensis
Pinus parviflora 'Glauca'
Pinus wallichiana 'Nana'
Pseudotsuga menziesii 'Glauca'

Abies concolor 'Candicans'
WHITE FIR
☼ 3   ↕ 70ft (20m) ↔ 22ft (7m)

The branches of this handsome conical conifer are clothed with spreading, needle-like leaves, colored a striking silver-white or blue-gray. Dislikes dry soils.

Chamaecyparis lawsoniana
'Pembury Blue'
☼ 6   ↕ 50ft (15m) ↔ 20ft (6m)

An excellent blue-gray cypress, 'Pembury Blue' is a conical tree, bearing numerous sprays of scalelike foliage on its loosely arching branches. Dislikes dry soils.

Cedrus libani subsp. *atlantica* f. *glauca*
BLUE ATLAS CEDAR
☼ 6   ↕ 78ft (24m) ↔ 50ft (15m)

This spectacular conifer is recognizable by its fast growth when young, its wide-spreading habit, barrel-shaped cones, and silver-blue needles. Dislikes dry soils.

Juniperus sabina 'Blue Danube'
SAVIN JUNIPER
☼ 5   ↕ 10in (25cm) ↔ 5ft (1.5m)

Its low, wide-spreading habit makes this a most effective conifer for the rock garden or scree. Branches have ascending tips and are crowded with light blue-gray foliage.

Picea pungens 'Koster'
BLUE COLORADO SPRUCE
☼ 2   ↕ 43ft (13m) ↔ 15ft (5m)

A striking spruce, this is one of several similar selections. It has scaly gray bark, whorled branches, and prickly, needle-like, silver-blue leaves fading to green.

193

TREES

I BELIEVE THAT ALL PLANTS, no matter how small, are important, but, I confess, trees are to me the most inspirational. This is partly due to their size, but more significant is the sense of continuity and permanence that they bring to the garden. To plant a tree, particularly a potentially large or long-lived one, is to express a belief in the future.

△ CRABAPPLE CHEER *The cherrylike crabapples of* Malus *'Red Sentinel', an excellent small tree, last well into winter.*

△ *Quercus canariensis*

THE BEAUTY OF TREES

- Provide a framework or backbone to to the garden to tie in other plants.
- Large trees give permanence and continuity to the garden.
- Give shade for plants and people.
- Deciduous trees change seasonally.
- Offer a variety of shapes and sizes.
- Some make excellent specimens.
- Offer protection from the elements, pollution, noise, and prying eyes.
- Give food and/or shelter for wildlife.

Trees are the anchors in many gardens, holding together diverse design elements. They can offer a seasonal display of flowers, fruit, or foliage, or an attractive habit, as well as provide a useful focal point for one's neighbors. The mountain ash (*Sorbus*), hawthorn (*Crataegus*), and ornamental crabapple (*Malus*) are examples that boast several of these attractive features.

ANNUAL ANTICIPATION
In cooler temperate climates, the number and variety of deciduous trees far exceeds their evergreen counterparts. Evergreen trees do, however, provide an excellent foil, often being used as background trees, screens, or windbreaks, though they should be considered

for prime sites where conditions suit. The miracle of renewal – bud flush, flowering, fruiting, and leaf fall – that deciduous trees annually enact is something we never tire of. All the trees in this section are deciduous unless otherwise stated.

BIG IS NOT ALWAYS BETTER
Trees vary in height and shape, providing plenty of candidates for every type and size of garden. Small trees need not be confined to small gardens, while a single large tree in place of several small ones can provide a welcome focus for all nearby. Whatever your priorities, available space should always be paramount. Large trees need space to develop; it is foolhardy to plant one where space is limited.

△ GLORIOUS GOLD *Striking and very reliable, golden* Robinia pseudocacacia *'Frisia' brightens dull corners in summer.*

◁ DUAL DELIGHT Amelanchier lamarckii's *lovely snow white spring blossoms are matched by its autumn tints.*

▷ NOBLE AUTUMN SPECIMEN *This Tulip Tree (*Liriodendron tulipifera *'Fastigiatum') is ideal for a large lawn.*

Bold Specimens for Large Gardens

TREES THAT ultimately grow to a large size – many native to forests – form an impressive sight in gardens big enough to accommodate them. Where conditions suit, some live to a great age, and may be enjoyed for years to come by future generations.

Catalpa speciosa
WESTERN CATALPA
☼ 4
Vigorous growth
↕ 70ft (20m) ↔ 50ft (15m)

The glossy, dark green leaves of this imposing tree are broad at the base, and each has a narrow point. Bell-shaped white flowers, spotted lightly inside, are carried in large heads in summer, followed by slender, pendulous pods.

Acer saccharinum
SILVER MAPLE
☼ 4
Vigorous growth
↕ 80ft (25m) ↔ 50ft (15m)

This handsome tree weeps and spreads with age. Its slender branchlets carry jagged leaves with silvery undersides that flash when disturbed by the wind. These turn yellow in autumn. Pendulous selections with more finely cut leaves are available.

Fagus sylvatica 'Aspleniifolia'
FERN-LEAVED BEECH
☼ 5
Vigorous growth
↕ 80ft (25m) ↔ 80ft (25m)

A tree that combines impressive stature and grace, this beech is often broader than it is tall and eventually forms a large, dome-shaped crown. The slender, spreading branchlets are clothed in narrow, toothed leaves that turn gold, then brown, in autumn.

Castanea sativa
SWEET, OR SPANISH, CHESTNUT
☼ ☼ 5
Vigorous growth
↕ 80ft (25m) ↔ 50ft (15m)

A magnificent tree that develops reddish brown, ridged bark in time. Clusters of slender summer flower spikes precede prickly capsules that contain the familiar edible chestnuts, and the leaves turn yellow in autumn. Best in rich acid soils.

Liriodendron tulipifera
TULIP TREE, TULIP POPLAR
☼ 5
Vigorous growth
↕ 80ft (25m) ↔ 50ft (15m)

This is one of the noblest ornamental trees, its impressive conical habit spreading with age. Tuliplike flowers appear in early summer, and its distinctively shaped leaves turn yellow in autumn. Seed-grown trees rarely flower until they are 15–20 years old.

T R E

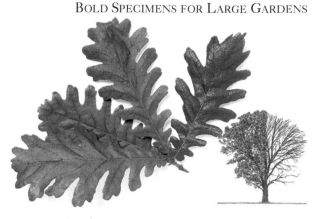

Nothofagus obliqua
ROBLÉ BEECH
☼ 7 PH
Vigorous growth
↕ 70ft (20m) ↔ 60ft (18m)

This elegant relative of the beech comes from the Southern Hemisphere and it develops a domed crown of slightly drooping branches. The deep green leaves turn red and orange in autumn. Happiest in moist but well-drained soils, in a sheltered site.

Quercus frainetto
HUNGARIAN OAK
☼ 6
Vigorous growth
↕ 70ft (20m) ↔ 60ft (18m)

One of the most handsome and distinct of all oaks in leaf, this species has large, glossy green leaves that are boldly and regularly lobed, and borne on stout shoots. Its habit is spreading, and the bark is darkly and deeply fissured. Tolerates most sites and soils.

> **OTHER BOLD SPECIMEN TREES**
>
> *Acer macrophyllum*
> *Acer saccharum*
> *Aesculus flava*
> *Aesculus hippocastanum*
> *Carya ovata*, see p.222
> *Cercidiphyllum japonicum*, see p.222
> *Cladrastis lutea*, see p.208
> *Corylus colurna*
> *Eucalyptus gunnii*
> *Fraxinus americana*
> *Gymnocladus dioicus*
> *Liquidambar styraciflua*
> *Magnolia acuminata*
> *Nyssa sylvatica*
> *Quercus macrocarpa*
> *Quercus virginiana*
> *Tilia tomentosa*
> *Zelkova serrata*

Quercus palustris
PIN OAK
☼ 5 PH
Vigorous growth
↕ 70ft (20m) ↔ 40ft (12m)

Good-looking and dome-shaped, Pin Oak is a superb tree for a large lawn. Spreading branches, the lowest of which are pendent, bear beautiful, sharply lobed leaves. Shining green in summer, they turn spectacular bronze, russet, or red in autumn.

Pterocarya x rehderiana
HYBRID WINGNUT
☼ 6
Vigorous growth
↕ 70ft (20m) ↔ 70ft (20m)

In summer, the branchlets of this walnut relative are draped with long catkins that are replaced by even longer strings of green, winged fruits. Its leaves turn a clear yellow in autumn. Thrives in deep soils, or in a moist situation. An imposing tree at all times.

Zelkova carpinifolia
CAUCASIAN ELM
☼ 6
Slow growth
↕ 100ft (30m) ↔ 80ft (25m)

This slow-growing tree is one to plant for your grandchildren to enjoy. Mature specimens develop a characteristic dense, broad-topped crown with strongly upswept branches and a short, stout stem. Its green leaves often turn orange-brown in autumn.

TREES

Medium-sized Trees

SOME OF THE LOVELIEST trees are found in the medium size range of 20–50ft (6–15m); they are suitable for many average-sized gardens. This selection encompasses the full variety of ornamental effects, from spring flowers, through attractive autumn foliage and berries, to attractive winter bark. All make fine shade or specimen trees.

Magnolia x *loebneri* 'Leonard Messel'
MAGNOLIA
☼ 5
Moderate growth
↕ 30ft (10m) ↔ 20ft (6m)

One of the loveliest of its kind, this magnolia is upright to vase-shaped in habit, becoming conical to rounded in maturity. The leafless branches are flooded during spring with fragrant, multi-petaled, pale lilac-pink flowers, a deeper color when in bud.

Aesculus x *neglecta* 'Erythroblastos'
SUNRISE HORSE CHESTNUT
☼ ☼ 5
Moderate growth
↕ 30ft (10m) ↔ 20ft (6m)

Grown principally for its spring foliage, this is a choice tree of upright habit, spreading later. The leaves are bright pink when they emerge, changing to yellow and then to green. In autumn the leaves turn orange and yellow. Not suitable for exposed sites.

Magnolia 'Wada's Memory'
MAGNOLIA
☼ 5
Moderate growth
↕ 30ft (10m) ↔ 22ft (7m)

This tree has a conical or oval crown. The fragrant white flowers that crowd its dense branches in spring are large, lax, and multi-petaled. Its leaves, aromatic when bruised, are dark green above and paler beneath. Spectacular when in full bloom.

Cornus macrophylla
BIGLEAF DOGWOOD
☼ ☼ 5
Moderate growth
↕ 40ft (12m) ↔ 30ft (10m)

The branches of this uncommon spreading tree grow in glossy, leafy layers. Flattened clusters of small, creamy white flowers are held above the foliage during summer, and are followed by blue-black berries in autumn. An attractive tree of loosely tiered habit.

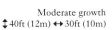

> **OTHER MEDIUM-SIZED TREES GROWN FOR FLOWERS**
>
> *Cladrastis lutea*, see p.208
> *Cornus kousa* var. *chinensis*
> *Davidia involucrata*
> *Koelreuteria paniculata*, see p.207
> *Magnolia* x *loebneri* 'Merrill'
> *Oxydendrum arboreum*, see p.205
> *Pterostyrax hispida*
> *Sorbus alnifolia*, see p.203
> *Stewartia pseudocamellia*, see p.205
> *Styrax obassia*

Malus hupehensis
TEA CRAB
☼ 5
Vigorous growth
↕ 25ft (8m) ↔ 25ft (8m)

The spreading branches of this dense, round-headed tree are crowded in spring with large, fragrant white flowers, pink in bud. Small, dark red fruits held on slender stalks follow and remain after the leaves have fallen, eventually to be eaten by birds.

Prunus jamasakura
HILL CHERRY
☼ 6
Moderate growth
↕ 40ft (12m) ↔ 40ft (12m)

This beautiful cherry has a vase-shaped, later spreading, crown. In spring, the branches are crowded with white or pink blossoms. The leaves are bronze at first, and color richly in autumn. When in full bloom, this tree is visible from a considerable distance.

Prunus avium 'Plena'
DOUBLE SWEET CHERRY
☼ 4
Vigorous growth
↕ 40ft (12m) ↔ 40ft (12m)

In spring, the rounded to spreading crown of this popular, strong-growing flowering cherry is heavily laden with drooping clusters of clear white, double flowers. The leaves turn an attractive red and yellow in autumn. Makes an excellent specimen tree.

OTHER MEDIUM-SIZED TREES GROWN FOR FOLIAGE

Acer triflorum, see p.200
Alnus glutinosa 'Imperialis'
Betula maximowicziana
Eucommia ulmoides
Gleditsia triacanthos cultivars
Parrotia persica, see p.223
Phellodendron amurense
Robinia pseudoacacia 'Frisia', see p.219
Sassafras albidum, see p.205
Tilia mongolica

Styrax japonica
JAPANESE SNOWBELL
☼ 5
Moderate growth
↕ 30ft (10m) ↔ 30ft (10m)

Neat, bright green leaves pack the spreading branches of this dense-headed tree. The undersides of its branches are crowded in early summer with drooping white, star-shaped flowers, each with a yellow beak of stamens.

199

Small Trees for Limited Space

SELECTING a single tree for a small space is a pleasant but difficult task because there are so many attractive candidates. Plant any of the suggestions here, alone as a specimen, or perhaps along your property line, where it can be enjoyed by neighbors or passersby.

Aesculus pavia 'Atrosanguinea'
DARK RED BUCKEYE
Slow growth
☼ 4
↕ 15ft (5m) ↔ 12ft (4m)

Because of its slow growth and compact, dome-shaped habit, this tree makes an ideal lawn specimen. The dark green leaves form an excellent backdrop for its red, tubular summer flowers. These are followed by smooth-skinned, pale brown fruits.

Acer palmatum var. *coreanum*
JAPANESE MAPLE
Vigorous growth
☼ ☼ 5
↕ 15ft (5m) ↔ 15ft (5m)

The slender branches of this reliable and easily grown tree are clothed with attractive green leaves that become a spectacular red-orange in autumn. Tiny, reddish purple flower clusters emerge with the leaves in spring. Dislikes dry soils.

Acer triflorum
THREEFLOWER MAPLE
Slow growth
☼ 5
↕ 25ft (8m) ↔ 22ft (7m)

The rugged, peeling gray-brown bark of this handsome maple is especially noticeable in winter. Its leaves, consisting of three hairy leaflets, give brilliant gold, orange, and red autumn tints. The small, greenish yellow flowers appear in clusters in late spring.

Cornus alternifolia   'Argentea'
VARIEGATED PAGODA DOGWOOD
Moderate growth
☼ 4
↕ 10ft (3m) ↔ 6ft (2m)

In time, distinct layers of slender branches with narrow leaves create a pagoda effect, making this a perfect specimen tree. You can prune and train it to a single stem or leave it with branches to the base. Its small clusters of white flowers appear in spring.

TREES

Cornus florida 'White Cloud'
FLOWERING DOGWOOD
☼ 5
Moderate growth
↕ 15ft (5m) ↔ 20ft (6m)

This low, bushy tree with a spreading crown needs space
to expand. It has two main seasons of interest – the first in spring,
when distinctive white flowerheads appear, and the second in
autumn, when dark green leaves become suffused red and purple.

Rhus trichocarpa
SUMAC
☼ 7
Moderate growth
↕ 22ft (7m) ↔ 22ft (7m)

In autumn, the large, deeply divided, ashlike green leaves of this
spreading tree provide purplish, then orange and red tints,
alongside the drooping clusters of bristly yellow fruits. The sap
of this sumac is poisonous and may cause an allergic reaction.

Eucalyptus pauciflora subsp. *niphophila*
SNOW GUM
☼ 7
Moderate growth
↕ 30ft (10m) ↔ 25ft (8m)

One of the most popular of all eucalypts, this is worth growing for
its evergreen gray-green leaves and its fluffy clusters of white
summer flowers. It is best known, however, for its beautiful bark
– green, gray, cream, and silver create a marbled effect.

OTHER SMALL TREES

Acer griseum, see p.226
Acer japonicum 'Aureum'
Amelanchier x *grandiflora*
Aralia elata
Carpinus caroliniana
Magnolia virginiana
Malus 'Red Jewel'
Ostrya virginiana
Prunus 'Okame'
Prunus 'Spire'
Viburnum prunifolium

△ *Sorbus vilmorinii*
'Pearly King'

Eucryphia glutinosa
EUCRYPHIA
☼ 8 PH
Moderate growth
↕ 20ft (6m) ↔ 15ft (5m)

This much-branched, rather bushy tree has shining, dark green
leaflets that turn orange and red in autumn. Clusters of fragrant,
roselike flowers occur from mid- to late summer. It prefers a
moist but well-drained soil with its roots shaded from the sun.

Sorbus vilmorinii
CHINESE MOUNTAIN ASH
☼ 6
Moderate growth
↕ 12ft (4m) ↔ 15ft (5m)

The arching branches of this elegant tree are clothed in neat
sprays of fernlike leaves that color orange or red in autumn. It
bears white flowers in late spring, and loose clusters of small pink
berries from autumn into early winter. 'Pearly King' is similar.

T R E E S

201

Trees Tolerant of Heavy Clay Soils

CLAY SOILS are frequently among the most fertile in gardens, although their physical characteristics do cause problems. Gardeners can take heart from the following selection of trees, all of which will grow happily in heavy clay, as long as it is not waterlogged.

Alnus incana
GRAY ALDER
☼ 2   Moderate growth
‡ 60ft (18m) ↔ 30ft (10m)

This is a tough and adaptable tree with a loosely conical habit. Its dark green leaves are strongly veined, and each has a downy gray underside. Drooping yellow catkins drape the branches in late winter or early spring. Gray Alder dislikes dry soils.

Catalpa bignonioides
CATALPA, INDIAN BEAN TREE
☼ 5   Moderate growth
‡ 40ft (12m) ↔ 50ft (15m)

Often broader than it is high, this is a bold, spreading tree. It has light green, heart-shaped leaves, purple-tinged when young, and bears large, loose heads of bell flowers with purple and yellow spots in summer. These are followed by long, thin seed pods.

Aesculus hippocastanum 'Baumannii'
DOUBLE HORSE CHESTNUT
☼ 4   Vigorous growth
‡ 100ft (30m) ↔ 50ft (15m)

A large tree with a spreading crown, Double Horse Chestnut has bold leaves, each divided into broad, fingerlike leaflets. It produces erect, conical spires of double white flowers in spring, which have red or yellow markings. Nonfruiting.

Cotoneaster frigidus
TREE COTONEASTER
☼ ☼ 7   Vigorous growth
‡ 30ft (10m) ↔ 30ft (10m)

Although it is most often multistemmed with a spreading crown, this cotoneaster can be trained to a single stem. It carries large leaves, and white flowerheads in early summer, to be followed in autumn and early winter by bold bunches of red fruit.

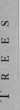

+ Laburnocytisus adamii
ADAM'S LABURNUM
☼ 5   Moderate growth   ↕ 25ft (8m) ↔ 22ft (7m)

This tree resembles a laburnum in habit and leaf, but the tassels of both yellow and pink flowers that are produced in late spring or early summer are accompanied by the occasional fuzzy clump of purple-flowered blooms.

Quercus robur
ENGLISH OAK
☼ 5   Slow growth   ↕ 80ft (25m) ↔ 80ft (25m)

A famous tree, and one that is very popular in English folk culture, the English Oak fully justifies its position as a symbol of toughness and longevity. Its rugged bark, wavy-lobed green leaves, and long-stalked acorns are among its credentials.

Magnolia x
soulangiana ▷

Magnolia x *soulangiana*
SAUCER MAGNOLIA
☼ 4   Moderate growth   ↕ 20ft (6m) ↔ 22ft (7m)

Fragrant, goblet-shaped white, pink, or purple-flushed blooms grace this magnolia in spring and often sporadically throughout summer. It has a spreading, low-branched crown and bold foliage. There are many excellent cultivars.

OTHER TREES TOLERANT OF HEAVY CLAY SOILS

Betula utilis var. *jacquemontii*,
see p.226
Carpinus betulus 'Fastigiata'
Crataegus viridis 'Winter King'
Eucalyptus glaucescens
Ilex opaca
Malus hupehensis, see p.199
Platanus acerifolia, see p.213
Prunus 'Okame'
Quercus palustris, see p.197
Salix pentandra
Sorbus aucuparia, see p.214
Tilia mongolica

Populus maximowiczii
POPLAR
☼ 4   Vigorous growth   ↕ 70ft (20m) ↔ 30ft (10m)

This poplar is a tall tree with ascending, then shortly spreading, branches. Its bold, heart-shaped, bright green leaves turn yellow in autumn. The spring catkins produced by female trees ripen to fluffy white in summer. Dislikes dry soils.

Sorbus alnifolia
KOREAN MOUNTAIN ASH
☼ ☼ 4   Moderate growth   ↕ 35ft (11m) ↔ 25ft (8m)

The crown of this tough and adaptable tree is conical or oval, and spreads later. Its bright green leaves become orange and red in autumn. White flower clusters are produced in late spring, and these are followed by bright red fruits in autumn.

TREES

203

Trees for Acid Soils

EW TREES WILL ACTUALLY FAIL to grow in alkaline soils, but quite a few perform poorly in such places, preferring to grow in soils of an acid or neutral reaction. The trees shown here grow best in acid soils, provided they are reasonably fertile and sufficient moisture is available during the growing season, usually summer.

Magnolia fraseri
FRASER'S MAGNOLIA
☀ 5 PH
Moderate growth
↕ 30ft (10m) ↔ 25ft (8m)

Uncommon in general cultivation, this attractive, loose-spreading magnolia is easily distinguished by its enormous green leaves. The large, fragrant flowers are carried from late spring into early summer, and may be followed by cylindrical red fruit clusters.

Cornus nuttallii
PACIFIC DOGWOOD
☀ ☀ 7 PH
Vigorous growth
↕ 43ft (13m) ↔ 25ft (8m)

The dark green leaves of this beautiful tree become yellow or red in autumn. Tiny spring flowers borne in tight clusters are surrounded by large white bracts and are followed by showy red fruit clusters. Thrives in moist but well-drained soils.

TREES TOLERANT OF BOTH HIGH ACIDITY AND HIGH ALKALINITY
Betula pendula
Crataegus monogyna
Fagus sylvatica, see p.215
Ilex aquifolium
Populus alba, see p.214
Populus canescens
Quercus cerris
Quercus robur, see p.203
Sorbus x *hybrida*
Sorbus intermedia

Eucryphia x *nymansensis*
EUCRYPHIA
☀ ☀ 8 PH
Moderate growth
↕ 43ft (13m) ↔ 20ft (6m)

From late summer into early autumn, the shoots of this compact, columnar evergreen tree are crowded with clusters of white rose-like flowers. Its leaves are typically divided into glossy green leaflets. Enjoys moist, well-drained soils, with its roots shaded.

Nothofagus procera
RAULI
☀ ☀ 7 PH
Vigorous growth
↕ 70ft (20m) ↔ 40ft (12m)

A straight-stemmed, good-looking tree with its shoots clothed in large, conspicuously veined leaves. These emerge bronze, then become green in summer, giving attractive orange and red tints in autumn. Rauli is not suitable for exposed sites.

T R E E S

OTHER TREES FOR ACID SOILS

Acer rubrum
Embothrium coccineum
Eucryphia glutinosa, see p.201
Franklinia alatamaha
Ilex opaca
Liquidambar styraciflua
Michelia doltsopa
Nothofagus dombeyi
Nyssa sylvatica
Styrax japonicum, see p.199
Styrax obassia

Oxydendrum arboreum
SOURWOOD
☼ ☼ 6 PH ▽   Moderate growth
↕ 40ft (12m) ↔ 25ft (8m)

This conical, later spreading, tree produces handsome, glossy green leaves that turn brilliant red or purple in autumn. Tiny, scented flowers appear in late summer and last into autumn. Thrives in moist, well-drained soils with its roots shaded.

Sassafras albidum
SASSAFRAS
☼ ☼ 5 PH ▽   Moderate growth
↕ 70ft (20m) ↔ 25ft (8m)

Famous for a medicinal tea brewed from its aromatic root bark, this handsome tree is clothed with variously lobed leaves that turn yellow, orange, or purple in autumn. Its rugged bark and pale branches are a winter attraction.

Quercus rubra
RED OAK
☼ 5 PH ▽   Vigorous growth
↕ 80ft (25m) ↔ 70ft (20m)

Suitable for planting as a specimen or a large screen, this bold-foliaged, spreading oak is free-growing. Its large, often deeply lobed leaves turn a deep bronze or brownish red in autumn, and sometimes change to a brighter red.

Stewartia pseudocamellia
JAPANESE STEWARTIA
☼ ☼ 5 PH ▽   Moderate growth
↕ 40ft (12m) ↔ 20ft (6m)

This superb decorative tree has many garden qualities. Spreading in habit, its reddish brown bark flakes with age to form patches that are attractive in winter. White flowers open from midsummer, and the leaves turn a striking orange or red in autumn.

TREES

Trees for Alkaline Soils

Having an alkaline soil in all or part of your garden does not mean your planting choices are limited. Free-draining, and warming faster than most other soils in spring, alkaline soils suit a range of ornamental trees. Many of the trees here will perform quite well in a range of soils, from slightly acid to alkaline.

Albizia julibrissin
MIMOSA, SILK TREE
☼ 6   Vigorous growth
                    ‡ 30ft (10m) ↔ 30ft (10m)

For most of its relatively short life, the Silk Tree is broader than tall, with spreading branches and finely divided, fernlike leaves. Its clusters of fluffy, pink-stamened flowers are produced in late summer and autumn. *A. julibrissin* 'Rosea' is a hardier selection.

Cercis siliquastrum
JUDAS TREE
☼ 6   Moderate growth
                    ‡ 30ft (10m) ↔ 30ft (10m)

Occasionally multistemmed, this more often single-stemmed, spreading tree has heart-shaped blue-green leaves. Rosy lilac pea flowers emerge in spring and are followed by flattened red seed pods. 'Bodnant' is a form with deep purple flowers.

OTHER TREES FOR ALKALINE SOILS
Acer campestre
Acer negundo 'Flamingo'
Acer platanoides, see p.215
Aesculus californica
Aesculus hippocastanum
Arbutus x *andrachnoides*
Fagus sylvatica, see p.215
Ligustrum lucidum
Malus 'Profusion'
Malus 'Red Sentinel', see p.224
Morus nigra
Paulownia tomentosa
Prunus 'Mount Fuji'
Prunus 'Shogetsu'
Prunus 'Ukon'
Quercus macrocarpa
Sophora japonica
Tilia tomentosa

△ *Crataegus orientalis*

Crataegus orientalis
ORIENTAL HAWTHORN
☼ 6   Slow growth
                    ‡ 18ft (5.5m) ↔ 18ft (5.5m)

This slow-growing ornamental hawthorn will eventually develop a dense, rounded crown clothed in deeply lobed, dark green leaves. Clusters of pretty white blossoms emerge in late spring, and its large, downy red fruits are produced in autumn.

Fraxinus ornus
MANNA ASH
☼ 6
Moderate growth
↕ 50ft (15m) ↔ 43ft (13m)

Typically round-headed, this attractive tree has much-divided, pale green leaves and produces large, branched heads of scented, creamy white flowers from late spring into early summer. Bronze-tinted fruits follow. A reliable tree of dense habit.

Malus floribunda
JAPANESE CRABAPPLE
☼ 5
Moderate growth
↕ 25ft (8m) ↔ 30ft (10m)

This is one of the most popular and reliable of all the flowering crabapples. Its dense, rounded crown is flooded in spring with pale pink flowers. Masses of pea-sized yellow, red-cheeked fruits are borne in autumn. Among the first crabapples to flower.

Koelreuteria paniculata
GOLDEN-RAIN TREE
☼ 5
Moderate growth
↕ 30ft (10m) ↔ 30ft (10m)

The leaves of this domed tree, which is sometimes broader than it is tall, are regularly divided into numerous toothed leaflets and turn yellow in autumn. Large, branched, yellow flowerheads in summer are followed by conspicuous, inflated seed pods.

Prunus x *yedoensis*
YOSHINO CHERRY
☼ 6
Moderate growth
↕ 25ft (8m) ↔ 30ft (10m)

Eventually broad-domed, this cherry has wide-spreading, arching branches. In early spring, these are profusely hung with drooping clusters of almond-scented, white or pale blush blossoms, pink in bud. One of the most reliable of all flowering cherries.

Laburnum alpinum
SCOTCH LABURNUM
☼ 5
Moderate growth
↕ 22ft (7m) ↔ 22ft (7m)

Scotch Laburnum is broad-headed, with a short, stocky stem and lush, deep green, three-parted leaves. Long, pendent chains of bright yellow pea flowers appear in late spring or early summer and are deliciously fragrant. All parts are poisonous if eaten.

Sorbus aria 'Lutescens'
WHITEBEAM
☼ 5
Moderate growth
↕ 35ft (11m) ↔ 25ft (8m)

This is an attractive ornamental tree with an erect to oval crown at first, later spreading. Its leaves are creamy white when they first emerge in spring and become gray-green as they mature. White flowers are produced from late spring into early summer.

TREES

Trees for Dry, Sunny Sites

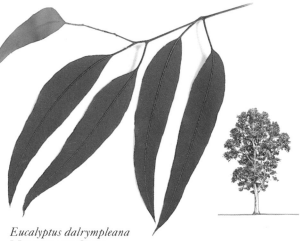

THOSE WITH gardens in dry, sunny places will be all too familiar with the problems that a summer drought can bring to trees. A fast-draining sandy or gravelly soil can be an added difficulty. Fortunately, some trees tolerate, if not relish, such conditions.

Eucalyptus dalrympleana
MOUNTAIN GUM
☼ 8
Vigorous growth
↕ 70ft (20m) ↔ 28ft (9m)

Columnar when young, the handsome Mountain Gum broadens later. Its evergreen leaves are rounded on younger trees, and elongated and drooping later. Leaves are joined by white flower clusters in late summer. Young creamy white bark is attractive.

Celtis australis
SOUTHERN NETTLE TREE
☼ 6
Moderate growth
↕ 60ft (18m) ↔ 50ft (15m)

Uncommon but easy to grow, this ornamental tree has smooth, pale gray bark. It is broadly columnar with a dome-shaped crown, although the branches on older trees are often pendulous. The surfaces of its slender, pointed leaves are rough to the touch.

Cladrastis lutea
YELLOWWOOD
☼ 4
Moderate growth
↕ 40ft (12m) ↔ 40ft (12m)

This excellent ornamental tree has numerous attractive features: a rounded or dome-shaped crown, ashlike leaves that become clear yellow in autumn, and large, branched, drooping heads of fragrant white pea flowers that are produced in summer.

Gleditsia triacanthos 'Sunburst'
SUNBURST HONEYLOCUST
☼ 3
Moderate growth
↕ 30ft (10m) ↔ 25ft (8m)

The stem and branches of this specimen tree are gray-brown. Its pretty, much-divided, glossy leaves are golden yellow when they emerge, darken to green later, then turn pale yellow in autumn. Honeylocusts are tolerant of extreme air pollution.

TREES

Maackia amurensis
MAACKIA
☼ 3
Slow growth
↕ 22ft (7m) ↔ 22ft (7m)

This wide-spreading tree with grayish brown bark has ashlike, deep green leaves, silver-blue when young. Dense, stubby spikes of flowers, white, tinged the palest slate blue, are produced in summer and held in clusters above the branches.

Pittosporum crassifolium 'Variegatum'
VARIEGATED KARO
☼ 9
Moderate growth
↕ 15ft (5m) ↔ 10ft (3m)

Unless trained to a single stem, this evergreen tree with its dense, bushy crown will remain shrubby. The leathery leaves are gray-green with a white margin. Small, scented, reddish purple flowers appear in spring. Karo is excellent for mild coastal areas.

Quercus canariensis
ALGERIAN OAK
☼ 8
Moderate growth
↕ 70ft (20m) ↔ 40ft (12m)

The habit of this distinct and handsome oak is broadly columnar when young, becoming more rounded with age. Its upswept branches are densely covered with large, regularly lobed leaves, which are usually retained into late winter.

Sophora japonica 'Violacea'
PAGODA TREE
☼ 5
Vigorous growth
↕ 60ft (18m) ↔ 60ft (18m)

The gray-brown bark of this round-headed tree is prominently ridged. Its ashlike leaves emerge late in the season, and the loose heads of small white, lilac-tinged pea flowers are borne from late summer into early autumn. Drooping seed pods follow.

OTHER TREES FOR DRY, SUNNY SITES

Arbutus x *andrachnoides*
Cercis siliquastrum, see p.206
Evodia daniellii
Fraxinus velutina
Genista aetnensis
Koelreuteria paniculata, see p.207
Ligustrum lucidum
Phellodendron amurense
Quercus alba
Quercus macrocarpa

Umbellularia californica
CALIFORNIA BAY, HEADACHE TREE
☼ 8
Moderate growth
↕ 40ft (12m) ↔ 30ft (10m)

A relative of sweet bay (*Laurus nobilis*), this dense, bushy-headed evergreen tree produces clusters of delicate yellowish flowers in spring. Its bright green, leathery leaves are pungent if crushed, and the vapor may cause nausea if inhaled.

T R E E S

209

Trees for Watersides

FEW SIGHTS, to me, are more appealing than a weeping willow growing on a river bank. Not many of us are fortunate enough to have a river running through our garden, but there is no reason why a suitable tree should not be planted next to a pool or stretch of water. As long as you maintain a sense of scale, the possibilities are endless.

Pterocarya fraxinifolia
CAUCASIAN WINGNUT
☼ 6
Moderate growth
↕ 80ft (25m) ↔ 70ft (20m)

Eventually a large, broad-spreading tree, this has much-divided, ashlike leaves and long, drooping tassels of green flowers. Its green winged fruits follow. Suckers that appear should always be removed, unless you want to encourage a grove.

Alnus rubra
RED ALDER
☼ 6
Vigorous growth
↕ 50ft (15m) ↔ 30ft (10m)

This is a fast-growing tree of conical habit. In early spring, before the leaves unfurl, its branches are draped with yellowish orange male catkins that can be up to 6in (15cm) long. Its toothed leaves are boldy veined. Older trees have pale gray bark.

OTHER TREES FOR WATERSIDES

Acer rubrum
Alnus glutinosa
Nyssa sylvatica
Populus maximowiczii, see p.203
Quercus bicolor
Salix alba var. *vitellina*
Salix matsudana 'Tortuosa', see p.227
Salix pentandra

△ *Salix* x *sepulcralis* 'Chrysocoma'

Betula nigra
RIVER BIRCH
☼ 4
Moderate growth
↕ 50ft (15m) ↔ 50ft (15m)

River birch is distinctive, quite unlike the more usual white-stemmed kinds. The bark of the stem and main branches is peeling and shaggy, pinkish gray in color, maturing to dark brown. Its leaves are diamond-shaped and pale beneath.

Salix x *sepulcralis* 'Chrysocoma'
GOLDEN WEEPING WILLOW
☼ 3
Vigorous growth
↕ 20m (70ft) ↔ 25m (80ft)

This is a popular subject for the waterside, but it is too large for the small gardens in which it is often planted. It has long curtains of weeping, golden yellow branches in winter. These are covered with slender, bright green leaves in spring and summer.

TREES

Weeping Trees

NOT EVERY GARDENER likes weeping trees. Some find them too messy or sad, but a well-sited weeping tree on a lawn, or by water or a border edge, can add both interest and dramatic effect. To attain a good height, such trees generally require further training to a stake for a few years, especially when bought as young, grafted plants.

Prunus subhirtella 'Pendula Rubra'
WEEPING SPRING CHERRY
☼ 5
Moderate growth
↕ 15ft (5m) ↔ 20ft (6m)

The dome-shaped crown of this beautiful, elegant cherry can be trained to a greater height than 15ft (5m) if desired. Masses of small, deep rose pink, single blossoms, carmine in bud, crowd its slender, weeping branches in spring.

Fagus sylvatica 'Pendula'
WEEPING EUROPEAN BEECH
☼ 5
Vigorous growth
↕ 60ft (18m) ↔ 70ft (20m)

The Weeping European Beech is a magnificent tree for a large lawn. Its arching or spreading branches are all draped with long, hanging branchlets, and it remains attractive throughout the year. Several other forms are also in cultivation.

OTHER WEEPING TREES
Betula pendula 'Youngii'
Cercidiphyllum japonicum 'Pendulum'
Morus alba 'Pendula'
Pyrus salicifolia 'Pendula', see p.220
Sophora japonica 'Pendula'

Salix caprea
'Kilmarnock' ▷

Prunus 'Cheal's Weeping'
CHEAL'S WEEPING CHERRY
☼ 6
Moderate growth
↕ 8ft (2.5m) ↔ 10ft (3m)

Normally low-domed, this small, weeping Japanese cherry tree is very popular in gardens where space is at a premium. In spring, the arching and pendent branches are crowded with bright pink, double flowers. It looks particularly effective by a small pool.

Salix caprea 'Kilmarnock'
KILMARNOCK WILLOW
☼ 5
Vigorous growth
↕ 6ft (2m) ↔ 4½ft (1.4m)

This dense-crowned cultivar of the goat willow is suitable for even the smallest garden. It has numerous weeping branches that, in spring, are studded with silver-gray male catkins that turn yellow as they mature.

TREES

Trees Tolerant of Air Pollution

Sites subject to air pollution would not seem to be ideal areas for growing trees. Given adequate soil preparation and after-care, however, a good variety of trees, both large and small, will perform just as well as they would in places enjoying clean air.

Fraxinus angustifolia
NARROW-LEAVED ASH
☼ 6
Vigorous growth
↕ 70ft (20m) ↔ 40ft (12m)

More elegant in habit than the European Ash *(Fraxinus excelsior)*, this large tree has spreading branches that form an attractive oval to rounded crown. Its leaves are regularly divided into narrow, smooth, glossy green leaflets that become yellow in autumn.

Amelanchier laevis
ALLEGHENY SERVICEBERRY
☼ ☼ 5
Moderate growth
↕ 20ft (6m) ↔ 20ft (6m)

Clusters of white flowers flood the branches of this small, often multistemmed tree or large shrub in spring. It has a dense, spreading habit, and leaves which are bronze in spring, changing to green in summer, and then red or orange in autumn.

Ilex x *altaclerensis* 'Belgica Aurea'
SILVER SENTINEL
☼ ☼ 6
Moderate growth
↕ 25ft (8m) ↔ 10ft (3m)

The bold leaves of this evergreen holly are lance-shaped with occasional spines. They are a mottled gray-green in color, and irregularly edged pale or creamy yellow. From autumn onward, this dense, compact columnar tree also bears red berries.

Crataegus laevigata 'Paul's Scarlet'
PAUL'S SCARLET HAWTHORN
☼ 5
Moderate growth
↕ 20ft (6m) ↔ 25ft (8m)

This is an attractive tree, with a dense, rounded or spreading crown. In late spring and early summer, the branches are covered in numerous clusters of double red flowers. The toothed leaves are glossy dark green. 'Punicea' is similar, with single crimson flowers.

OTHER TREES TOLERANT OF AIR POLLUTION

Acer pseudoplatanus
Aesculus x *carnea* 'Briotii'
Ailanthus altissima
Alnus cordata, see p.215
Carpinus betulus
Catalpa bignonioides, see p.202
Celtis occidentalis
Fraxinus americana
Ginkgo biloba, see p.174
Koelreuteria paniculata, see p.207
Magnolia x *soulangiana*, see p.203
Malus cultivars
Phellodendron amurense
Platanus occidentalis
Populus alba
Quercus rubra
Sophora japonica
Tilia cordata

△ *Crataegus laevigata* 'Paul's Scarlet'

TREES

Prunus dulcis 'Roseoplena'
DOUBLE ALMOND
☼ 7   Moderate growth
                       ↕ 25ft (8m) ↔ 25ft (8m)

In late winter and early spring, the spreading branches of this tree are studded with double, pale pink flowers. These emerge ahead of the dark green, lance-shaped, long, and pointed leaves, brightening the dullest of late winter days.

Laburnum x *waterei* 'Vossii'
VOSS'S LABURNUM
☼ 5   Moderate growth
                       ↕ 22ft (7m) ↔ 22ft (7m)

The crown of this tree, the most commonly planted laburnum, is spreading and crowded with leaves composed of three leaflets. Long, tapering chains of pea flowers hang from its branches in late spring or early summer. All parts are poisonous if eaten.

Pyrus calleryana 'Chanticleer'
ORNAMENTAL PEAR
☼ 6   Moderate growth
                       ↕ 40ft (12m) ↔ 20ft (6m)

Tough and hardy, this compact, conical tree has rounded, glossy green leaves that turn reddish purple in autumn. The branches are hidden by beautiful white blossoms in spring, at which time the tree is clearly visible from afar.

Platanux x *acerifolia*
LONDON PLANE
☼ 5   Moderate growth
                       ↕ 100ft (30m) ↔ 70ft (20m)

This enormous tree develops a massive splotchy stem and a large spreading crown. Broad, maplelike leaves with five big, toothed lobes are carried in summer. From summer onward, strings of bristly, spherical fruits hang on stalks, like baubles.

Robinia pseudoacacia
BLACK LOCUST
☼ 3   Vigorous growth
                       ↕ 70ft (20m) ↔ 40ft (12m)

The shoots of this tough and adaptable tree are prickly, and its leaves ashlike with oval leaflets. Drooping clusters of white pea flowers are fragrant and occur from late spring into early summer. Develops rugged bark in time, and will sucker if pruned hard.

Trees Tolerant of Coastal Exposure

ONLY THE TOUGHEST TREES will survive the twin problems of strong winds and salt spray in seaside gardens. The following are among the most tolerant, and are well worth considering if only as an outer planting to provide shelter for shrubs and perennials.

Populus alba
WHITE POPLAR, ABELE   Vigorous growth
☼ 4   ↕ 70ft (20m) ↔ 43ft (13m)

This well-known, spreading tree has imposing, gray-fissured bark. The leaves, which vary in shape from rounded and toothed to lobed and maplelike, are dark green above and covered below with a white felt, making a striking contrast when blown by wind.

Hippophae rhamnoides
SEA BUCKTHORN   Moderate growth
☼ 3   ↕ 20ft (6m) ↔ 20ft (6m)

Due to its bushy nature, careful pruning and training are needed to make a single- or few-stemmed tree. Narrow, silver-gray leaves crowd the thorny branches. Plant both male and female plants to produce brilliant orange berries that may last all winter.

OTHER TREES TOLERANT OF COASTAL EXPOSURE
Alnus rubra, see p.210
Populus x *canadensis* 'Robusta'
Quercus ilex
Tilia cordata

Salix alba
WHITE WILLOW   Vigorous growth
☼ 2   ↕ 70ft (20m) ↔ 43ft (13m)

A handsome willow of conical habit at first, this soon spreads to be as broad as it is tall. Its narrow silvery leaves shimmer in the sun. Suited to damp places, but do not plant near underground drains, water systems, or buildings because of its invasive roots.

Phillyrea latifolia
PHILLYREA   Slow growth
☼ 8   ↕ 25ft (8m) ↔ 25ft (8m)

This little-known, but valuable, evergreen tree is rather like a small version of the Holly Oak *(Quercus ilex)*. The narrow, glossy, dark green leaves are leathery and toothed. Its tiny cream-yellow flowers are borne in dense clusters from late spring into summer.

Sorbus aucuparia
EUROPEAN MOUNTAIN ASH   Moderate growth
☼ ☼ 3   ↕ 30ft (10m) ↔ 22ft (7m)

The leaves of this gray-barked tree of spreading habit resemble those of an ash, often turning red or yellow in autumn. Clusters of white spring flowers are followed by drooping bunches of orange-red berries, maturing to bright red. Better in cooler areas.

TREES

Trees for Screening or Windbreaks

I N ADDITION TO CONIFERS, various medium-sized to large broad-leaved trees make a good line of defense against persistent winds, and can screen unattractive views or unsightly objects. Many also have ornamental features.

Fagus sylvatica
EUROPEAN BEECH
☼ [5]
Moderate growth
↕ 120ft (35m) ↔ 50ft (15m)

One of the temperate world's most beautiful trees, this matures to form a dome-shaped crown. Smooth gray bark in winter and pale green leaves in spring, turning shiny midgreen in summer and golden yellow in autumn, make this a tree for all seasons.

Acer platanoides
NORWAY MAPLE
☼ [3]
Vigorous growth
↕ 80ft (25m) ↔ 50ft (15m)

One of the most adaptable and reliable of all trees, Norway Maple develops a rounded crown. Yellow-green flower clusters emerge in midspring, before the leaves appear, followed by green winged fruits. The leaves may turn yellow in autumn.

OTHER TREES FOR SCREENING OR WINDBREAKS

Acer pseudoplatanus
Fraxinus americana
Maclura pomifera
Populus x *canadensis* 'Robusta'
Quercus imbricaria
Quercus phellos

△ *Prunus serotina*

Alnus cordata
ITALIAN ALDER
☼ [6]
Vigorous growth
↕ 80ft (25m) ↔ 35ft (11m)

This handsome columnar tree becomes conical later. Bunches of long yellow male catkins drape the branches in late winter or early spring. In summer, its conelike fruits develop among the large, rounded leaves with shining, dark green upper surfaces.

Prunus serotina
BLACK CHERRY
☼ ◐ [3]
Moderate growth
↕ 50ft (15m) ↔ 43ft (13m)

This free-growing tree has an oval crown of pendulous or arching branches. Its deep green, glossy leaves are deciduous, becoming yellow or red in autumn. Small white spring flowers are carried in drooping tassels, and give way to shining black fruits.

Evergreen Trees

APART FROM CONIFERS, evergreen trees are greatly outnumbered by deciduous trees in temperate climates. This makes evergreens all the more desirable in the garden, especially in winter when their rich green, colored, or variegated foliage offers a striking contrast to bare twigs or winter-flowering shrubs. They also provide effective year-round screening.

Pittosporum tenuifolium
KOHUHU
☀ 9   Moderate growth
                                       ↕ 20ft (6m) ↔ 15ft (5m)

Columnar when young, Kohuhu is later dome-shaped and compact. Slender branchlets bear glossy leaves and small, honey-scented, bell-shaped purple flowers appear in late spring. It is excellent as a screen or single specimen, especially in coastal areas.

OTHER EVERGREEN TREES
Arbutus unedo
Drimys winteri
Eucalyptus glaucescens
Ilex opaca
Ilex pedunculosa
Ligustrum lucidum
Magnolia grandiflora
Prunus lusitanica, see p.141
Quercus agrifolia
Quercus virginiana
Trachycarpus fortunei, see p.217

Maytenus boaria
MAITEN
☀ ☀ 9   Moderate growth
                                       ↕ 30ft (10m) ↔ 25ft (8m)

This unusual and elegant tree has an effect not unlike a weeping willow. Erect when young, it gradually broadens into a round-headed tree, its branches well clothed with narrow, glossy green, toothed leaves. Tiny spring flowers are of little ornamental merit.

Myrtus luma
LUMA
☀ ☀ 9   Vigorous growth
                                       ↕ 22ft (7m) ↔ 15ft (5m)

Luma is a splendid year-round performer. From midsummer into autumn the glossy, dark green leaves of this dense-habited tree are interspersed with masses of small white flowers. Golden brown bark peels with age to reveal patches of creamy new bark.

Rhododendron arboreum
TREE RHODODENDRON
☀ 7   Slow growth
                                       ↕ 40ft (12m) ↔ 10ft (3m)

This magnificent, slow-growing rhododendron broadens as it ages. The leaves are leathery and dark green on top, silver or brownish beneath. Red, pink, or occasionally white bell-shaped flowers are carried in dense, globular heads in spring.

Trees with Bold Leaves

YOU CAN TRANSFORM your garden by growing a tree with bold foliage. A single specimen with leaves of impressive size is worth planting in its own right, creating a tropical effect in the most mundane planting. Bold foliage can also be effective when contrasted with smaller-leaved subjects. Many bold-foliaged trees have the further bonus of attractive flowers and fruits.

Toona sinensis
CHINESE TOON TREE
☼ 6
Vigorous growth
↕ 50ft (15m) ↔ 30ft (10m)

This fast-growing tree has large, much-divided leaves that can grow up to 24in (60cm) long. These are bronze-red when young and turn yellow in autumn. In summer, mature trees carry large, drooping heads of small, fragrant white flowers.

> ### OTHER TREES WITH BOLD LEAVES
> *Aralia elata* 'Variegata'
> *Catalpa bignonioides*, see p.202
> *Firmiana simplex*
> *Liriodendron tulipifera*, see p.196
> *Paulownia tomentosa*

Kalopanax pictus
CASTOR ARALIA
☼ 5
Moderate growth
↕ 40ft (12m) ↔ 30ft (10m)

A handsome tree, this has prickly stems and trunk, and maple-like leaves that turn yellow in autumn. Rounded clusters of tiny whitish flowers in late summer are followed by blue-black berries. Thrives in moist, well-drained soils.

Magnolia hypoleuca
JAPANESE BIG-LEAF MAGNOLIA
☼ 5 PH
Vigorous growth
↕ 70ft (20m) ↔ 30ft (10m)

The large, firm leaves of this magnificent conical tree, broadest in their upper halves, are carried in impressive whorls at the ends of the branches. Strongly fragrant, bowl-shaped flowers are borne in summer and followed by cylindrical red fruit clusters.

Trachycarpus fortunei
CHUSAN PALM, WINDMILL PALM
☼ 8
Slow growth
↕ 25ft (8m) ↔ 8ft (2.5m)

This is probably the hardiest palm suitable for cool, temperate regions, especially in coastal areas. It is a familiar sight, with its shaggy, fibrous bark, rounded head of fan-shaped, many-fingered leaves, and sprays of fragrant creamy flowers in early summer.

Trees with Variegated Leaves

BESIDES the novelty appeal they afford, trees with variegated leaves are valuable when used as a contrast against plain green or darker-leaved subjects. This is particularly true of foliage whose variegation consists of a strong white or yellow margin against green.

Ilex x *altaclerensis* 'Camelliifolia Variegata'
HIGHCLERE HOLLY

☼ ☼ 6   Slow growth
                                                                 ↕ 25ft (8m) ↔ 10ft (3m)

This broadly columnar evergreen is densely packed with short-spreading branches that reach all the way down to the base. Its oblong leaves are glossy dark green, and each has a broad yellow margin. Bears red berries when pollinated.

Liriodendron tulipifera 'Aureomarginatum'
VARIEGATED TULIP TREE

☼ 5   Vigorous growth
                                                               ↕ 60ft (18m) ↔ 35ft (11m)

Strong-growing and erect, this tree spreads with age. Its peculiarly shaped leaves are dark green with yellow margins in full sun, and pale to light green in shade. They turn a golden color in autumn. Established trees produce cup-shaped, greenish white flowers.

Cornus controversa 'Variegata'
JAPENESE PAGODA DOGWOOD

☼ 5   Slow growth
                                                                 ↕ 30ft (10m) ↔ 30ft (10m)

As a lawn specimen, this beautiful tree is unmatched. Frequently broader than it is high, it develops a tabulated, or tiered, crown of spreading branches, ideally to ground level. These are clothed with slender-pointed leaves, broadly margined creamy white.

OTHER VARIEGATED TREES
Acer negundo 'Flamingo'
Acer platanoides 'Drummondii'
Cornus florida 'Welchii'
Fagus sylvatica 'Tricolor'
Liquidambar styraciflua 'Variegata'

Quercus cerris 'Variegata'
VARIEGATED TURKEY OAK

☼ 6   Moderate growth
                                                               ↕ 30ft (10m) ↔ 40ft (12m)

This broad-spreading oak needs to be given plenty of space to develop and is one of the most effective hardy, variegated trees. Its branches are crowded with bristle-toothed, deeply lobed, dark green, glossy leaves, each with an irregular, creamy white margin.

TREES

Trees with Golden or Yellow Leaves

FLOWERING DISPLAYS ASIDE, no trees bring a brighter effect to the garden than those with golden or yellow foliage. A single tree of this kind, especially in a lawn, immediately attracts attention, as well as providing a bold contrast to a plain or dark background.

Ptelea trifoliata 'Aurea'
GOLDEN HOP TREE
☼ ☼ 4
Moderate growth
↕ 10ft (3m) ↔ 10ft (3m)

The aromatic, three-parted leaves of this small, round-headed or bushy tree are soft yellow when young, maturing through yellow-green to green. It is less harsh on the eye than most other golden trees. Greenish summer flowers are followed by winged fruits.

Acer shirasawanum 'Aureum'
GOLDEN FULLMOON MAPLE
☼ ☼ 5
Slow growth
↕ 18ft (5.5m) ↔ 15ft (5m)

This beautiful maple is upright to begin with, and spreads later. Its rounded, many-lobed leaves are golden yellow, often with a thin scarlet edge. It is one of the best golden-leaved trees but may be susceptible to sun scorch, particularly in hot, dry sites.

Quercus rubra 'Aurea'
GOLDEN RED OAK
☼ ☼ 5 PH
Slow growth
↕ 50ft (15m) ↔ 30ft (10m)

Although it is seldom planted, Golden Red Oak is a lovely tree, with a spreading crown of large, boldly lobed leaves. These are a clear, soft yellow when they emerge, becoming green later. It prefers a site that is sheltered from cold winds.

Catalpa bignonioides 'Aurea'
GOLDEN CATALPA
☼ 5
Moderate growth
↕ 30ft (10m) ↔ 30ft (10m)

Eventually, Golden Catalpa grows to be domed or round-headed. The large, heart-shaped leaves are bronze-purple when young and mature to bright yellow. Its bell-shaped white flowers with purple and yellow spots are produced in summer.

Robinia pseudoacacia 'Frisia'
GOLDEN BLACK LOCUST
☼ ☼ 4
Moderate growth
↕ 50ft (15m) ↔ 25ft (8m)

This is one of the most popular and commonly planted golden-leaved trees. Its much-divided, ashlike leaves are a rich golden color when young, maturing through yellow to greenish yellow. They then become orange-yellow in autumn.

TREES

Trees with Blue-gray or Silver Leaves

COMPARED with the abundance of shrubs, there are very few trees with blue-gray or silver leaves suitable for gardens in cool, temperate climates. Fortunately, the few that are encompass a wide range of sizes. Their presence can contribute much to the garden.

Pyrus salicifolia 'Pendula'
WEEPING WILLOW-LEAVED PEAR
☼ 5
Vigorous growth
↕ 25ft (8m) ↔ 20ft (6m)

This is a popular small tree that will form a domed or mushroom-shaped crown of arching and weeping branches, each clothed in narrow gray, downy leaves. The white flowers produced in spring are followed by small green fruits. Easy and reliable.

Elaeagnus 'Quicksilver'
OLEASTER
☼ 4
Moderate growth
↕ 15ft (5m) ↔ 15ft (5m)

Although it has a bushy habit, this oleaster can be trained on a single stem to form a small tree (as can many large shrubs), with a loose, spreading crown of narrow silver-gray leaves. Fragrant, star-shaped, creamy yellow flowers open in late spring or summer.

OTHER TREES WITH BLUE-GRAY OR SILVER LEAVES
Elaeagnus angustifolia
Eucalyptus coccifera
Eucalyptus glaucescens
Eucalyptus gunnii
Populus alba, see p.214
Populus alba 'Raket'
Pyrus nivalis
Salix alba f. *argentea*
Salix exigua, see p.153
Tilia petiolaris

△ *Sorbus thibetica*
'John Mitchell'

Eucalyptus perriniana
SPINNING GUM
☼ 8
Vigorous growth
↕ 20ft (6m) ↔ 12ft (4m)

The stems of this small evergreen tree are darkly blotched and they have a white sheen. The leaves on juvenile trees are round and a shimmering silver-blue, but as the tree matures, its leaves are larger and longer, and their color more blue-green.

Sorbus thibetica 'John Mitchell'
HIMALAYAN WHITEBEAM
☼ ☼ 6
Vigorous growth
↕ 40ft (12m) ↔ 30ft (10m)

This broad, eventually round-headed, tree produces large leaves that are gray-green above and become green and white-felted beneath. Leaves of young, vigorous trees can be more than 6in (15cm) long. Clusters of white flowers appear in late spring.

Trees with Purple, Red, or Bronze Leaves

PURPLE- OR BRONZE-LEAVED trees in a garden do not appeal to all gardeners, and there is no doubt that such a strong color can be an eyesore in the wrong place. Used with discretion, however, purple foliage can be very effective, especially when contrasted with shades of silver or blue-gray.

Acer platanoides 'Crimson King'
NORWAY MAPLE
☼ 3   Vigorous growth
↕ 60ft (18m) ↔ 50ft (15m)

One of the most commonly planted trees of this color, 'Crimson King' is a large tree with sharply-toothed, deep crimson-purple leaves. Even the clusters of small, deep yellow flowers that occur in spring have a reddish tinge. Displays rich autumn color.

Fagus sylvatica f. *purpurea*
PURPLE BEECH, COPPER BEECH
☼ 5   Vigorous growth
↕ 100ft (30m) ↔ 75ft (22.5m)

This striking, round-headed beech is the largest tree of its color. The oval, wavy-margined leaves are shiny purple, turning a rich coppery color in autumn. 'Riversii' is also an excellent selection, with rich autumn tints, and is one of the most commonly planted.

> **OTHER TREES WITH PURPLE, RED, OR BRONZE LEAVES**
>
> *Acer palmatum*, many cultivars
> *Gleditsia triacanthos* 'Rubylace'
> *Malus* 'Liset'
> *Prunus virginiana* 'Schubert'

△ *Prunus cerasifera* 'Nigra'

Cercis canadensis 'Forest Pansy'
REDBUD
☼ 6   Moderate growth
↕ 25ft (8m) ↔ 25ft (8m)

This is a small, often multistemmed, tree with a broad, rounded crown. It has relatively large, heart-shaped leaves that are a rich reddish purple. The small pink pea flowers, which are borne in spring, are not always freely produced.

Prunus cerasifera 'Nigra'
PURPLE-LEAVED PLUM
☼ 5   Moderate growth
↕ 30ft (10m) ↔ 30ft (10m)

In spring, the branches of this commonly planted, dense-headed tree are flooded with pink flowers. These are followed by its red leaves that turn to blackish purple. 'Pissardii' is a very similar and an equally popular cultivar with white, pink-budded blooms.

TREES

Trees for Autumn Color

FEW SIGHTS warm the heart more than a Japanese maple in autumn, its canopy a blaze of color. The foliage of many other trees, however, offers equally rich tints, and also more subtle shades of yellow, pink, and purple. These are some of the most reliable.

Amelanchier lamarckii
SNOWY SERVICEBERRY   Moderate growth
☼ ☀ 4   ↕ 70ft (20m) ↔ 50ft (15m)

A superb tree, Snowy Serviceberry has two main seasons of interest: spring, when the bushy crown is a cloud of white blossoms, and autumn, when it is ablaze with red and orange foliage. Dislikes dry soils. A most reliable tree for autumn color.

Acer palmatum 'Osakazuki'
JAPANESE MAPLE   Moderate growth
☼ ☀ 5   ↕ 20ft (6m) ↔ 20ft (6m)

This beautiful tree is commonly acknowledged to be one of the most impressive and reliable of its kind. It is rounded and bushy, with seven-lobed leaves that turn a brilliant scarlet in autumn. All the Japanese maples dislike exposed sites and dry soils.

Carya ovata
SHAGBARK HICKORY   Moderate growth
☼ ☀ 4   ↕ 70ft (20m) ↔ 50ft (15m)

The bold, divided, ashlike leaves of this robust tree, which has an ultimately spreading crown, turn a rich golden yellow in autumn. Its grayish brown bark peels in vertical plates. This is the most reliable member of a colorful group of hickories.

Acer rubrum 'Schlesingeri'
RED MAPLE   Moderate growth
☼ 4   ↕ 50ft (15m) ↔ 40ft (12m)

'Schlesingeri' is an old selection, but still one of the earliest and best of its color. The three- to five-lobed leaves turn wine-red and have contrasting pale undersurfaces, which are eye-catching even when shed and lying on the ground.

Cercidiphyllum japonicum
KATSURA TREE   Vigorous growth
☼ ☀ 5   ↕ 60ft (18m) ↔ 50ft (15m)

This is a lovely tree of graceful, spreading habit, with slender branches. Its rounded, paired leaves are bronze when they first unfurl, changing through blue-green in summer to yellow, pink, or purple in autumn, with a sweet fragrance. Dislikes dry soils.

Nyssa sinensis
CHINESE TUPELO
☼ ☀ 7
Moderate growth
↕ 40ft (12m) ↔ 30ft (10m)

Erect or conical when young, this tree spreads with maturity. Its long, narrow leaves emerge purplish, turn green, and become a brilliant scarlet in autumn, perhaps equal to the American tupelo *(N. sylvatica)* in autumn effect. Dislikes dry soils.

Cotinus 'Grace'
SMOKE TREE
☼ ☀ 5
Vigorous growth
↕ 15ft (5m) ↔ 15ft (5m)

This can be a small, bushy, round-headed tree or a large, multi-stemmed shrub. The striking leaves are wine purple in summer, coloring to a brilliant orange-red later. Large plumes of purplish pink flowers are produced in summer.

OTHERS FOR AUTUMN COLOR

Acer saccharum
Fraxinus americana
Nyssa sylvatica
Oxydendrum arboreum, see p.205
Phellodendron amurense
Prunus sargentii
Quercus coccinea

Parrotia persica
PERSIAN IRONWOOD
☼ ☀ 5
Moderate growth
↕ 22ft (7m) ↔ 40ft (12m)

Persian Ironwood will eventually become a broad, spreading tree with mottled bark. It produces small red flower clusters in late winter or early spring, and its glossy green leaves turn yellow, orange, and red-purple in autumn. Dislikes dry soils.

Liquidambar styraciflua 'Lane Roberts'
SWEET GUM
☼ ☀ 5
Moderate growth
↕ 70ft (20m) ↔ 35ft (11m)

One of the darkest and most reliable of all the autumn-coloring trees, this handsome specimen of conical, later spreading, habit has shining green maplelike leaves that turn through a range of colors from pale orange to deep red-purple. Dislikes dry soils.

Rhus typhina 'Dissecta'
CUTLEAF STAGHORN SUMAC
☼ 4
Vigorous growth
↕ 10ft (3m) ↔ 15ft (5m)

Generally wider than it is tall, this low-crowned tree has deeply divided, fernlike leaves that are large and downy. They turn orange-red in autumn, when dense, conical clusters of red fruits are borne. Sensitive skin may react to the sap of this sumac.

Trees with Autumn-to-winter Fruit

MANY TREES produce attractive fruits during autumn, but few carry them into winter, when they are of most ornamental value to gardeners, frequently hanging from or clinging to the often leafless branches. Birds, too, appreciate these during the winter months.

Malus 'John Downie'
CRABAPPLE
☼ 5
Moderate growth
↕ 25ft (8m) ↔ 15ft (5m)

This ornamental crabapple is erect at first, and spreads with maturity. White blossoms are carried in spring. The slightly elongated, red-flushed orange crabapples that crowd the branches from autumn onward are edible.

Malus 'Professor Sprenger'
CRABAPPLE
☼ 5
Moderate growth
↕ 18ft (5.5m) ↔ 18ft (5.5m)

From autumn onward, this free-fruiting crabapple with a dense, dome-shaped crown bears little, rounded orange-red fruit. Its pink-budded white flowers open in spring, and the glossy green leaves become yellow in autumn.

Ilex x *altaclerensis* 'Lawsoniana'
HIGHCLERE HOLLY
☼ ☼ 6
Moderate growth
↕ 30ft (10m) ↔ 15ft (5m)

This is a dense evergreen holly with a wide, columnar habit that broadens further with age. It has large, yellow-splashed leaves and a heavy crop of red berries from autumn onward. Plant a male form nearby for pollination.

OTHER TREES WITH AUTUMN-TO-WINTER FRUIT

Arbutus unedo
Crataegus phaenopyrum
Crataegus viridis 'Winter King'
Idesia polycarpa
Ilex aquifolium, many cultivars
Ilex opaca
Malus 'Donald Wyman'
Malus 'Winter Gold'
Melia azedarach
Phellodendron amurense

Malus 'Red Sentinel'
CRABAPPLE
☼ 5
Moderate growth
↕ 18ft (5.5m)) ↔ 18ft (5.5m)

One of the best fruiting crabapples for the smaller garden, this develops a compact, rounded crown. White flowers are borne in spring, and the autumn clusters of glossy-skinned, cherrylike fruits mature to bright red, lasting well into winter.

TREES

Photinia davidiana
STRANVAESIA

☼ ☼ 6   Moderate growth
↕ 15ft (5m) ↔ 15ft (5m)

Although it is often grown as a large evergreen shrub, this can be trained on a single stem to form a small tree. White flowers are produced in early summer, and the clusters of bright red berries that appear in autumn last through the winter months.

Sorbus forrestii
MOUNTAIN ASH

☼ ☼ 7   Moderate growth
↕ 20ft (6m) ↔ 20ft (6m)

Each leaf of this small, rounded tree is composed of numerous blue-green leaflets. Flattened heads of white flowers are carried in late spring, and the large bunches of small white berries that emerge in the autumn persist all through winter.

Sorbus cashmiriana
KASHMIR MOUNTAIN ASH

☼ ☼ 5   Moderate growth
↕ 25ft (8m) ↔ 25ft (8m)

Erect when young, this openly branched tree has divided leaves that become gold or russet in autumn. Blush pink flowers open in early summer, and the clusters of marble-sized white berries decorate the branches from autumn onward.

Sorbus 'Joseph Rock'
MOUNTAIN ASH

☼ ☼ 7   Vigorous growth
↕ 30ft (10m) ↔ 18ft (5.5m)

One of the showiest of all mountain ashes, 'Joseph Rock' has the characteristic vase-shaped crown that spreads with age. Its rich green, regularly divided leaves color brilliantly in autumn, when the yellow berries, carried in drooping bunches, ripen.

Sorbus commixta
JAPANESE MOUNTAIN ASH

☼ ☼ 6   Vigorous growth
↕ 30ft (10m) ↔ 18ft (5.5m)

This is a handsome tree with ascending, eventually spreading, branches. It has white flowers in spring, and regularly divided leaves that color richly in autumn. Large bunches of red berries are borne from autumn onward.

Sorbus scalaris
MOUNTAIN ASH

☼ ☼ 5   Moderate growth
↕ 30ft (10m) ↔ 30ft (10m)

The glossy green leaves of this wide-spreading tree grow in neat rosettes, turning red and purple in autumn. Flattened white flowerheads appear in late spring, and its large, densely packed bunches of red berries persist from autumn into winter.

Ornamental Bark or Shoots in Winter

THE BARK of many trees is attractive or interesting when examined closely, but some trees have colored or peeling bark that is especially ornamental. Others boast colored or unusually twisted shoots that have visual appeal, particularly in winter.

Arbutus menziesii
MADRONE
☼ 7
Moderate growth
‡ 50ft (15m) ↔ 40ft (12m)

Madrone is a handsome evergreen tree with a spreading crown of dark green leaves. The smooth reddish bark peels away to reveal its pea green, new bark. White urn-shaped flowers are produced in early summer; these are followed by orange-red fruits.

Acer griseum
PAPERBARK MAPLE
☼ ☼ 5
Moderate growth
‡ 30ft (10m) ↔ 25ft (8m)

Famous for its peeling, papery orange-brown bark, this maple has the characteristic three-parted leaves that turn orange and red in autumn. The branches are ascending at first, spreading later. It is excellent for growing in a border or a large lawn.

△ *Betula utilis*
var. *jacquemontii*

Acer palmatum 'Senkaki'
CORALBARK MAPLE
☼ ☼ 6
Moderate growth
‡ 20ft (6m) ↔ 20ft (6m)

In their first year, the winter shoots of this stunning Japanese maple, borne on ascending branches, are an attractive coral-pink, darkening later. The neatly lobed leaves are orange-yellow in spring, mature to green, and then turn yellow in autumn.

Betula utilis var. *jacquemontii*
WEST HIMALAYAN BIRCH
☼ ☼ 6
Vigorous growth
‡ 50ft (15m) ↔ 25ft (8m)

This strong-growing birch is popular for the white bark of its stem and branches. Its leaves turn yellow in autumn. 'Silver Shadow' and 'Grayswood Ghost' are selections with similarly white bark, as is 'Jermyns', whose catkins drape the branches in spring.

OTHER TREES WITH ORNAMENTAL
BARK OR SHOOTS IN WINTER

Acer pensylvanicum 'Erythrocladum'
Betula nigra, see p.210
Betula 'Whitespire'
Myrtus luma, see p.216
Platanus occidentalis
Pseudocydonia sinensis
Salix alba var. *vitellina*
Stewartia pseudocamellia, see p.205
Syringa reticulata
Ulmus parvifolia

△ *Prunus serrula*

△ *Eucalyptus
pauciflora* subsp.
niphophila

Prunus serrula
PAPERBARK CHERRY
☼ 6
Moderate growth
↕ 30ft (10m) ↔ 30ft (10m)

Its mahogany red, polished and peeling bark makes this one of the most popular of all cherry trees. Small, inconspicuous white flowers are produced in spring. Its slender, lance-shaped, pointed green leaves become yellow in autumn.

Eucalyptus pauciflora subsp. *niphophila*
SNOW GUM
☼ 8
Moderate growth
↕ 30ft (10m) ↔ 25ft (8m)

The leathery gray-green leaves of this evergreen grow on glossy shoots, bloomy white when young. The bark of its main branches and stem flakes to form a patchwork of gray, cream, and green. Fluffy summer flowerheads are white. Plant when small.

△ *Salix
matsudana*
'Tortuosa'

Prunus maackii
MANCHURIAN BIRD CHERRY
☼ ☼ 2
Moderate growth
↕ 40ft (12m) ↔ 30ft (10m)

Conical at first, this tree eventually spreads. Its smooth, glossy, yellowish brown or amber bark peels in bands like that of a birch. Small white flower spikes are produced in spring, and its leaves turn yellow in autumn. 'Amber Beauty' also has attractive bark.

Salix matsudana 'Tortuosa'
DRAGON'S CLAW WILLOW
☼ 6
Vigorous growth
↕ 50ft (15m) ↔ 30ft (10m)

Erect when young, and spreading later, this willow is easy to recognize. Its long, twisted branches and shoots are clothed with narrow, contorted leaves. When the branches are bare in winter, the dramatic outline of this tree is very striking.

T R E E S

Multipurpose Trees

WHEN CHOOSING a suitable tree for your garden, it makes sense to consider those offering more than one attraction. This is particularly important in small gardens, where space is limited. Fortunately, many trees offer a combination of ornamental features such as attractive flowers, fruit, and foliage, or impressive autumn color and winter bark.

Photinia villosa
ORIENTAL PHOTINIA
☼ ☀ 5 PH ▼   Moderate growth   ↕ 15ft (5m) ↔ 15ft (5m)

This versatile, wide-spreading shrub or small tree has dark green leaves that are bronze-tinted when young, turning a magnificent fiery orange-red in autumn. Clusters of white flowers open in spring, and small red fruits are carried from late summer onward.

△ *Acer capillipes*

Acer capillipes
SNAKEBARK MAPLE
☼ 5   Moderate growth   ↕ 30ft (10m) ↔ 25ft (8m)

Bark and autumn color are the principal attributes of this most attractive maple with spreading branches, and three-lobed leaves that color richly. The bark on its stems and main branches is a dark green color, with silvery or pale green striations.

Stewartia monadelpha
TALL STEWARTIA
☼ 7 PH ▼   Moderate growth   ↕ 30ft (10m) ↔ 25ft (8m)

Upright and conical when it is young, this stewartia spreads with age. Small white flowers are carried among the green leaves in summer. The foliage becomes orange and red in autumn, and its bark peels, giving a splotchy effect. Dislikes dry soils.

Malus baccata var. *mandschurica*
MANCHURIAN CRAB
☼ 3   Vigorous growth   ↕ 40ft (12m) ↔ 40ft (12m)

The slender branches of this round-headed tree are covered with scented white blossoms in spring. Its small, rounded red fruits are carried from autumn into winter, and the mottled, flaking bark provides yet another attraction. Reliable and tough.

△ *Malus baccata* var. *mandschurica*

> ### OTHER MULTIPURPOSE TREES
>
> *Acer griseum*, see p.226
> *Arbutus unedo*
> *Betula nigra*, see p.210
> *Cornus kousa*
>   *Lagerstroemia indica*
>   *Magnolia grandiflora*
> *Malus x zumi* 'Calocarpa'
> *Prunus sargentii*
> *Salix x sepulcralis* 'Chrysocoma', see p.210
> *Ulmus parvifolia*

T R E E S

Columnar Trees

TREES OF COLUMNAR habit are uniquely useful. They are easily accommodated where space is at a premium, such as in small gardens or those that are long and narrow. They are also effective architecturally for breaking up otherwise low or horizontal plantings, as well as for providing a focal point. Most offer other ornamental features.

<table>
<tr><td>OTHER COLUMNAR TREES</td></tr>
<tr><td>

Carpinus betulus 'Fastigiata'
Fagus sylvatica 'Dawyck Purple'
Liriodendron tulipifera 'Fastigiata'
Malus baccata 'Columnaris'
Populus alba 'Raket'
</td></tr>
</table>

△ *Prunus* 'Amanogawa'

Acer rubrum 'Columnare'
COLUMNAR RED MAPLE
☼ 4   Moderate growth
↕ 50ft (15m) ↔ 15ft (5m)

This cultivar is slender and columnar at first, and its long, upright branches are loosely packed to the stem. These branches broaden later, covered in leaves that turn yellow, orange, and red in autumn. *A. rubrum* 'Bowhall' is another excellent cultivar.

Prunus 'Amanogawa'
JAPANESE CHERRY
☼ 6   Moderate growth
↕ 30ft (10m) ↔ 12ft (4m)

The branches of this cherry are closely held at first, but they spread out with maturity. Large, fragrant, semidouble pale pink flowers crowd its branches in spring. The leaves often give rich autumn tints. One of the most striking of all flowering cherries.

Acer saccharum 'Temple's Upright'
SUGAR MAPLE
☼ 3   Slow growth
↕ 40ft (12m) ↔ 15ft (5m)

The ascending branches of this broad, columnar tree are densely clothed with large, five-lobed leaves that turn yellow and orange in autumn. Performs best where summers are warm and winters are cold, such as in northern Europe and the Midwest.

Quercus robur f. *fastigiata*
CYPRESS OAK
☼ 5   Slow growth
↕ 60ft (18m) ↔ 20ft (6m)

Cypress Oak is a broad, columnar form of English Oak. Its ascending branches are thickly clothed with the bright green foliage. *Q. robur* 'Fastigiata Koster' is a very attractive compact selection. Both are long-lived.

Index

Plants that are illustrated in the book are indicated by this symbol ▣

A

Abele ▣ 214
Abelia floribunda 98
   A. x *grandiflora* 165
   A. triflora 127, 168
Abeliophyllum distichum 98, 166
Abies balsamea 'Nana' ▣ 188
   A. concolor 174, 185, 187
   A. concolor 'Candicans' ▣ 193
   A. concolor 'Glauca Compacta' ▣ 188
   A. grandis 174
   A. koreana ▣ 150, ▣ 180, 182
   A. lasiocarpa 'Compacta' 189
   A. magnifica 174
   A. nordmanniana ▣ 174
   A. nordmanniana
      'Golden Spreader' ▣ 188
   A. pinsapo 'Glauca' 193
Abutilon megapotamicum ▣ 92, ▣ 98
   A. pictum 'Thompsonii' 144
Acacia, Rose ▣ 99
Acacia baileyana 152
   A. dealbata 99, ▣ 158
Acaena 'Blue Haze' 28, 72
Acantholimon glumaceum 38
Acanthus hungaricus 20
   A. mollis ▣ 30
   A. mollis 'Holland's Gold' 71
   A. spinosus ▣ 18, 37, 85, 90
Acca sellowiana, see *Feijoa sellowiana* ▣ 99
Acer campestre 206
   A. capillipes ▣ 228
   A. griseum 201, ▣ 226, 228
   A. japonicum 'Aureum',
      see *A. shirasawanum* 'Aureum'
      151, 201, ▣ 219
   A. macrophyllum 197
   A. negundo 'Flamingo' 206, 218
   A. palmatum 221
   A. palmatum 'Aureum' 151
   A. palmatum 'Bloodgood' 155
   A. palmatum 'Corallinum' ▣ 142
   A. palmatum var. *coreanum* ▣ 200

A. palmatum 'Garnet' ▣ 154
A. palmatum var. *heptalobum* ▣ 156
A. palmatum 'Osakazuki' ▣ 222
A. palmatum 'Red Pygmy' ▣ 154
A. palmatum 'Senkaki' ▣ 226
A. palmatum 'Septemlobum', see
   A. palmatum var. *heptalobum* ▣ 156
A. pensylvanicum 'Erythrocladum' 227
A. platanoides 206, ▣ 215
A. platanoides 'Crimson King' ▣ 221
A. platanoides 'Drummondii' 218
A. pseudoplatanus 212, 215
A. rubrum 205, 210
A. rubrum 'Columnare' ▣ 229
A. rubrum 'Schlesingeri' ▣ 222
A. saccharinum ▣ 196
A. saccharum 197, 223
A. saccharum 'Monumentale',
   see *A. saccharum* 'Temple's
   Upright' ▣ 229
A. saccharum 'Temple's Upright' ▣ 229
A. shirasawanum 'Aureum'
   155, 201, ▣ 219
A. triflorum 199, ▣ 200
Achillea argentea,
   see *Tanacetum argenteum* 57, ▣ 73
   A. clavennae 28
   A. 'Coronation Gold' 37, 48
   A. 'Gold Plate' ▣ 85
   A. ptarmica 'The Pearl' 48
acid soils 10, 12
   perennials 34–5
   shrubs 124–5
   trees 204–5
Aconite, Winter ▣ 60, ▣ 84
Aconitum x *bicolor*,
   see *A.* x *cammarum* 'Bicolor' ▣ 20
   A. 'Blue Sceptre' 91
   A. 'Bressingham Spire' 33
   A. x *cammarum* 'Bicolor' ▣ 20
   A. carmichaelii 'Arendsii' 90
   A. lycoctonum, see *A. vulparia* ▣ 90
   A. vulparia ▣ 90
Acorus gramineus 'Ogon' 64
   A. gramineus 'Variegatus' 71
Actaea rubra 35, 44
Actinidia arguta 96
   A. kolomikta ▣ 94, 102
Adam's Laburnum ▣ 203
Adam's Needle, Variegated ▣ 69
Adiantum pedatum ▣ 34, 45
Aegopodium podagraria
   'Variegatum' ▣ 30
Aeonium arboreum 'Schwarzkopf',
   see *A.* 'Zwartkop' ▣ 64
   A. 'Zwartkop' ▣ 64
Aesculus x *carnea* 'Briotii' 212
   A. flava 197
   A. hippocastanum 197, 206
   A. hippocastanum 'Baumannii' ▣ 202
   A. x *neglecta* 'Erythroblastos' ▣ 198
   A. parviflora ▣ 110
   A. pavia 'Atrosanguinea' ▣ 200
Aethionema grandiflora ▣ 56
African Daisy ▣ 51, ▣ 63

Agapanthus Headbourne Hybrids
   50, 62, 91
   A. orientalis, see *A. praecox*
      subsp. *orientalis* ▣ 50
   A. praecox subsp. *orientalis* ▣ 50
Agave americana 65
   A. americana 'Variegata' ▣ 64
Agrostemma githago 'Milas' ▣ 26
Ailanthus altissima 212
air pollution 48–9, 136 7, 212–13
Ajuga reptans 'Atropurpurea' ▣ 74
   A. reptans 'Braunherz' 75
   A. reptans 'Catlin's Giant' 48
Akebia quinata 96, ▣ 102
   A. trifoliata 96
Albizia julibrissin ▣ 206
Alcea rosea ▣ 22
   A. rosea 'Chater's Double' 23
Alchemilla mollis 25
Alder
   Gray ▣ 202
   Italian ▣ 215
   Red ▣ 210
Aleppo Pine ▣ 184
Algerian Oak ▣ 209
alkaline (limy) soils 12
   perennials 36–7
   shrubs 126–7
   trees 204, 206–7
Allegheny Serviceberry ▣ 212
Allium aflatunense ▣ 80
   A. albopilosum,
      see *A. christophii* ▣ 40, 50, 81
   A. christophii ▣ 40, 50, 81
   A. cyathophorum var. *farreri* ▣ 58
   A. farreri, see *A. cyathophorum*
      var. *farreri* ▣ 58
   A. karataviense 40, 59
   A. moly 40, 41
   A. narcissiflorum 79
   A. oreophilum ▣ 58
   A. ostrowskianum, see *A. oreophilum* ▣ 58
   A. schoenoprasum 63, ▣ 86
   A. schoenoprasum 'Forescate' 86
Almond
   Double ▣ 213
   Dwarf Russian ▣ 127
Alnus cordata 212, ▣ 215
   A. glutinosa 210
   A. glutinosa 'Imperialis' 199
   A. incana ▣ 202
   A. oregona, see *A. rubra* ▣ 210
   A. rubra ▣ 210, 214
Aloe arborescens 'Variegata' ▣ 64
Alopecurus pratensis 'Aureovariegatus' 70
Aloysia triphylla ▣ 144
Alpine Eryngo ▣ 39
Alpine Phlox ▣ 57
Alpine Pink ▣ 56
Alstroemeria 'Ligtu Hybrids' ▣ 80
Althaea officinalis ▣ 86
Alyssum saxatile, see *Aurinia saxatilis* ▣ 54
Amaranthus caudatus ▣ 22
   A. caudatus 'Viridis' 22
   A. tricolor 'Illumination' 22

241

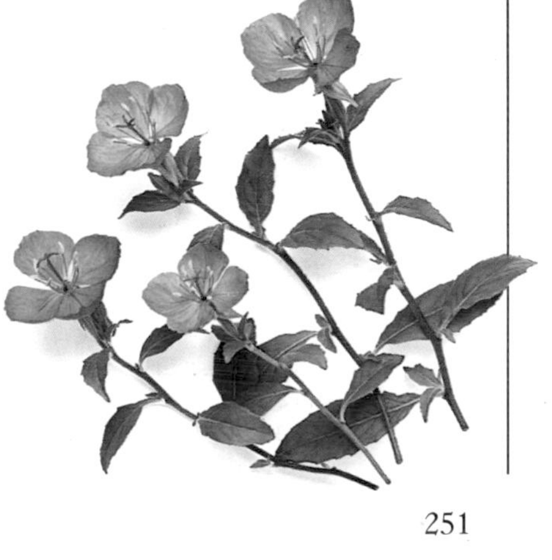

Acknowledgments

ROY LANCASTER'S CREDITS:
A number of people have either directly or indirectly influenced the preparation of this book, none more so than my wife, Sue, whose unfailing support, including the typing of my scribbled notes and lists, helped bring it to fruition.

Sarah Drew, Jacqueline Postill, Martin Puddle, and James Wickham all made helpful comments based on their considerable collective experience dealing with customers' problems and questions at garden centers.

Five years of traveling the length and breadth of Britain with Channel Four Television's *Garden Club* has taken me to a multitude of gardens large and small, while also introducing me to some helpful and resourceful gardeners. In acknowledging their contribution

I should also like to thank the present and former members of the *Garden Club* team, who have helped me in so many ways.

They include John Bennett, Matthew Biggs, Adrian Brennard, Karen Brown, Derek Clarke, Penny Cotter, Mary Foxall, Tony Griggs, Margaret Haworth, Elaine Hinderer, Sylvia Hines, Paddy McMullin, Ken Price, Rebecca Pow, Rebecca Ransome, Jo Redman, Sue Shepherd, Richard Stevens, and Steve Stunt.

Finally, I thank my publishers, especially Mary-Clare Jerram for asking me to compile this book, and Lesley Malkin and Colin Walton, my editor and designer respectively, whose enthusiasm and professionalism greatly impressed and encouraged me. I could not have asked for better.

DORLING KINDERSLEY would like to thank Barbara Ellis, Lyn Saville, and Ian Whitelaw for additional editorial assistance; Gloria Horsfall and Sue Caffyn for design assistance; Jane Parker for compiling the index; Ann Kay for proofreading; Dr. Alan Hemsley for his assistance in finding and identifying plants to photograph; Charles Cresson for providing hardiness zone information; David Roberts and the cartography department for the zone map, and Julia Pashley for additional picture research. Thanks also to the A-Z team, particularly Ina Stradins, Helen Robson, and Susila Baybars, for their patience with our shared resources, and to Rebecca Davies for all her trips to the post office.

ARTWORK CREDITS

Aspect Illustration by
Karen Cockrane 13

Tree Illustrations by
Laura Andrew, Marion Appleton, David Ashby, Bob Bampton, Anne Child, Tim Hayward, Janos Marffy, David More, Sue Oldfield, Liz Pepperell, Michelle Ross, Gill Tomlin, Barbara Walker

PHOTOGRAPHY CREDITS

Key: t=top, b=bottom, c=center, l=left, r=right

All photographs by
Clive Boursnell, Deni Bown, Jonathan Buckley, Andrew Butler, Eric Crichton, Andrew de Lory, Christine Douglas, John Fielding, Neil Fletcher, John Glover, Derek Hall, Jerry Harpur, Sunniva Harte, Neil Holmes, Andrew Lawson, Howard Rice, Robert Rundle, Juliette Wade, Colin Walton, Matthew Ward, and Steve Wooster, **except:**

Garden Picture Library:
Lynne Brotchie: 92 bl
Brian Carter: 93
Robert Estall: 194 br
John Glover: 13 tr, 14 bl, 108 br, 194 bl
M. Lamontagne: 195
Marianne Majerus: 2
Gary Rogers: 13 br
Ron Sutherland: 4
Brigitte Thomas: 9 b, 172 bl, 173
Steven Wooster: 13 bl, 92 br

John Glover: 85 bc, 174 tc, 187 tc, 213 bl

Derek Gould: 165 bl

Andrew Lawson: 219 tr

Roy Lancaster:
8 bl, 8 br, 9 tr, 9 tc, 12 bl, 31 tl, 31 cl, 31 bl, 42 tr, 45 tl, 49 bl, 67 br, 69 br, 83 cr, 84 bl, 85 bl, 85 tc, 85 tr, 86 bc, 87 bc, 87 tr, 87 br, 96 tr, 102 bl, 104 bl, 104 bc, 105 bl, 105 tr, 106 tl, 106 bl, 107 tl, 107 tr, 107 cr, 111 tl, 113 cr, 117 cr, 128 bl, 128 tc, 129 tl, 129 tr, 133 cl, 135 bc, 138 tl, 140 tl, 141 tc, 151 cr, 156 tl, 156 bc, 156 tr, 157 tl, 157 br, 161 br, 162 bc, 163 tl, 163 bl, 164 tr, 169, tl, 169 bl, 172 tr, 172 br, 174 bl, 176 tl, 179 br, 181 tr, 184 tl, 185 cl, 187 tl, 190 bl, 190 bc, 191 tl, 191 br, 192 tc, 192 tr, 194 tr

Nature Photographers Ltd:
Brinsley Burbage: 187 tr

Clive Nichols:
Chenies Manor Garden, Buckinghamshire: 109
Dartington Hall Garden, Devon: 14 br
Longacre, Kent: 14 cl

Photos Horticultural:
77 cl, 83 bl, 141 cr, 165 bc, 177 tc, 178 tr, 186 cr, 187 br, 191 bc, 193 bc, 207 bl, 212 bl, 213 tr, 229 cr

Harry Smith Collection / Polunin:
210 cl, 215 br

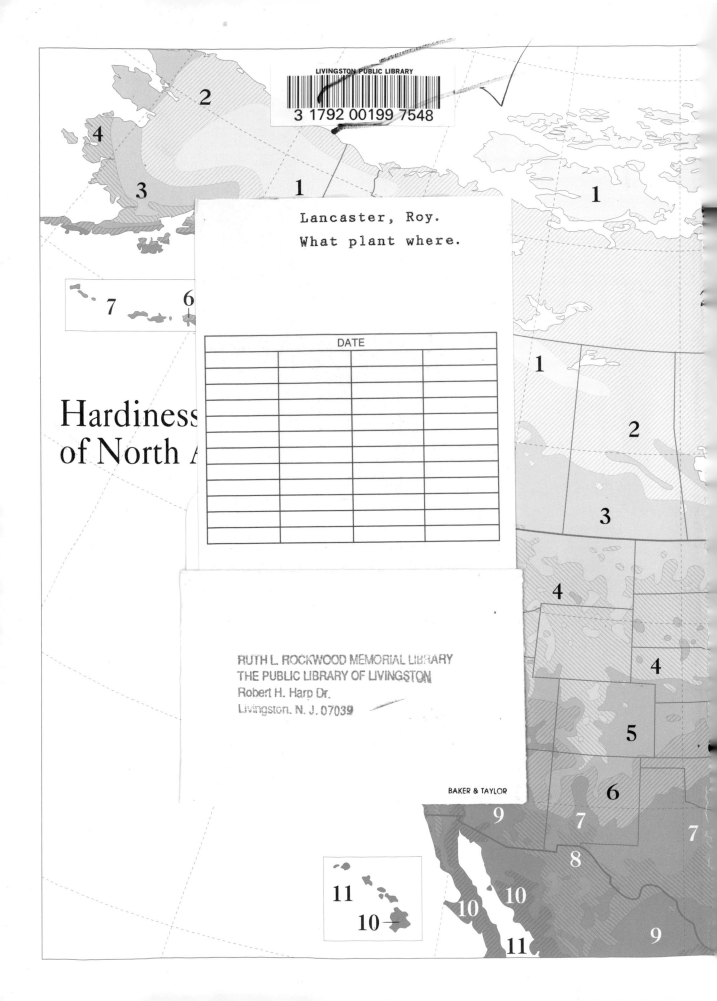

Lancaster, Roy.

What plant where.

Hardiness
of North A

DATE			

BAKER & TAYLOR